The Great Arizona Almanac

Facts About Arizona

1st Edition

Dean Smith

WestWinds Press™

First edition published 2000

ISBN 1-55868-523-5
ISSN 1529-6415

Key title: The Great Arizona Almanac

WestWinds Press™
An imprint of Graphic Arts Center Publishing Company
P.O. Box 10306, Portland, OR 97210, 503-226-2402; www.gacpa.com

President/Publisher: Charles M. Hopkins
Editorial Staff: Douglas A. Pfeiffer, Timothy W. Frew, Ellen Harkins Wheat, Tricia Brown, Jean Andrews, Jean Bond-Slaughter
Production Staff: Richard L. Owsiany, Susan Dupere
Editor: Dean Smith
Associate Editors: Wes Holden and Kathy Franklin
Cover and interior design: Michelle Taverniti
Cover illustration: Gary Bennett
Page composition/editorial assistance: Fay L. Bartels
Maps: Gray Mouse Graphics

Printed in the United States of America

Contents

Acknowledgments, 5
Map of Arizona, 6–7
Miscellaneous Facts About Arizona, 8

Adobe, 9
Agriculture, 9
Air Conditioning, 10
Air Travel, 11
Ajo, 11
American Indians, 11
Apache Junction, 20
Archaeology, 20
Area Codes, 23
Arizona Strip, 24
Arts, 24
Astronomy, 27
Auto Racing, 28
Baseball, 29
Basketball, 30
Battleship *Arizona,* 31
Benson, 31
Biosphere II, 31
Birds, 32
Bisbee, 34
Bisbee Deportation, 34
Buffalo Soldiers, 34
Bullhead City, 35
Butterfield Overland Mail, 35
Cacti, 35
Calendar of Events, 37
Caliche, 41
Camel Experiment, 42
Camping, 42
Canyon de Chelly, 44
The Capital on Wheels, 45
Casa Grande, 45
Casinos, 46
Central Arizona Project, 46
Chambers of Commerce, 47
Chandler, 50
Chiles, 50
Civil War in Arizona, 51
Clifton, 52
Climate, 52
Cochise, 56
Colossal Cave, 56
Congressional Representatives, 56
Coronado, 58
Cottonwood, 58
Counties, 58
Cowboys, 64
Crime Rate, 65

Dams, 66
Disasters, 67
Douglas, 68
Dude Ranches, 68
Economy, 70
Elected Officials, 72
Endangered and Threatened Species, 74
Energy, 75
Entertainers, 76
Ethnic Distribution, 77
Fairs & Festivals, 78
Famous Arizonans of the Past, 83
Fish and Fishing, 84
The Five C's, 86
Flagstaff, 88
Florence, 88
Food, 88
Football, 90
Forests, 90
Fountain Hills, 91
Gadsden Purchase, 92
Geography, 93
Geronimo, 95
Ghost Towns, 95
Gila Trail, 96
Gilbert, 97
Glendale, 97
Globe, 97
Gold, 98
Goldwater, Barry, 98
Golf, 98
Governors of the State, 99
Grand Canyon, 99
Green Valley, 101
Grey, Zane, 101
Guadalupe Hidalgo Treaty, 102
Gunfighters of the Old West, 102
Health Care, 104
Highways, 109
History—A Brief Overview, 109
Hockey, 117
Hogan, 117
Holbrook, 118
Honeymoon Trail, 118
Horse Racing, 118
Hunt, George W.P., 119
Hunting, 119
Insects and Spiders, 120
Jackass Mail, 121
Japanese Internment, 121
Jerome, 121
Kartchner Caverns, 122

Kingman, 123
Labor Force, 123
Lake Havasu City, 123
Lakes, 123
Leaders, Politicians, and Government
    Figures, 125
Libraries, 126
Literature, 126
London Bridge, 128
Lost Dutchman Mine, 129
Magazines, Selected General Interest
    Periodicals, 129
Mammals, 130
Mesa, 131
Meteor Crater, 132
Military, 132
Military Posts, 133
Mining, 134
Miranda v. Arizona, 135
Montezuma Castle, 136
Monument Valley, 136
Moon Walkers, 137
Mountains, 137
Movies, 138
Museums and Historical Societies, 140
National Parks and Monuments, 143
Native Arts and Crafts, 147
Newspapers, 149
Nogales, 151
Oak Creek Canyon, 152
OK Corral, 152
Outdoor Recreation, 152
Page, 153
Painted Desert, 153
Payson, 153
Peoria, 154
Petroglyphs, Pictographs, and Geoglyphs,
    154
Phoenix, 155
Pima County Cities, 157
Pioneers and Settlers, 157
Pioneers Home and Disabled Miners
    Hospital, 160
Place Names—Where Did That Name
    Come From?, 160
Plants, 161
Politics, 163
Population Trends, 164
Poston, Charles, 165
Pow Wow, 165
Prescott, 165
Prisons, 166
Pronunciation Guide, 167
Public Transportation, 167

Radio Stations, 167
Railroads, 169
Ranching, 170
Reptiles and Amphibians, 171
Retirement Communities, 172
Rio Salado, 173
Rivers, 173
Rocks, Minerals, and Gemstones, 175
Rodeos, 177
Safford, 177
Saguaro National Park, 177
Salt River Project, 178
San Xavier del Bac Mission, 179
Scottsdale, 179
Sedona, 179
Sierra Vista, 180
Skiing and Snowboarding, 180
Speed Limits, 181
State Government, 181
State Parks, 184
Statehood Battle, 187
Steamboats on the Colorado, 188
Taliesin West, 189
Taxes, 189
Television Stations, 190
Tempe, 190
Tennis, 190
Tombstone, 191
Tourism, 191
Trees and Shrubs, 195
Tubac, 196
Tucson, 197
Union Membership, 198
Universities and Colleges, 199
Western Maricopa Cities, 203
White Mountain Communities, 204
Window Rock, 204
Winslow, 204
World War II, 204
Yuma, 205
Zanjero, 205
Zip Codes, 206
Zoos and Gardens, 208

News Highlights, 1999–2000, 209
Suggested Reading, 213
Web Sites to Check Out for Additional
    Information, 214
Index, 215

Acknowledgments

Arizona Chamber of Commerce
Arizona Corporation Commission
Arizona *Daily Star* newspaper
Arizona Department of Commerce
Arizona Department of Game and Fish
Arizona Department of Tourism
Arizona Department of Transportation
Arizona Diamondbacks
Arizona Dude Ranch Association
Arizona Hall of Fame Museum
Arizona Highways magazine
Arizona Historical Foundation
Arizona Historical Society
Arizona Mining and Mineral Museum
Arizona Pioneers Home and Disabled
    Miners Hospital
Arizona Public Service Company
Arizona Republic newspaper
Arizona Secretary of State
Arizona Sonora Desert Museum
Arizona State Department of Agriculture
Arizona State Department of Economic
    Security
Arizona State Library, Archives and Public
    Records
Arizona State Mine Inspector
Arizona State Parks Board
Arizona State University Libraries
Arizona State University News Bureau
Diane Bain
Biosphere II
Todd Bostwick
Boyce Thompson Arboretum State Park
Randy Britton
Department of Mines and Mineral
    Resources,
Desert Botanical Garden
Kathy Franklin

KTAR/Ed Phillips *Arizona Almanac*
Heard Museum
Wes Holden
Scott Harelson
Bea and Noller Herbert
Islamic Center, Tempe
League of Arizona Cities and Towns
David Manning
Mesa Chamber of Commerce
Meteor Crater Enterprises
Metropolitan Tucson Convention and
    Visitors Center
Northern Arizona University Libraries
Office of Governor Jane Dee Hull
Old Tucson
Phoenix Coyotes
Phoenix International Raceway
Phoenix Mercury
Phoenix Suns
Prescott Chamber of Commerce
Rillito Downs
Saguaro National Park
Salt River Project
Susie Sato
Sharlot Hall Museum
Gary Shoemaker
Southwest Gas Company
Southwest Studies, Scottsdale Community
    College
Gail Steiger
James Tallon Photography
Tempe Chamber of Commerce
Marshall Trimble
Tucson Electric Power Company
Tucson Metropolitan Chamber of
    Commerce
Turf Paradise
University of Arizona Libraries
University of Arizona News Bureau

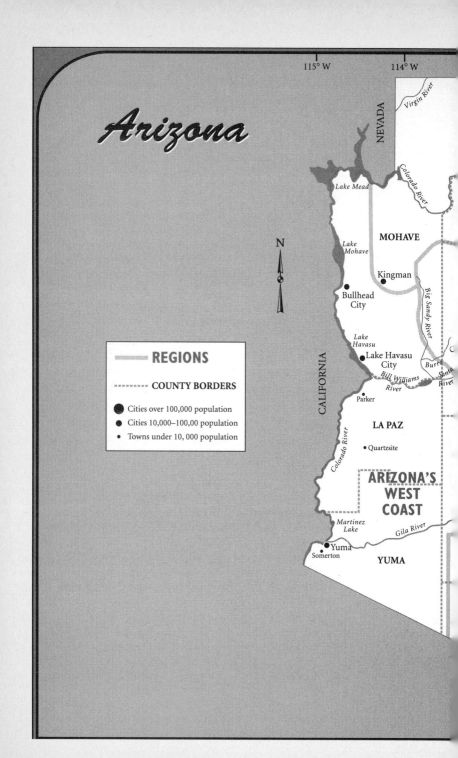

Arizona

115° W   114° W

NEVADA

Virgin River

Lake Mead

Colorado River

MOHAVE

Lake Mohave

Kingman

Bullhead City

Big Sandy River

Lake Havasu

Lake Havasu City

Burro

Santa River

Bill Williams River

CALIFORNIA

Parker

REGIONS

COUNTY BORDERS

● Cities over 100,000 population
● Cities 10,000–100,00 population
• Towns under 10, 000 population

LA PAZ

• Quartzsite

ARIZONA'S WEST COAST

Colorado River

Martinez Lake

Gila River

Yuma

Somerton   **YUMA**

N

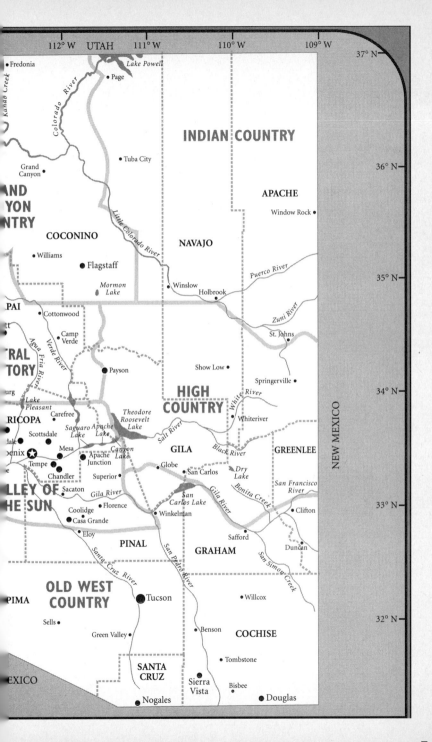

Miscellaneous Facts About Arizona

Nickname: *Grand Canyon State (also called the Copper State).*

Motto: *Ditat Deus (God Enriches).*

Capital: *Phoenix.*

Counties: *15.*

Path to statehood: *Obtained from Mexico in Mexican Cession of 1848. Organized in 1850 as the western half of New Mexico Territory. Southern quarter of Arizona bought from Mexico via Gadsden Treaty, 1854. Arizona Territory made a separate territory, Feb. 24, 1863. Admitted as the 48th state, Feb. 14, 1912.*

Courtesy Office of Secretary of State

Dimensions: *Roughly 350 miles wide and 400 miles long; 114,000 square miles. Sixth largest of American states in area.*

Neighbors: *Bounded by Mexico on the south, California and Nevada on the west, Utah on the north, New Mexico and the southwestern tip of Colorado on the east.*

Highest point: *12,670 feet, at top of Mount Humphreys near Flagstaff.*

Lowest point: *70 feet above sea level on Colorado River near Yuma.*

State population: *(1999 est.) 4,924,350.*

Most populous cities *(Year 2000 estimates, within city limits): Phoenix, 1,300,000; Tucson, 480,000; Mesa, 380,000.*

State amphibian: *Arizona tree frog.*

State bird: *Cactus wren.*

State colors: *Blue and old gold.*

State fish: *Apache trout.*

State flag: *A copper star rising from a field of blue, topped by 13 red and yellow rays of sun.*

Courtesy Office of Secretary of State

State flower: *Saguaro blossom.*

State fossil: *Petrified wood.*

State gem: *Turquoise.*

State mammal: *Ringtail.*

State neckwear: *Bola tie.*

State reptile: *Arizona ridgenosed rattlesnake.*

State tree: *Paloverde.*

Temperature Records: *Highest, 128°F at Lake Havasu City, 1994; Lowest, −40°F at Hawley Lake, 1971.*

Largest Native American reservation area: *Navajo, with capital at Window Rock. (See page 14)*

Major league sports teams: *Phoenix Suns, basketball; Arizona Cardinals, football; Arizona Diamondbacks, baseball; Phoenix Coyotes, ice hockey; Phoenix Mercury, women's basketball.*

Nation's *largest producer of copper.*

Tucson founded *in 1775, year of Paul Revere's ride.*

Old Oraibi, *founded about* A.D. *1000, oldest continuously inhabited town in United States.*

Women *were elected to all five major state offices in 1998 (first and only state in which this is true).* ✷

Adobe Adobe is a building material commonly associated with Arizona and the Southwest. The word can also refer to structures built of these bricks made from sun-dried mud and straw. Although "adobe" has Spanish and Arabic origins, Native Americans in the Southwest built earthen homes and walls long before Europeans came to North America. Arizona's arid climate and sunny days are ideal for drying and curing adobe bricks.

Before the advent of air conditioning, adobe walls kept the temperature inside a building from changing more than a few degrees throughout the day. While adobe buildings may seem vulnerable to the eroding effects of rainfall, they actually hold up quite well in places that receive fewer than 15 inches of rain per year, especially when a hard roof like Mexican tile is used.

Fruits and Vegetables

Principal table crops grown in Arizona include lettuce, cantaloupes, broccoli, watermelons, cauliflower, citrus, and honeydew melons. The total value of fruits and vegetables grown in Arizona totaled $712 million in 1995, according to a study by the Arizona Department of Agriculture.

Arizona ranks third in the nation in the total production of all vegetables and fruits, and second in the nation in the annual production of broccoli, cantaloupes, cauliflower, head lettuce, leaf lettuce and romaine lettuce. The state is third in growing honeydews and citrus, fourth in dry onions and grapefruit, fifth in watermelons, and sixth in grapes. ✳

Agriculture (SEE ALSO THE FIVE C'S; ZANJERO) In the mid-1860s, settlers in Arizona's southern river valleys discovered that prehistoric Indians had made their

Number of Farms in Operation and Total Acreage (in millions)

County	1982 Farms	1982 Acres	1987 Farms	1987 Acres	1992 Farms	1992 Acres	1997 Farms	1997 Acres
Apache	296	6.2	380	5.8	332	5.8	288	*
Cochise	785	2.0	836	2.1	831	2.1	824	1.3
Coconino	232	5.9	294	5.9	285	5.9	199	6.2
Gila	163	1.1	157	1.2	143	1.2	148	*
Graham	308	1.9	323	1.8	317	1.8	281	1.2
Greenlee	121	0.1	102	0.1	107	0.1	99	0.1
La Paz	**	**	109	0.2	101	0.2	97	0.3
Maricopa	2,403	1.4	2,334	1.4	1,856	0.7	1,643	0.7
Mohave	223	2.2	236	1.9	212	1.9	212	1.0
Navajo	331	7.3	376	7.7	375	7.7	310	3.9
Pima	539	3.5	520	3.2	448	3.2	419	2.9
Pinal	605	2.4	730	2.0	611	1.9	541	1.3
Santa Cruz	133	0.4	179	0.3	164	0.3	156	0.2
Yavapai	474	2.5	484	2.4	463	2.1	453	0.8
Yuma	721	0.5	609	0.3	528	0.2	465	0.2
Total	7,334	37.4	7,669	36.3	6,773	35.1	5,835	20.1

* Not reported to avoid disclosing individual operations; distorting total.
** La Paz County did not exist for the 1982 census.
Source: Arizona Department of Agriculture

living by digging canals and bringing river water to their crops. Jack Swilling and other entrepreneurs formed canal companies, re-dug the ancient canals, and started growing crops on thousands of acres of desert land. Completion of the Theodore Roosevelt dam in 1911 ushered in decades of lucrative farming in central Arizona. Today most of Arizona's farm production comes from irrigated lands.

Despite the fact that millions of acres of productive farmland have been taken over by developers of housing tracts, Arizona's agricultural production annually contributes some $6.5 billion to the economy. According to U.S. Department of Agriculture statistics, the state had 35.4 million acres of land devoted to agriculture in 1996. The state's leading cash crops are cotton, dairy products, head lettuce, and cantaloupes. Pima (long staple) cotton accounts for

Irrigated lettuce field at Mohawk in western Arizona. Photo by James Tallon.

73,000 bales annually, second highest in the nation. Upland cotton production is ninth in the U.S., with 770,000 bales.

Arizona ranks first in the nation in farm size. The average farm is 4,720 acres, compared with the national average of 470 acres.

Air Conditioning

Few technological advances have affected the growth of Arizona as much as the development of air conditioning. By making desert summers more livable, air conditioning has changed the course of history in the state.

Until the early 1930s, when crude evaporative coolers began to make an appearance on homes and business buildings, Arizonans in desert areas were forced to survive in 100-plus degree temperatures throughout the long summers. Many slept on their lawns, covered with damp sheets, and battled mosquitoes through hot summer nights. People retreated behind thick adobe walls, swam in irrigation canals, and ate their meals in the breeze of electric fans. Because of the summer heat, relatively few people in other states were brave enough to settle in Arizona.

But the advent of evaporative (often called "swamp") coolers, still in use in many homes, lowered inside temperatures as much as 20 degrees. Not long thereafter, refrigerated air conditioners made their appearance in theaters, department stores, and eventually in residences. They are infinitely more effective. Today no commercial enterprise can long survive without refrigerated air conditioning, and all but the most modest homes maintain summer temperatures in the 75- to 80-degree range.

With the advent of air conditioning,

migration to Arizona's desert cities, particularly in Maricopa and Pima counties, skyrocketed. Greater metro Phoenix, for example, had a population of less than 100,000 in the early 1940s, but now has nearly 3 million.

Air Travel
Ever since 1919, when Tucson opened the nation's first municipal airport, civilian flying has been an important part of Arizona life. Today almost every city in the state has an airport or landing strip.

Phoenix Sky Harbor International Airport is the largest in Arizona, and one of the nation's busiest. Sky Harbor ranked sixth among American airports in 1998 in the number of takeoffs and landings, and ninth in total passengers, with 31.7 million. In addition to 20 major airlines that have operations at the airport, there are spacious facilities for general (private) aviation, as well as the adjoining Arizona Air National Guard operation.

Largest of the airline facilities at Sky Harbor are those of America West, which has its national headquarters in nearby Tempe, and Southwest Airlines has a regional hub here. These two lines occupy Terminal 4, recently named for Senator Barry Goldwater.

Other major general aviation facilities in the metro Phoenix area include: Phoenix Deer Valley Airport to the north side; Phoenix-Litchfield Airport to the west; Scottsdale Municipal Airport; Mesa Municipal Airport; and Chandler Municipal Airport.

Tucson International Airport is located at Valencia Road and Tucson Boulevard. The facility is operated by the Tucson Aviation Authority, with a nine-member governing board. TIA is served by American, America West, Continental, Delta, Northwest/KLM, Southwest, United/Lufthansa, and several smaller airlines. The airport served 3.47 million passengers in 1998. The Arizona Air National Guard also has an operational facility at TIA.

Ryan Field, home of a World War II Army pilot training school, came under control of the Tucson Airport Authority in 1951. Today more than 20 tenants, including flight schools, maintenance shops, and other flight services, are housed at Ryan Field.

Ajo
In Spanish, ajo means "garlic," but the pleasant mining town of Ajo in Pima County deserves a more appealing name. Wild garlic plants that grew in the surrounding hills were responsible for the naming of the community. The Arizona Mining and Trading Company, established in 1854, was the first incorporated mining property in Arizona Territory. Today the New Cornelia open-pit copper mine remains the principal source of the town's economy.

The heart of Ajo (estimated population 3,000) is the plaza, a Spanish Colonial Revival town square built in 1917 at the direction of mining pioneer John Greenway and his wife Isabella, who later became the only woman elected to Congress by Arizona.

American Indians
(SEE ALSO ARCHAEOLOGY; CASINOS; COCHISE; GERONIMO; HOGAN; NATIVE ARTS AND CRAFTS; POW WOW) Earliest evidence of humans in Arizona has been radiocarbon-dated at about 11,500 years ago at the mammoth hunting location known to

archaeologists as the Lehner Ranch Site in southeastern Arizona. Those Paleo-Indians retreated eastward, following the big game animals, about 5,500 B.C., and, later, Nomadic hunter-gatherers, called the Archaic Culture, moved into the area from the west. Four sedentary cultures began to appear from the background of the Archaic about the year A.D. 1: the Patayan along the Colorado River in western and northwest Arizona; the Anasazi in the high mesa country to the north; the Hohokam in the desert basins of central and southern Arizona; and the Mogollon in Arizona's eastern mountains, New Mexico and south-ward into northern Mexico. The latter three became the more prominent.

Pre-historic Indigenous People

Anasazi People. It is likely that some of the migrating Archaic hunter/gatherers with a matrilineal culture pattern became more sedentary, and, even today, live in mesa-top villages in northeastern Arizona. Archaeologists mistakenly named them *Anasazi*, from a Navajo word meaning "enemy ancestors." Understandably, the Hopi, who are the descendants, prefer *Hisatsinom*, meaning "their ancestors." Nonetheless, these earliest Anasazi began settling in the area before the birth of Christ. They lived in clusters of pit houses; their primary methods of hunting were snares and throwing sticks with which they acquired small game; and they used a hunting spear called an *atlatl*, to bring down big game.

The Anasazi, or Pueblo people, flourished until the early 1200s, when a series of droughts and weather-related calamities throughout the entire region put pressure on all peoples in the Southwest. By then the Anasazi had developed unique dry-land agriculture techniques to a high degree and grew corn, beans, squash, and, later on, even cotton. They were also noted for their fine pottery, basketry and the dramatic cliff dwellings that survive today. In the Navajo National Monument are two of the most important of these in Arizona, Keet Seel and Betatakin. Dr. Byron Cummings of the University of Arizona was one of the pioneers in the discovery and preservation of these cliff communities.

The Anasazi also built the larger Mesa Verde cliff dwellings not far from Four Corners in southwestern Colorado. All of these well-preserved archaeological treasures are visited by hundreds of thousands of people from around the world each year.

Why the Anasazi culture underwent such drastic changes is not as much of a mystery as popularly portrayed in some journals. A series of long term changes in weather patterns was only one thing that put pressure on their lifestyle. And later on, diseases from the Spanish were devastating as well.

Although never a monolithic group, their cyclical Kachina ceremonies held the culture together, more than other Indian group

Hopi kachina doll. Courtesy Office of the Secretary of State.

in America has managed to do. Today Kachina dolls are a signature symbol of the Anasazi.

The Hopi in Arizona and other Pueblo peoples in New Mexico still speak six distinct languages, and they are proud to say that the

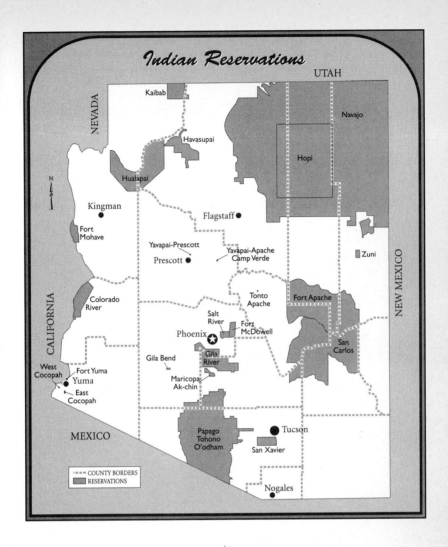

Indian Reservations

(Map of Arizona showing Indian Reservations, county borders, and surrounding states: Nevada, Utah, New Mexico, California, and Mexico. Labeled reservations and cities include: Kaibab, Havasupai, Navajo, Hopi, Hualapai, Kingman, Flagstaff, Fort Mohave, Yavapai-Prescott, Prescott, Yavapai-Apache Camp Verde, Zuni, Colorado River, Tonto Apache, Fort Apache, Salt River, Fort McDowell, Phoenix, San Carlos, Gila Bend, Gila River, West Cocopah, Fort Yuma, Yuma, East Cocopah, Maricopa Ak-chin, Papago Tohono O'odham, San Xavier, Tucson, Nogales. Legend: County Borders, Reservations.)

descendants of the *Hisatsinom* (Anasazi) still live here.

Hohokam People. The prehistoric people called the Hohokam lived in Arizona's central desert region for centuries, from about A.D. 1–1450. Ethnographer Frank Russell is credited with translating *Hohokam* as a Pima Indian word meaning "that which has perished." It has been estimated that 20,000 to 50,000 Hohokam lived in the Phoenix area alone by the 1200s. They irrigated thousands of acres of crops through extensive canal systems that tapped water from the Salt and Gila Rivers, as well as smaller streams. In fact, they dug more canals and moved more water than any other group in North America. Pioneers in the Salt River Valley in the 1860s rediscovered the ancient Hohokam canals, cleaned them out and used them as the basis for today's irrigation water system.

Indian Tribes and Reservations

Reservation Name	People	Enrolled Population	Number of Acres
Ak-Chin Indian Community	Tohono O'odham Pima (Akimel O'odham)	571	21,840
Cocopah Indian Tribe	Cocopah	774	6,009
Colorado River Indian Tribes	Mohave, Chemehuevi, Hopi and Navajo	3,100	268,691*
Fort McDowell Indian Community	Yavapai, Mohave-Apache and Apache	849	24,680
Fort Mojave Indian Tribe	Mohave (Pipa Aha Macav)	1,120	32,679**
Fort Yuma-Quechan Tribe	Quechan	2,475	43,561*
Gila River Indian Community	Maricopa (Xalychidom Pipaash) and Pima	11,550	371,933
Havasupai Tribe	Havasupai	700	188,077
Hopi Tribe	Hopi	8,000	1,561,213
Hualapai Tribe	Hualapai	1,532	992,463
Kaibab Paiute Tribe	Paiute	350	120,431
Navajo Nation	Navajo (Dine)	230,000	9,101,396***
Pascua Yaqui Tribe	Yaqui	9,021	895
Salt River Pima-Maricopa Indian Community	Pima and Maricopa	6,000	52,600
San Carlos Apache Tribe	Apache (Indeh)	10,000	1,834,781
San Juan Southern Paiute Tribe	Paiute	250	0
Tohono O'odham Nation	Tohono O'odham	18,000	2,846,541
Tonto Apache Tribe	Tonto Apache	95	85
White Mountain Apache Tribe	Apache	12,000	1,664,972
Yavapai-Apache Tribe	Yavapai and Apache	1,200	653
Yavapai Prescott Reservation	Yavapai	139	1,399

*Includes land in Arizona and California
**Includes land in Arizona, Nevada and California
*** Includes land in Arizona, New Mexico and Utah

Source: U.S. Bureau of Indian Affairs, Arizona Secretary of State.

The Hohokam's primary "cash crop" was cotton. Growing cotton requires great amounts of two things: heat and water. They were blessed with both of them via the sun-drenched desert and the Salt and Gila Rivers, and with the resulting cotton they wove beautiful and useful textiles.

By A.D.1150 the Hohokam were moving their expanding and complex society into larger and larger communities. The tall adobe structure known as Casa Grande Ruins National Monument, near Coolidge, began about 1300. But like the Anasazi and others, the Hohokam suffered from their growing population, decreasing resources, and profound weather changes that finally, painfully caused them to give up their vast agricultural struggle. When Spanish explorers entered the area in the 1500s, only a few scattered Pima and Papago villages dotted the desert riverbanks and arroyos. Their inhabitants had gone back to hunting and gathering and planting small plots of corn in the muddy bottomlands. The Spanish called them Papago and Pima. Today these people prefer to be recognized by the names *Tohono O'odham* and *Akimel O'odham* and they still live along the Salt and Gila Rivers.

Mogollon People. The Mogollon didn't begin to emerge from the Archaic, hunter/gatherer culture in Arizona's central and eastern high country until about A.D. 200. Similar to other peoples in Arizona, whose origins are still debated by archaeologists, they likely experienced influences from Mexico. By 1000 they had perfected agricultural techniques necessary for living where the growing season is short, and by the mid-1100s were flourishing. They had communities of pit houses on high mesas, and, later on, also built cliff dwellings and pueblo-style villages. Their cultural change was slow. The Mogollon and Anasazi had been living together possibly since A.D. 600, with the Mogollon adopting many Anasazi traits and eventually blending with their Colorado Plateau neighbors. By about A.D. 1400 the culture recognized as Mogollon was gone from Arizona's eastern mountain region.

A cultural icon for which the Mogollon are justifiably remembered worldwide is their distinctive Mimbres black-on-white pottery.

Today's Tribal Communities

All Arizonans who have an indigenous heritage are referred to as Native Americans or American Indians, but when speaking of specific people it is best to use their tribe or clan name. The federal government officially recognizes 21 communities (tribes) on 20 reservations in Arizona.

Nearly 20 million acres, about 27 percent of Arizona's total land, make up these Indian homelands. Arizona Indian peoples are citizens of the United States, but the reservations remain centers where various Indian nations preserve their cultures, traditions, and languages. About half of registered tribal members live off the reservations, moving to cities in search of work. Many maintain contact with their roots by returning home for family celebrations, ceremonies, dances, tribal fairs, and rodeos.

Thousands of visitors come from all over the globe to Arizona Indian country to view the ceremonies, arts, and lifestyles of the Native people. Tribes try to satisfy the interest of visitors and benefit economically when possible, while not allowing visitors to intrude on their privacy—often a difficult balancing act. Some villages permit visitors, but when a community does not welcome guests, its wishes should be respected. Visitors should never take photographs, videos or tape recordings on reservations without first receiving permission.

Ak-Chin Indian Community. The 571 members of the *Akimel O'odham* (Pima), *Tohono O'odham* (Papago) and Maricopa tribes belong to this community on the Maricopa Ak-Chin Indian Reservation, 17 miles south of Phoenix. Ak-Chin Farms Enterprises grow crops on 15,000 irrigated acres. Harrah's Phoenix Ak-Chin Casino

Looking Back

1539

The Spaniard Marcos de Niza and the slave Esteban were the first non-Indians to enter what is now Arizona.

Kachinas

The Hopi Indians of northeastern Arizona and, to a lesser extent, the Zunis of New Mexico are the Native Americans most identified with kachinas—representations of gods believed to control the various phases of life. They represent the sun, animals, plants, birds, and many other entities. Kachina authority Barton Wright says that the Hopis do not worship their kachinas, but instead consider them friends. Hopi men fashion kachina masks and wear them in their intricate ceremonial dances. The men who impersonate kachinas often carve small wooden replicas of them and present them to infants and other family members. The art of kachina-making is an ancient one. Spanish explorers of the 16th century reported seeing them hung in Hopi dwellings. The better kachina "dolls" are extremely colorful, artistically constructed from cottonwood roots, with feathers and other materials, and are highly prized by those who receive them. They range in size from a few inches to several feet in height.

Thousands of collectors have assembled sizable arrays of kachinas, many of which are worth large sums of money. One of the most famous collectors was the late Senator Barry Goldwater, who started acquiring kachinas in the early 1930s during frequent visits to the Indian reservations of Arizona. He paid small sums for them in those early days, or traded personal items for them, and eventually had what is believed to be the largest private collection in existence. Senator Goldwater presented most of his kachina collection to the Heard Museum in Phoenix. ✦

stays open 24 hours a day. 42507 W. Peters and Nall Road, Maricopa 85239, or call (520) 568-2227.

Cocopah Tribe. There are 774 Cocopahs that live on this reservation, about 13 miles south of Yuma. It's divided into three parcels of land, and the tribe cultivates several crops. Attractions: Cocopah Casino, Cocopah Bend RV Park, 18-hole golf course. County 15 and Avenue G, Somerton 85350, or call (520) 627-2102.

Colorado River Indian Tribes. 225,995 acres of Colorado River Indian Reservation (CRIT) lie near Parker, on the east side of the Colorado River, and 42,696 acres are in California, on the west side. The entire reservation houses 3,100 members of the Mohave, Chemehuevi, Hopi and Navajo tribes. Agriculture, recreation on the Colorado River, light industry, and the Blue Water Casino form their economic base. In September, the CRIT hold National Indian Days

festivities near Parker. Route 1, Box 23-B, Parker 85344, or call (520) 669-9211.

Fort McDowell Mohave-Apache Community. The 849 community members include those of the Yavapai, Mohave-Apache, and Apache tribes. The Fort McDowell Indian Reservation lands lie near Fountain Hills, 36 miles northeast of Phoenix. The original Fort McDowell was an important outpost for the U.S. Cavalry during the Apache Wars (1865–1891). The area around the Verde and Salt Rivers offer many recreational activities. Floating down the river on an inner tube has long been a popular summer pastime for Phoenix-area residents. Attractions: River Recreation, Fort McDowell Casino. Fort McDowell, P.O. Box 17779, Fountain Hills 85269, or call (480) 837-5121.

Fort Mohave Indian Tribe. Situated on Arizona's northwest border, the Fort Mohave Indian Reservation is home to the *Pipa Aha Macav* (Mohave) people. They have 23,669 acres in Arizona, 5,582 acres in Nevada, and 3,428 acres in California. Agriculture, recreational activities along the Colorado River, and the Avi Hotel and Casino support their 1,120 people. 500 Merriman Ave., Needles, CA 92363, or call (760) 629-4591.

Gila River Indian Community. The Gila River Indian Reservation is the state's oldest, established by Congress in 1859 for members of the *Xalychidom Pipaash* (Maricopa) and *Akimel O'odham* (Pima) tribes. Tribal Headquarters are at Sacaton, about 25 miles south of Phoenix. The community supports itself with agriculture, two casinos, three industrial parks, retail stores, arts and crafts, and recreation and tourism. They also own and operate a sports complex at Firebird Lake for boat races and drag races, and Compton Terrace, an open-air entertainment center. P.O. Box 97, Sacaton 85247, or call (520) 562-3311.

Havasupai Tribe. There are 700 Havasupais (*Havasuw 'Baaja*) that live on 188,077 acres of their ancestral lands outside the southwest corner of Grand Canyon National Park. They rely on farming and tourism. The only way to get to the Havasupai Indian Reservation is on foot, horseback, mule, or helicopter (permits and reservations are required). The tribe offers 24 first-class rooms at Havasupai Lodge and a campground near Havasu Falls. P.O. Box 10, Supai 86435, or call (520) 448-2961.

Hopi Tribe. The Hopi Indian Reservation with its 1,561,213 acres lies

Navajo child cuddles her goat. From Arizona by Fred Hirschmann.

Hubbell Trading Post, on the Navajo Reservation. From What Is Arizona Really Like? *by Reg Manning.*

in northeastern Arizona, completely surrounded by the Navajo Nation. More than 8,000 people live in the 12 pueblos, or villages, on First Mesa, Second Mesa and Third Mesa. Old Oraibi, on Third Mesa, established about A.D. 1000, is the oldest continuously inhabited town in the United States. The Hopi operate a motel, restaurant and cultural museum on Second Mesa, and support themselves through agriculture, arts and crafts (including pottery, baskets, jewelry and kachina dolls), and tourism. Ceremonial dances, performed on weekends throughout the summer, attract many visitors. Keep in mind, these ceremonies are sacred—no cameras, no videos, no recording, no drawings. P.O. Box 123, Kykotsmovi 86039, or phone (520) 734-2441.

Hualapai Indian Tribe. The 1,532 Hualapai live on 992,463 acres of the Hualapai Indian Reservation along the Colorado River and the Grand Canyon, 50 miles east of Kingman. Employment comes from tribal services, education, tourism, cattle ranching, timber, and arts and crafts. The Hualapai River Runners raft people down the Colorado River from May 1 to Oct. 31. P.O. Box 179, Peach Springs 86434, or call (520) 769-2216.

Kaibab-Paiute Tribe. These 250 Arizona Paiutes are part of the Southern Paiute Nation. The Kaibab Indian Reservation lies north of the Grand Canyon and south of the Utah border along Kanab Creek. The tribe operates several businesses, including Pipe Springs National Monument Visitor Center and Pipe Springs RV Park. Their economy also depends on agriculture, livestock and tourism. HC 85, Box 2, Fredonia 86002, or call (520) 643-7245.

Navajo Nation. The 9,101,396 acres of the Navajo Indian Reservation extend into three states, northeastern Arizona, northwestern New Mexico, and southeastern Utah, making this the largest reservation in the United States. The *Diné* (Navajo) have 230,000 enrolled members, making them the country's second largest tribe. Their land is known for its scenic wonders, including Monument Valley Tribal Park, and Canyon de Chelly, Navajo, and Rainbow Bridge National Monuments. The Nation operates many businesses on the reservation, and Navajos still pursue traditional activities such as raising livestock, arts and crafts (including weaving and silver jewelry), and tourism. A popular event is the Navajo Nation Fair and

Rodeo at Window Rock, in September. P.O. Box 663, Window Rock 86515, or phone (520) 871-6436 or (520) 871-7371.

Pascua Yaqui Tribe of Arizona. Yaquis are relative newcomers to Arizona, migrating from Mexico about 100 years ago. The 895-acre Pascua Yaqui Indian Reservation, the state's newest, is located about 15 miles southwest of Tucson. Most of the tribe's 9,021 members live off the reservation, including a large contingent in the town of Guadalupe, between Phoenix and Tempe. The tribe operates several businesses, including the Casino of the Sun in Tucson. Their Easter Ceremonies involve special dances, beginning on Ash Wednesday and continuing every Friday night for seven weeks. 7474 S. Camino de Oeste, Tucson 85746, or call (520) 883-2838.

Quechan Tribe. The Fort Yuma Indian Reservation of the *Quechan* (pronounced Kwuh-tsan) people straddles the Colorado River near Yuma, bordering on Arizona, California and Mexico. River recreation, other tourism, and a 300-seat Bingo hall form the economic base. P.O. Box 1899, Yuma 85366-1899, or call (619) 572-0213.

Salt River Pima-Maricopa Indian Community. Many years ago this reservation, east of Scottsdale and along the Salt River, was established for Maricopa and Pima families when Coolidge Dam literally dried up their source of livelihood—the lower Gila River bottom. Today the 6,000-member Salt River Indian community leases land to The Pavilions (which, at 140 acres, is the nation's largest retail commercial development on Indian lands), provides recreational opportunities on the Salt River, and operates Casino Arizona. 10005 E. Osborn Road, Scottsdale 85256, or call (480) 850-8000.

San Carlos Apache Tribe. Located in eastern Arizona, the 1,834,781-acre San Carlos Indian Reservation ranges from desert land at 2600 feet near Tribal Headquarters to heavily wooded land above 7000 feet at Point of Pines Lake. San Carlos is home to more than 10,000 *Indeh* (Apache) people. Residents work for the tribal government, in cattle ranching and recreational tourism. The tribe also mines peridots, makes jewelry with the beautiful green stones, operates the Apache Gold Casino, and hosts the All-Indian Rodeo and Fair in November. P.O. Box O, San Carlos 85550, or call (520) 475-2361.

San Juan Southern Paiute Tribe of Arizona. Also part of the Southern Paiute Nation, the San Juan Paiutes have a tribal government but no land for a reservation. (This issue is currently in litigation.) The people live mainly in Navajo communities in northern Arizona. Livestock, farming and basketry are the major economic activities. P.O. Box 1989, Tuba City 86045, or call (520) 283-4587.

Tohono O'odham Nation of Arizona. The home of the *Tohono O'odham*, the Papago Indian Reservation has 2,846,541 acres broken into four reservation parcels in south central Arizona. Tribal Headquarters are at Sells, 60 miles west of Tucson. The tribe's 18,000-plus members, traditionally farmers, also raise cattle, conduct tourist operations, and mine. Attractions include Mission San Xavier del Bac, just south of Tucson, and Kitt Peak National Observatory. The Tohono O'odham operate the Desert Diamond Casino near Tucson and host the O'odham Tash Rodeo at Casa Grande the first weekend in February. P.O. Box 837, Sells 85634, or call (520) 383-2221 or (520) 622-2441.

Tonto Apache Tribe of Arizona. The 95 Tonto Apaches have Arizona's smallest reservation, with 85 acres near Payson, 90 miles northeast of Phoenix. They produce beautiful beadwork and baskets and operate the Mazatzal Casino and Restaurant. Tonto Reservation No. 30, Payson 85541, or call (520) 474-5000.

White Mountain Apache Tribe. This 1,664,972-acre reservation in east-central Arizona houses its 12,000 members in nine communities. Its official name is the Fort Apache Indian Reservation. Agriculture, livestock, tribal businesses and tourism are the main economic activities. Hunting, fishing and winter sports at the tribe's Sunrise Ski Resort are the major outdoor pastimes for tourists. The tribe also operates Hon Dah Casino. From May through September, members perform the Sunrise Dance Ceremony (to attend, special arrangements are required), and the White Mountain Apache Fair and Rodeo is held in September at Whiteriver. P.O. Box 700, Whiteriver 85941, or call (520) 338-4346.

Yavapai-Apache Nation. Lying 55 miles south of Flagstaff in the Verde Valley, the 653-acre reservation, called Camp Verde Indian Reservation and made up of three separate tracts of land, is home for the 1,200 tribal members. Popular nearby attractions are Montezuma Castle National Monument, Montezuma Well and Tuzigoot National Monument. The tribe operates the Cliff Castle Lodge & Casino and Camp Verde RV Park. P.O. Box 1188, Camp Verde 86322, or call (520) 567-3649.

Yavapai-Prescott Tribe. The 139 members have 1,399 acres on the Yavapai Indian Reservation next to Prescott, where they operate several businesses, including Frontier Village retail center, Prescott Resort and Convention Center, and two casinos. Local gift shops display the fine work of Yavapai basket makers. 530 E. Merritt Street, Prescott 86301, or call (520) 445-8790.

Apache Junction

From a small suburb of Mesa, populated at one time principally by retirees and winter visitors, Apache Junction is now a city of 24,480 and is attracting scores of new residents each month. Its post office was opened in 1950, but the community was unincorporated until 1978, when its modern era of maturation began. Apache Junction lies mostly in northern Pinal County, but a portion of it extends into eastern Maricopa County.

Archaeology (SEE ALSO PETROGLYPHS, PICTOGRAPHS, AND GEOGLYPHS)

Arizona's State Historic Preservation Office has published a brochure, *Archaeological Parks and Sites in Arizona,* providing information on federal, state and municipal archaeological parks in the state. "The parks and sites listed provide a number of diverse experiences for both children

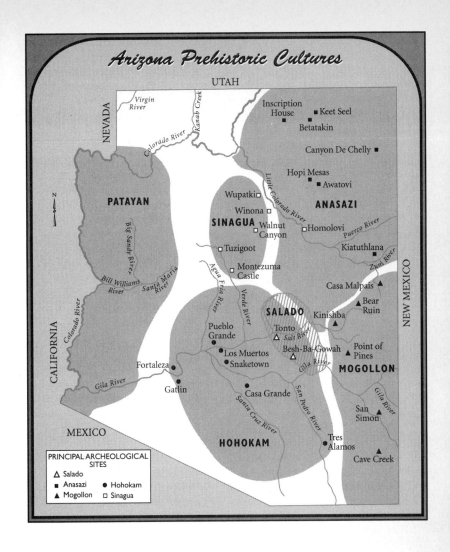

Arizona Prehistoric Cultures

UTAH

NEVADA

CALIFORNIA

NEW MEXICO

MEXICO

Virgin River

Kanab Creek

Colorado River

Big Sandy River

Bill Williams River

Santa Maria River

Colorado River

Gila River

PATAYAN

Inscription House ■ ■ Keet Seel

■ Betatakin

Canyon De Chelly ■

Hopi Mesas
■ Awatovi

Wupatki □

Winona □

Little Colorado River

ANASAZI

SINAGUA □ Walnut Canyon

□ Homolovi

Puerco River

□ Tuzigoot

Kiatuthlana ■

Zuni River

Agua Fria River

□ Montezuma Castle

Casa Malpais ▲

● Bear Ruin

Verde River

Pueblo Grande ●

Tonto △ Salt River

Besh-Ba-Gowah △

Kinishba ▲

SALADO

Point of Pines ▲

● Los Muertos

● Snaketown

Fortaleza ●

MOGOLLON

Gila River

Gila River

● Gatlin

● Casa Grande

Santa Cruz River

San Pedro River

San Simon ▲

HOHOKAM

Tres Alamos ●

Cave Creek ▲

PRINCIPAL ARCHEOLOGICAL SITES

△ Salado
■ Anasazi   ● Hohokam
▲ Mogollon   □ Sinagua

and adults," says the brochure, "including the viewing of ruins, exhibits, lectures and hands-on activities." Featured are these sites:

Apache County.

Canyon de Chelly National Monument. Spectacular prehistoric pueblo ruins built at the base of soaring canyon walls. One of Arizona's treasures, this site features cliff dwellings, a museum, and guided tours. It is 3 miles off U.S. Route 191 in far northeastern Arizona near Chinle.

Casa Malpais Archaeological Park and Museum. Mid-13th century ruins overlook the Little Colorado River valley on the outskirts of Springerville.

Lyman Lake State Park. The park and lake are located in an area where Anasazi and Mogollon petroglyphs

Keet Seel cliff dwelling. From *Arizona* by Fred Hirschmann.

abound. This 3-mile-long lake is 13 miles south of St. Johns.

Petrified Forest National Park. Prehistoric indigenous people carved hundreds of human, animal, and geometric designs on boulders throughout the park, off Interstate 40 east of Holbrook.

Cochise County.

Fort Bowie National Historic Site. Established in 1862, it was an important point on the wagon route across southern Arizona. The adobe ruins can be reached by a 3-mile round-trip foot trail. It starts 12 miles south of Bowie.

Coconino County.

Elden Pueblo. This prehistoric Sinagua ruin has more than 60 rooms. It is on U.S. Highway 89, 2 miles past the junction with Interstate 40 in Flagstaff.

Tusayan Ruin and Museum. The small pueblo was built by the Anasazi about A.D. 1200. It is on East Rim Drive of Grand Canyon National Park.

Walnut Canyon National Monument. The Sinagua people lived in these cliff dwellings in the 12th and 13th centuries. The monument is 7 miles east of Flagstaff on Interstate 40, then 3 miles south from Exit 204.

Wupatki National Monument. These pueblos were occupied as early as A.D.1120 The visitor center is on the 36-mile loop road passing through Sunset Crater and Wupatki. The loop road begins 15 miles north of Flagstaff off State Route 89.

Gila County.

Besh-Ba-Gowah Archaeological Park. The Salado culture may be studied in these pueblo ruins from the

13th and 14th centuries. The park is near Globe, on Jess Hayes Road.

Gila Pueblo. This Salado pueblo was occupied A.D. 1225–1400. The main complex has more than 200 rooms. The pueblo is near Globe, 3 miles south of U.S. Routes 60–70.

Tonto National Monument. A popular site, Tonto has two 13th-century Salado cliff dwellings 3 miles southeast of Roosevelt Dam off State Route 88. They are built in cliff overhangs.

Maricopa County.

Park of the Canals. This park contains ancient Hohokam villages and canal networks, and also features relics of early Mormon settlers' canals. It is on Horne Road in Mesa.

Pueblo Grande Museum and Cultural Park. One of the state's most visited archaeological sites, Pueblo Grande is on East Washington Street in Phoenix. A Hohokam village and canals have been restored here.

Mohave County.

Pipe Spring National Monument. Pipe Spring, a ranch and fort settled by Mormon pioneers in 1863, is on the Honeymoon Trail leading to the Mormon Temple in St. George, Utah. It is 14 miles west of Fredonia, Arizona.

Navajo County.

Homolovi Ruins State Park. The park contains six pueblos and was one of the last stopping places during the Hopi migrations. It is east of Winslow.

Navajo National Monument. Well-preserved Anasazi cliff dwellings, including the famous Keet Seel and Betatakin sites, are in the monument, 22 miles southwest of Kayenta off U.S. Route 160.

Pinal County.

Casa Grande Ruins National Monument. Features a four-story caliche structure surrounded by ruins of a farming village dating to A.D. 900. It is near Coolidge off State Route 87.

Santa Cruz County.

Tubac Presidio State Historic Park. The park highlights the cultures of American Indians, Spaniards, Mexicans, Mexican Americans and Anglo Americans in Arizona's development. Tubac was the first European settlement in Arizona, dating to 1752. The park is in the town of Tubac just off Interstate 17, south of Tucson.

Tumacacori National Historic Park. The Jesuit *visita* (smaller than a mission) was opened to the Indians in 1691, and a later Franciscan church is still standing. Tumacacori is 45 miles south of Tucson and 15 miles north of Nogales off Interstate 19.

Yavapai County.

Montezuma Castle National Monument. Sinagua cliff dwellings and irrigation systems are here. The Visitor Center is just off Interstate 17, 90 miles north of Phoenix.

Tuzigoot National Monument. One of Arizona's most important archaeological sites, Tuzigoot pueblo flourished in the 11th century. It had 97 ground-floor rooms. Easily accessible, it is 2 miles east of Clarkdale.

Area Codes
Until September 1999, Arizona had only two telephone area codes: 602 for metropolitan Phoenix and 520 for the remainder of the state. Now there are four: 602 for central Phoenix, 480 for East Maricopa County cities, 623 for

 West Maricopa County cities; and 520 for the rest of Arizona.

Arizona Strip

Anyone who craves isolation will be happy in the Arizona Strip country—the huge expanse of land between the Grand Canyon and the Utah border. It covers roughly the same area as the state of New Jersey, has fewer than 5,000 people, and is cut off from the rest of Arizona by the mile-deep canyon gorge.

If you live in the village of Colorado City, just south of the Utah line, you are in Mohave County, and must travel some 300 miles, through bits of Utah and Nevada, to reach your county seat of Kingman. The community of Littlefield, tucked into the most remote corner of northwestern Arizona, was settled in 1864, the same year Prescott was established.

Much of this is high desert country, but it also contains Mount Trumbull, a peak soaring 8,028 feet above sea level. Hardy souls may travel on a *very* rough road for 65 miles from Fredonia to Toroweap Point, on the north rim of the Grand Canyon, where they may walk, or crawl, to the edge and look straight down 3,000 feet to the Colorado River. It's a breathtaking experience. This is a fair-weather, summertime trip only! A high-clearance vehicle is a must, and be prepared for any circumstance.

Arts

(SEE ALSO NATIVE ARTS AND CRAFTS; TALIESIN WEST) Many noted painters, photographers, sculptors and other artists have come from Arizona, moved to the state at some point in their lives, or have drawn inspiration from its environment and colorful history. Here are a few of those famous for their work in the fine arts.

Artists

Painters. The 19th-century artists loved Arizona's unusual landscapes and clear light. These include **Henry Cheever Pratt** (1803–1880), who painted *Basin of the Rio Gila.* **Thomas Moran** (1837–1926) went on the Powell expeditions to record the Grand Canyon and painted such scenes as *Chasm of the Colorado.* The Grand Canyon has been a popular subject for artists ever since. **John Mix Stanley**'s (1814–1872) *Chain of Spires Along the Gila River* hangs in the U.S. Capitol Building. The war against Geronimo was immortalized in the pages of *Harper's Weekly* by the illustrations of artist **Frederic Remington** (1861–1909). Images of the Southwest and cowboy life were captured by the paintings of **Charlie Russell** (1864–1926) and many other "cowboy artists," such as **Charlie Dye** (1906–1973), **John Hampton** (1918–), **George Phippen** (1916–1966) and **Joe Beeler** (1931–).

Ettore "Ted" De Grazia (1909–1982), born in Morenci, achieved national recognition for his paintings and sculptures of American Indian children and angels. Navajo women are the preferred subjects of painter, sculptor and lithographer **R. C. Gorman** (1932–), from Chinle. **Fritz Scholder** (1937–), graduate of the University of Arizona, lives in Scottsdale and features Arizona themes in many of his paintings. **Charles Loloma** (1921–1991), born in Hotevilla, was a potter, weaver, silversmith and jewelry artist.

Photographers. **Timothy H. O'Sullivan** (1840–1882) took some of the earliest photographs of Arizona in the 19th century. **C. S. Fly** (1849–1901), owner of a legendary photography studio in Tombstone, captured Geronimo and his war party in some of the most famous photos of the time. Although he pursued photography as a hobby, not a profession, **Barry Goldwater**'s (1909–1998) photographs of Arizona are nationally respected. The photographs of **Ansel Adams** (1902–1984) helped *Arizona Highways* magazine become popular nationwide. The pictures of **Josef Muench** (1904–1998) also formed the backbone of early issues. His son, **David Muench** (1936–), is among the many photographers who contribute to *Arizona Highways* today. He has published several stunning books of Arizona pictures. **A. C. Vroman** (1856–1916), whose dramatic images of Hopi and Pueblo people can be seen in the book *Dwellers at the Source*, first visited Arizona in 1895.

Architects. Arizona's most famous architect is, of course, **Frank Lloyd Wright** (1867–1959). He founded his winter studio and school, Taliesin West, near Scottsdale. He also designed Grady Gammage Auditorium on the ASU campus. **Mary Elizabeth Jane Colter** (1869–1958), one of America's first women architects, designed many of the buildings at Grand Canyon National Park and other western sites through her work for the Fred Harvey Company. **Paolo Soleri**'s (1919–) architectural school and experimental city of the future, Arcosanti, is near Cordes Junction. Sales of his famous bells and wind chimes help to fund this project.

Cartoonists. Several decades ago, Americans enjoyed **J. R. Williams'**

Grady Gammage Memorial Auditorium, Tempe, designed by Frank Lloyd Wright. Photo by James Tallon.

(1888–1957) "Out Wickenburg Way" comic strip in their daily newspapers. Today they look forward to reading Phoenician **Bil Keane**'s (1922–) "Family Circus" strip. Popular World War II cartoonist **Bill Mauldin** (1921–), creator of "Up Front" featuring GIs Willie and Joe, graduated from Phoenix High School. He won the Pulitzer Prize in 1945 and in 1959. Two *Arizona Republic* editorial cartoonists have won Pulitzer Prizes, **Reg Manning** (1905–1986) and **Steve Benson** (1954–).

Performing Arts Centers and Companies

Actors Theatre of Phoenix, P.O. Box 1924, Phoenix 85001

America West Arena, 201 E. Jefferson St., Phoenix 85004

Ardrey Auditorium, P.O. Box 6040, Northern Arizona University, Flagstaff 86011

Arizona Early Music Society, 6609 E. Crimson Sage Drive, Tucson 85750

Arizona Jewish Theatre Company, 4800 N. Central, No. 106, Phoenix, 85012

Arizona Opera, 4600 N. 12th St., Phoenix 85014

Arizona Performing Arts Theater, dba Murder Ink Productions, 623 W. Southern, Suite 1, Mesa 85210

Arizona Theatre Company, 808 N. First St., Phoenix 85004

Arizona Theatre Company, P.O. Box 1631, Tucson 85702

Ballet Arizona, 3645 E. Indian School Road, Phoenix 85018

Berger Performing Arts Center, 1200 W. Speedway, Tucson 85703

Blockbuster Desert Sky Pavilion, 2121 N. 83rd Ave., Phoenix 85035

Celebrity Theater, 440 N. 32nd St., Phoenix 85008

Centennial Hall, 1020 E. University Blvd., Tucson 85721

Chandler Center for the Arts, 250 N. Arizona Ave., Chandler 85224

Childsplay, P.O. Box 517, Tempe 85280

Cobre Valley Center for the Arts, 101 N. Broad St., Globe 85502

Coconino Center for the Arts, 2300 N. Fort Valley Road, US Highway 180 North, Flagstaff 86002

Ethington Theater, Grand Canyon University Campus, 3200 W. Camelback Road, Phoenix 85017

Flagstaff Symphony, P.O. Box 122, Flagstaff 86002

Gammage Auditorium, Arizona State University Campus, Box 879105, Tempe 85287-0105

Paul V. Galvin Playhouse, Arizona State University Campus, Tempe 85287-2102

Great Arizona Puppet Theater, 302 W. Latham St., Phoenix 85011

Herberger Theater Center, 222 E. Monroe, Phoenix 85004

Kerr Cultural Center, 6110 N. Scottsdale Road, Scottsdale 85253

Lyric Opera Theatre, Arizona State University Campus, Tempe 85287

Mesa Arts Center & Galeria Mesa, 155 N. Center St., Mesa 85211

Mesa Symphony Orchestra, P.O. Box 1308, Mesa 85211

Mesa Youtheatre, 155 N. Center St., Mesa 85211

Nelson Fine Arts Center, Arizona State University Campus, Tempe 85287

Orpheum Theater, 200 W. Washington St., Phoenix 85003

Playhouse Theatre, Arrowhead Towne Center, 75th Avenue and Bell Road, Glendale 85308

Phoenix Boys Choir Association, 1131 E. Missouri Ave., Phoenix 85014

Phoenix Symphony, 455 N. Third St., Suite 390, Phoenix 85004-2167

Phoenix Symphony Hall & Civic Plaza, 225 E. Adams, Phoenix 85004

Phoenix Theatre, 100 E. McDowell Road, Phoenix 85004

Pima Community College Center for the Arts, 2202 W. Anklam Road, Tucson 85709-0225

Prescott Fine Arts Association, 208 N. Marina, Prescott 86301

Red River Music Hall, 730 N. Mill Ave., Tempe 85281

Scottsdale Center for the Arts, 7380 E. Second St., Scottsdale 85251

Scottsdale Symphony Orchestra, 3817 N. Brown, Scottsdale 85252

Sedona Arts Center, North Highway 89A and Art Barn Road, P.O. Box 569, Sedona 86339

Southwest Shakespeare Company, P.O. Box 30595, Mesa 85275-0595

Stagebrush Theatre, 7020 E. Second St., Scottsdale 85251-5555

Sundome Center for Performing Arts, 19403 R.H. Johnson Blvd., Sun City West 85375

Kitt Peak National Observatory. Photo by James Tallon.

Tempe Little Theater, P.O. Box 24718, Tempe 85285-4718

Tempe Performing Arts Center, 136 E. Sixth St., Tempe 85280

Tucson Arizona Boys Choir, P.O. Box 12034, Tucson 85732

Tucson Convention Center—TCC, 260 S. Church, Tucson 85702-3053

Tucson Jazz Society, P.O. Box 85101, Tucson 85754-5101

Tucson Kitchen Musician Association, P.O. Box 26531, Tucson 85726

Tucson Symphony Orchestra, 433 S. Stone Ave., Tucson 85701

U of A Presents, 888 N. Euclid, Room 203, Tucson 85721

Valley Youth Theatre, P.O. Box 15601, Phoenix 85060

West Valley Fine Arts Council, 387 Wigwam Blvd., P.O. Box 754, Litchfield Park 85340

Astronomy (SEE ALSO

MOON WALKERS) Tucson is recognized by many international astronomers as the astronomy capital of the world. The presence of the University of Arizona and its renowned Department of Astronomy faculty, along with the clear air and the absence of excessive lighting in the area, are among the factors which have brought the world's most advanced telescopes and many highly ranked astronomers to southern Arizona.

Among the state's most important observatories are:

Flandrau Science Center. Also on the University of Arizona campus is a sophisticated planetarium and education facility, the Flandrau Science Center. Visitors to Tucson should place a trip to Flandrau high on their list. Write to them at: Flandrau Science Center; University of Arizona Campus, Cherry Avenue and University Boulevard, Tucson 85721.

Kitt Peak National Observatory. On the top of Kitt Peak, 56 miles southwest of Tucson, is the Kitt Peak National Observatory, which has the world's largest collection of optical telescopes. At Kitt Peak there are 22 optical telescopes, two radio telescopes, and the most advanced auxiliary equipment available. The Association of Universities for Research in Astronomy, a consortium of prominent universities, is the principal operator. The University of Arizona plays a key role in research here. For more information, write: National Optical Astronomy Observatories, Kitt Peak, 950 N. Cherry Ave., P.O. Box 26732, Tucson 85726-6732.

Lowell Observatory. On Mars Hill in Flagstaff is an observatory that has been in the scientific news for more than a century. Famed astronomer Percival Lowell made significant discoveries about Mars in this facility during the 1890s, and in 1930 Clyde Tombaugh discovered the planet Pluto here. Address: Lowell Observatory, 1400 W. Mars Hill Road, Flagstaff 86001.

Steward Observatory. On the campus of the University of Arizona is the Steward Observatory, which has been among the national leaders in research and astronomical studies for many decades. Address: Steward Observatory, 933 N. Cherry Ave., Tucson 85721.

Fred Lawrence Whipple Observatory. Mount Hopkins, which soars 8,300 feet above sea level, is the site of a world-class observatory jointly operated by the Smithsonian Institution and the University of Arizona. Located 37 miles south of Tucson, it houses one of the largest telescopes on the planet—a 256-inch diameter multiple mirror telescope completed in 1979. It combines the light collected by six 70-inch telescopes. Write to: Fred Lawrence Whipple Observatory, P.O. Box 97, Amado 85645.

Auto Racing
Daredevil race car driver Barney Oldfield and other pioneers of the sport competed in an annual race from Los Angeles to Phoenix in the early 1920s. Auto racing has continued to thrill thousands of fans since that time in Phoenix, Tucson and other Arizona cities.

Nationally known Phoenix International Raceway, west of Phoenix, has a fast 1-mile track and hosts several Indy and NASCAR races each year, attracting America's premier drivers and some of the largest crowds for any Arizona sporting event. Information about upcoming racing schedules may be obtained by calling (602) 252-3833.

Manzanita Speedway in Phoenix is one of the oldest in the state, and schedules a variety of stock car and other races during its season. Information is available at (602) 276-7575.

Firebird International Raceway south of Chandler has achieved prominence in recent years, both for its auto and speedboat racing. Racing schedules are available by calling (520) 796-6000.

Tucson Raceway Park hosts NASCAR racing. Call (520) 762-9200.

Tucson's Southwestern International Raceway, (520) 762-9700, features NHRA drag racing.

The Bondurant School of High Performance Driving in Chandler has earned an excellent reputation for training race-car drivers.

Raceways.
American Sand Drag Association, 2045 N. Winterhaven, Mesa 85213
Canyon Raceway, 9777 W. Carefree Highway, Peoria 85382
Firebird International Raceway,

NASCAR racing at Phoenix International Raceway. Courtesy Phoenix International Raceway.

20000 Maricopa Road, Chandler 85226

Kingman Motor Sports Park, Kingman Off Road Competition Club, P.O. Box 6463, Kingman 86402

Manzanita Speedway, 3417 W., Broadway Road, Phoenix 85041

Phoenix Greyhound Park, 3801 E. Washington St., Phoenix 85034

Phoenix International Raceway, 115th Avenue and Baseline Road, Avondale 85323

Rillito Park Racetrack, 4502 N. First Ave., Tucson 85713

Tri-City Speedway, P.O. Box 1192, Safford 85548

Tucson Greyhound Park, 2601 S. Third Ave., Tucson 85713

Tucson Raceway Park, Pima County Fairgrounds, P.O. Box 18759, Tucson 85731

Turf Paradise Race Course, 1501 W. Bell Road, Phoenix 85023

Yuma Speedway, 3450 W. County 15th St., Yuma 85365

Baseball The Arizona-Texas League brought professional baseball to Arizona in the 1920s, and for decades teams representing Tucson, Phoenix, Bisbee-Douglas, and Globe-Miami competed in it and in the Arizona-Mexico League. Later the Class AAA Phoenix and Tucson teams were members of the Pacific Coast League, bringing Arizona nearer to the major league level. During many of those years, baseball had to share attention with softball, which often drew bigger crowds. Both men's and women's softball teams were competitive with the best in America.

Jerry Colangelo, who earlier had brought top-flight basketball and hockey franchises to Phoenix, led the move to obtain a National League baseball team (christened the Arizona Diamondbacks) to the capital city.

They made their debut in 1998, playing in the domed, air conditioned, Bank One Ballpark in downtown Phoenix. Buck Showalter, former New York Yankees manager, was chosen to manage the "D-Backs," as they are affectionately called. Their first season was predictably short on victories, but in 1999 the management invested more than a hundred million dollars to obtain super-star pitcher Randy Johnson, reliever Matt Mantei, third-baseman Matt Williams, second-baseman Jay Bell, outfielders Steve Finley and Luis Gonzalez, and other proven talents.

The 1999 Diamond-backs season, the second in its history, was a record-breaking one. The franchise won 100 games in the 162-game season. This was the earliest any expansion team had reached the 100-win milestone. They also won the National League's Western Division title, the earliest division win by a new team.

Arizona collegiate teams have ranked with the nation's best for many years. The Arizona State University Sun Devils, playing in Packard Stadium on the Tempe campus, have won five NCAA baseball championships. The University of Arizona Wildcats, whose home park is Sancet Field in Tucson, have won the national baseball championship three times.

One of the most popular tourist attractions in the state is the Cactus League, which now brings 10 major league baseball teams to Arizona each year for spring training. The Arizona Diamondbacks, Chicago White Sox, and Colorado Rockies play their Cactus League home games in Tucson;

> ### Looking Back
>
> **March 8, 1947**
>
> **The first Cactus League baseball game was played in Arizona, Indians vs. Giants.**

the San Diego Padres and Seattle Mariners in Peoria; the Milwaukee Brewers in Maryvale; the San Francisco Giants in Scottsdale; The Oakland A's in Phoenix; the Chicago Cubs in Mesa; and the Anaheim Angels in Tempe.

Basketball

Although the Southwest has rarely been ranked among the national hotbeds of basketball, Arizona teams have achieved considerable success during the past three decades. On both the professional and collegiate levels, winning squads have attracted enthusiastic followings and necessitated the building of huge stadiums for the sport.

In Phoenix, America West Arena's 19,000 seats are usually filled when the Phoenix Suns host National Basketball Association opponents. The University of Arizona in Tucson sells out all its home games in the McKale Center. Arizona State University in Tempe has its Wells Fargo Arena and Northern Arizona University plays both football and basketball in the Walkup Skydome in Flagstaff.

The Phoenix Suns have had several of professional basketball's great players: Connie Hawkins, Charles Barkley, Kevin Johnson, Danny Ainge, and Jason Kidd, to name but a few.

The Phoenix Mercury was one of the first entrants in the professional Women's National Basketball Association. Coached by former star Cheryl Miller, the Mercury plays home games in America West Arena.

Lute Olson has coached the University of Arizona Wildcats to national prominence and one national collegiate championship. His teams have won many Pacific 10 Conference titles and the Wildcat basketball program is rated among the most successful in America.

Arizona State University, also a Pacific 10 member, is bidding to regain the basketball prominence it enjoyed two decades ago. Rob Evans, who recently left his successful program at the University of Mississippi to coach Arizona State, is making notable strides in his rebuilding efforts.

Northern Arizona University in Flagstaff is enjoying winning seasons and a growing body of support in the state. Grand Canyon University in Phoenix, once a national power in the small college ranks, also has a substantial contingent of loyal fans.

Battleship *Arizona*

(*SEE ALSO* WORLD WAR II) Early in the morning of Dec. 7, 1941, swarms of Japanese bombers attacked Pearl Harbor in Oahu, Hawaii and sank or severely damaged many of the capital ships of America's Pacific fleet. The battleship USS *Arizona* sustained the most damage, and sank within a few yards of land, with most of its officers and crew still aboard. The ship is now a shrine for many thousands of tourists who visit the *Arizona* Memorial each year.

Not all of the ship lies beneath the water, however. Portions of the hull are now in the Arizona capitol building in Phoenix, along with an anchor which is the heart of a monument, at the center of the capitol complex, honoring those who went to their deaths with the ship.

Benson (*SEE ALSO* KARTCHNER CAVERNS)

Benson, 45 miles east of Tucson on Interstate 10, was founded in 1880 as a railroad camp housing workers laying track for the Southern Pacific Railroad. It was the shipping point for Tombstone and its surrounding communities. Located on the banks of the San Pedro River, along the first wagon road and stagecoach route across southern Arizona, the area is rich in territorial history. This Cochise County city of 4,605 people was a railroad town for many decades. It is a pleasant residential community and has recently experienced growth because of the opening of nearby Kartchner Caverns State Park in 1999.

Biosphere II

Biosphere II, located near Oracle, 25 miles north of

Tucson, is a research and teaching facility of Columbia University. Inside its three-acre glass and frame structure is 7 million cubic feet of space devoted to the study of the Earth's complex ecosystems. It maintains several wilderness ecosystems, including a rain forest, desert, savanna, marsh, ocean and a separate agriculture area. The Human Habitat section includes an exhibit on climatic change that has toured the nation for seven years.

Scientists at the facility conduct tests on the effects of controlled environments on plants and soils. A special emphasis in the research program is the study of how greenhouse warming will impact our planet, and measures that may be taken to prevent ecological disaster.

Biosphere I, in this same facility, was an experiment started in 1991, in which eight scientists lived inside the glass enclosure without leaving it for several months. One of their goals was to determine whether humans could live in a self-sustaining environment and thus prepare the way for colonizing other planets. No humans live in Biosphere II. Visitors are welcome to inspect the research in progress.

Birds
Arizona is a bird watcher's paradise, with 475 native species of birds, both year-round and migratory. The rivers and lakes, with their abundant animal and plant life, attract many waterfowl.

Thousands of Canada and snow geese winter in wildlife refuges along the lower Colorado River and summer in marshes at higher, forested elevations. Ducks of many kinds can be found all over the state. Wading birds such as egrets and herons live in many areas year-round. Sandhill cranes winter in the Willcox Playa Wildlife Area and in the Cibola National Wildlife Refuge along the southern end of the Colorado River. Wildlife refuges along the Colorado River even attract marine birds such as pelicans.

In the mountains one can see such birds as wild turkeys, piñon and Steller's jays, western and mountain bluebirds, grouse, woodpeckers, mountain chickadees, red-winged blackbirds, wrens, flycatchers, cardinals, robins and orioles, to name a few. Of the 19 species of hummingbirds that are found in the United States, 13 can be seen in Arizona. Birds of prey include eagles, hawks, falcons, ospreys, and owls. About 250 northern bald eagles winter in Arizona's secluded canyon areas.

Cliffs and large trees along rivers attract about 60 so-called "southwestern" bald eagles to the central deserts. Other desert birds include Gila woodpeckers and numerous species of doves, quails, hawks, and owls. Even a few brightly colored Elegant Trogons, a tropical bird, nest in southeastern Arizona forests.

Gambel's quail (*Lophortyx gambelii*). These fat little gray, black, and white birds with the bobbing single black plume atop the rust-colored patch on their heads are found in dry areas below 6,000 feet throughout the state. They are very adaptable and can tolerate a water loss of up to half their body weight. Although they can fly, these birds live on the ground and like to eat buds, mesquite beans, seeds, cactus fruits, and insects. Various representations of a mother Gambel's quail with several babies following behind are popular decorative items.

Roadrunner (*Geococcyx californianus*). Commonly known as the Greater Roadrunner, this is a type of cuckoo that can dash across a road at 15 miles per hour. Their speed helps them escape predators and catch insects, scorpions, lizards, and snakes—even rattlesnakes. This brown-and-white speckled bird, which grows to a length of 2 feet, adapts well to very hot and very cool desert weather.

Great Roadrunner. Illustration by Robert Williamson.

They *coo* and make a clattering sound, but, unlike the famous cartoon Roadrunner, they do not beep. The parents produce a nest of three to eight eggs twice a year, winter and summer, and take turns sitting on them.

Cactus wren (*Campylorhynchus brunneicapillus*). Arizona's state bird nests and roosts in the spiny branches of various species of cacti and thorny trees, to protect their young from predators. You can find hundreds of them in the deserts below 4,000 feet. These brown and white birds are the largest wrens in North America, 8 inches long. They eat spiders, lizards, fruit, and seeds, but they are particularly fond of grasshoppers.

Turkey vulture (*Cathartes aura*). With their 6-foot wingspan, these birds of prey are among America's largest birds. People also call them buzzards or carrion crows. They have coloring somewhat like that of a turkey—a dark brown body, red head, and white-tipped wings and tail. They can soar slowly over open country or woodlands looking for rotting dead animals, which the vultures actually locate through their sense of smell rather than sight. In mid-March folks in Superior celebrate the annual return of a flock of migrating turkey vultures that spend the summer in a eucalyptus grove there. When they leave for Mexico in September, everyone turns out for "Bye Bye Buzzards," to bid the birds *adios* for the winter.

Bisbee

Copper was discovered in 1877 in Cochise County, 8 miles north of the Mexican border. The mining camp that sprang up was named Bisbee after Judge DeWitt Bisbee, one of the co-owners of the Copper Queen mine. The Lavender Pit, a huge open pit mine, was for many years one of the nation's top copper producers. But the ore was exhausted and the mine closed in 1975.

Although many hundreds of miners and their families moved out, the city has continued to survive. Today there are more than 6,500 residents in Bisbee, the seat of Cochise County government. Its 5,490-foot elevation provides for pleasant year-around temperatures. The Copper Queen Hotel, mine tours on a narrow gauge railroad, a thriving retirement and art colony, and a picturesque setting with homes perched precariously on steep hillsides make it a popular tourist attraction.

Bisbee Deportation

Early in the morning of July 12, 1917, an angry army of vigilantes swarmed through Bisbee. They rounded up nearly 2,000 suspected members of the Industrial Workers of the World (IWW), who were believed to have fomented a strike of copper miners against the Phelps Dodge Company, and held them under guard at the ball park in nearby Warren. America had just entered World War I and any wartime strike was deemed by many to be grossly unpatriotic.

Lavender Pit copper mine, Bisbee. Photo by James Tallon.

Two men died in the confrontation, one union member and one vigilante. Twelve hundred of the union men (only a third of them proved to be IWW members) were loaded onto boxcars and shipped to New Mexico without warning to their families or means of sustenance when they arrived. They were unloaded on the desert after 15 hours without a drink of water and left to fend for themselves. A short time before, in the mining community of Jerome, local men had rounded up a much smaller group of IWW strike instigators and sent them in boxcars to Kingman.

Some 200 of the Bisbee vigilantes were later charged in a state court for kidnapping, but they were acquitted.

Buffalo Soldiers

Buffalo soldiers were United States Army units of African American soldiers. The units were formed to protect settlers in the western United States from hostile Indians, gunslingers, cattle rustlers, and Mexican revolutionaries. Their name, which they used proudly, was given to them by Indians who thought their hair resembled buffalo fur and their courage reminded them of this powerful, sacred animal.

In Arizona, these soldiers served with the 9th and 10th Cavalry units. Based at Fort Huachuca, they patrolled against lawbreakers, but their main function was to fight in the Apache Wars. From 1879–1880, buffalo soldiers pursued and helped to contain Chief Victorio and his Apache followers. From 1885–1886, their mission was to capture Geronimo and the Chiricahua Apaches who were with him.

Buffalo soldiers suffered racial discrimination, receiving inferior equipment and lower pay than white soldiers. However, they served with valor and distinction. At least 10 of them earned the Congressional Medal of Honor for bravery through their service in Arizona Territory.

Bullhead City

One of the fast-growing Colorado River communities is Bullhead City in Mohave County. Incorporated in 1984, it now is home to nearly 30,000 residents. Water sports enthusiasts find Bullhead City a fine place to enjoy the river, the lakes, and the sunshine. Perhaps its most powerful draw is its location across the Colorado from Laughlin, Nevada, a popular gambling and resort city. Bullhead City got its name from Bullhead Rock, now mostly submerged in nearby Lake Mohave, impounded by Davis Dam.

Butterfield Overland Mail

(SEE ALSO JACKASS MAIL) John Butterfield launched his Butterfield Overland Mail line in September 1858. It traversed some 2,700 miles, starting from St. Louis, dipping down through Texas to El Paso and across Arizona, through Tucson and Fort Yuma, to southern California and up the coast to San Francisco. Concord stage coaches and the smaller Celerity wagon were used for the 25-day trek. Stage stations were set up about every 20 miles.

Apache raiders were a constant threat during the two-and-a-half year operation of the line through Arizona. The outbreak of the Civil War and the advent of the faster Pony Express caused the route to be shifted northward, and thus shortened, in March 1861. But by that time, more than a hundred Americans and half a hundred Mexicans had lost their lives to raiders while they were passengers on the line.

The Butterfield experiment was instrumental in focusing the eyes of the nation on little-known Arizona and hastened the time of its settlement.

Cacti

"Where the bold saguaros raise their arms on high . . ." begins the Arizona State University *Alma Mater*. A cactus silhouetted against a mountain and a blazing desert sunset; these are images closely associated with Arizona. Cacti, like other native Arizonans, have found ways to survive in land with searing summer temperatures and little rainfall.

Native cactus plants are not found in Europe, Africa, or Australia. Since scientists have discovered only two fossils so far, we don't know much about early cacti. The oldest, from about 50 million to 65 million years ago, was found in Utah. The other, a 2-million-year-old specimen, came from Arizona. Both were early forms of prickly pear.

Cacti adapt to the dry climate in several ways. Their roots grow very close to the surface, to quickly collect even the smallest bit of moisture that comes their way. Instead of leaves, they have hard spines or thorns. Their green stems produce food for the plant and lose less water than leaves would because of a waxy coating.

Many animals and birds use cacti for food and for protected places to raise their young. Arizona's Indians have long used their fruit and stems for food and medicine. The brightly colored flowers of many varieties usually can be seen throughout the deserts from mid-April through August. Depending on the amount of November–December rainfall and

Prickly pear cactus. Illustration by Robert Williamson.

winter frosts, some spring blooms are more spectacular than others.

Arizona and federal laws prohibit removing, disturbing or destroying any cactus on public lands. Some cacti commonly seen are hedgehogs, barrels, pincushions, cholla, and Arizona Queen-of-the-Night (night-blooming *Cereus*). Some common spiny desert plants that *are not* in the cactus family are agaves, yuccas, Joshua trees and ocotillos. More interesting plants you will see in the desert are:

Teddybear cholla (*Opuntia bigelovii*). Cholla are related to prickly pears. There are many types of cholla in the Arizona deserts, but this species is one type people call "jumping cactus." They don't really jump, but their joints, densely covered with fine, golden, barbed spines, detach easily from the plant when a passerby brushes them even slightly. A hiker would swear the cactus jumped on him and fastened itself firmly into his skin. Some of the spines get so firmly implanted, it takes pliers to get them out! So the teddybear cholla is one plant you don't want to cuddle up with.

Organ Pipe Cactus (*Lemaireocereus thurberi*). The many stems of this rare plant rise from the ground 5–25 feet, and the whole cactus grows several feet in diameter. The lavender-white flowers open only at night in May, June and July. The edible red fruit is about the size of a small plum. Organ Pipe Cactus National Monument was established in southwestern Arizona to preserve these plants, which also grow in northern Mexico.

Parry's Century Plant (*Agave parryi*). Century plants are in the agave family. This one has grayish-green leaves with hooked spines along the edges. They grow up to 20 inches long. The plant lives for 25–35 years, not a century, before sending up a single flower stalk. These can grow as much as a foot in one day and reach 18–20 feet in height. The reddish-orange buds turn into yellow flowers. Once the seeds are set, the plant dies. Agave hearts may be roasted, mashed, fermented, and distilled to make mescal and tequila liquors.

Prickly Pear Cactus (Genus *Opuntia*, many species). The large, paddle-shaped pads of these plants may look like leaves, but they are actually modified stems. Large, sharp spines grow from the pads, and surrounding each spine is a cluster of fine, barbed spines, yellow or red in color, called *glochids*. The barbs make them difficult to remove if you get them in your skin. In spring, prickly pears grow brilliantly colored red, yellow, orange or purplish flowers, which later turn into red or purple edible fruit called *tunas*. This fruit is used to make syrup, candy, jelly, soups, stews and salad dressing. You can also cook and eat the pads, called *nopalitos*.

Saguaro (*Carnegiea gigantea*). These are the largest cacti in the United States and are only found in the Sonoran Desert, in Arizona and Mexico. Occasionally they grow as high as 50–60 feet in wind-protected valleys, and can weigh up to 12 tons. Saguaros may live for 200–300 years, although they lack the tree-type rings that would make exact dating possible. They develop their first "arms" after about 75 years and a few have been seen to grow as many as 50 before they die. The waxy creamy-white saguaro blossoms (Arizona's state flower) bloom for the first time when the cactus is about 25–50 years old. They can be seen in May and June. The brilliant red fruit ripens in July. Tohono O'odham and Akimel O'odham people harvest them. They eat them raw or make syrup or jelly. The juice can also be fermented into a wine used for ceremonies celebrating the coming of summer rains.

Calendar of Events

(SEE ALSO FAIRS AND FESTIVALS)
Here is a sampling of the many events held each month throughout the state:

January

Alpine—*Sled Dog Races at Williams Valley Winter Recreation Area.*

Bullhead City—*PRCA Turquoise Circuit Rodeo.*

Casa Grande—*Arizona Old-Time Fiddlers Jam and Country Store Bazaar and Car Show at Pinal County Fairgrounds.*

Mesa—*High Noon's Wild West Collector's Show and Auction at Centennial Hall.*

Phoenix—*Arizona National Boat Show and Fishing Expo at Bank One Ballpark; Fiesta Bowl Parade.*

Quartzsite—*Events throughout January and February: Prospector's Panorama; Tyson Wells Rock/Gem/Mineral Show; Hi Jolly Daze; Hobby, Craft and Gem Show; Rock and Roll Classic Car Show; Main Event; Sports, Vacation and RV Show; and Pow Wow, Gem and Mineral Show—most at Main Event Rodeo Grounds.*

Scottsdale—*Barrett-Jackson Auction at WestWorld, world's largest antique/ classic car auction; Jaycee's Parada Del Sol Rodeo Parade; Phoenix Open at Tournament Players Club of Scottsdale; Professional Golfers Association Tour event; Arizona Sun Country Circuit Quarter Horse Show at WestWorld.*

Superior—*Australia Day at Boyce Thompson Arboretum.*

Tempe—*Tostitos Fiesta Bowl Football Classic at Sun Devil Stadium.*

Tucson—*Doubletree Copperbowl Tennis Open at Randolph Tennis Center.*

Willcox—*Wings Over Willcox Sandhill Crane Celebration.*

February

Avondale—*SKOAL Bandit Racing Copper World Classic at Phoenix International Raceway.*

Buckeye—*Helz-A-Poppin' Senior Pro Rodeo*

Florence—*Tour of Historic Florence.*

Laveen—*Old Fashioned BBQ and Laveen Country Challenge Bike Tour.*

Phoenix—*Native American Hoop Dance Championship at Heard Museum.*

Safford—*Oldtime Fiddlers' Contest at Graham county Fairgrounds.*

Salome—*Great Arizona Outback Chili Cook-Off at Indian Hills Airpark; Tortilla Toss, Coyote Howling Contest.*

Scottsdale—*All-Arabian Horse Show at WestWorld; Jaycee's Parada Del Sol Rodeo Week.*

Tucson—*Gem & Mineral Show; La Fiesta de los Vaqueros at Tucson Rodeo Grounds; America's largest PRCA rodeo; Chrysler Classic at Omni Tucson National Golf Resort and Spa; Touchstone Energy Tucson Open*

Calendar of Events continued

at Omni Tucson National Golf Resort and Spa—PGA Tour event.

Yuma—"An Evening Under Western Skies" at Territorial Prison State Historic Park; Jaycee's Silver Spur Rodeo Parade and Rodeo.

March

Cottonwood—Verde Valley Gem and Mineral Show at Mingus Union High School.

Globe/Miami—Copper Dust Stampede Rodeo and Parade at Gila County Fairgrounds.

Mesa—Cox Communications Air Show Spectacular at Williams Gateway Airport; Chicago Fest at the corner of Main and Macdonald Streets.

Phoenix—Celebrity Golf Tournament at Arizona Biltmore; Indy Racing League at Phoenix International Raceway; Standard Register Ping LPGA Tour Event at Legacy Golf Course.

Picacho Peak—Civil War Battle Re-enactment at Picacho Peak State Park.

Scottsdale—AKC Dog Show and Obedience at WestWorld; Franklin Templeton Tennis Classic presented by U.S. West at Scottsdale Princess Resort; Association of Tennis Professionals (ATP) Tour tournament; The Tradition at Desert Mountain presented by Countrywide, a Senior PGA Tour championship.

Tucson—LPGA Welch's/Circle K Championship at Randolph North Golf Course.

Window Rock—Woozhchiid Pro-Indian Rodeo at Fairgrounds.

April

Bylas—Mount Turnbull Rodeo; all-Indian rodeo.

Chandler—Gila River Casino Lakefest at Firebird International Raceway; hydroplane races.

Lake Havasu City—Western Outdoor Bass Tournament at Windsor Beach in Lake Havasu State Park.

Mesa—Jesus the Christ Easter Pageant at Arizona (Mormon) Temple Gardens; largest annual Easter pageant in the world.

Phoenix—Sunday on Central from McDowell to Osborn Roads.

Scottsdale—PRCA Professional Rodeo Series at Rawhide; Xerox Southwest Salsa Challenge at Scottsdale Stadium.

Tempe—ASU Spring Competition Pow Wow; Native American dance competition.

Tucson—Yaqui Easter Lenten Ceremony at Old Pascua Village.

Winslow—Easter Egg Hunt at City Park.

May

Jerome—Paseo de Casas; historic Victorian home and public buildings tour.

Payson—PRCA Spring Rodeo at the Rodeo Grounds; world championship cowboys.

Tucson—Allstate Celebrity Golf and Tennis Classic at Randolph Tennis Center; NASCAR Winston Racing Series Season at Tucson Raceway Park, Saturday nights through October.

Williams—Rendezvous Days; re-enacts reunion of Mountain Men, black powder shoot.

June

Flagstaff—Pine Country Pro Rodeo at Coconino County Fairgrounds.

Sonoita—Quarter Horse Show at the Santa Cruz County Fairgrounds.

Springerville/Eagar/Greer—Cowboy Golf on the Range and Highland Valley Western Art Show and Sale at Aspen Meadows Lodge (golfers must play on horseback and may use cow patties for tees).

July

Ajo—Fourth of July at Ajo Plaza.

Benson—Fourth of July Celebration at Lions Park.

Cave Creek—July 3rd Fireworks Extravaganza.

Calendar of Events *continued*

Chloride—Old-Fashioned Fourth of July BBQ and Fireworks Display at City Park.
Clarkdale—Starlight Tours on the Verde Canyon Railroad.
Eagar/Springerville—Round Valley Western July Fourth Celebration.
Flagstaff—Fourth of July Community Parade in historic downtown.
Florence—Fourth of July Festivities by Florence Community Services.
Fredonia—Old Fashioned Fourth.
Gila Bend—Fourth of July Celebration at the High School Football Field.
Glendale—Hometown Fourth of July at Community College Stadium, F-16 flyover.
Holbrook—Fourth of July; BBQ at the Fire Station.
Lake Havasu City— Independence Day Fireworks Display at Spectator Point.
Overgaard—Fourth of July at Tall Timbers Navajo County Park.
Page—Old-Fashioned Fourth at City Park; fireworks over Lake Powell.
Parker—Fireworks Over the River at Parker Strip.
Payson—Family Fun Fourth and Community BBQ at Green Valley Park and High School.
Phoenix—Fabulous Phoenix Fourth at Wesley Bolin Plaza.
Prescott—Indian Art Market at Sharlot Hall Museum (attracts artists from all over the Southwest).
Quartzsite—Fourth of July Celebration in Town Park.
Salome—Fourth of July Picnic and Fireworks at La Paz County Centennial Park.
San Carlos—Indian Festival at San Carlos Lake; bass fishing tournament.
Sedona— Fourth of July Fireworks at Lion's Park.
Sierra Vista—Fourth of July Celebration at Veterans Memorial Park, Army Band Concert.
Taylor—July Fourth Celebration; firing of the anvil, pancake breakfast, BBQ, rodeo.
Tempe—12 News Volvo Fourth of July Fireworks Spectacular presented by Kiwanis Club and City of Tempe; Military Warbird Fly-Bys.
Tombstone—Fireworks by Tombstone Lion's Club.
Tucson—Tucson's Old-Fashioned Fourth of July Celebration.
Whiteriver—Fourth of July Celebration.
Wickenburg—Fireworks and Family Fun.
Williams—Main Street Celebration and Independence Day Fireworks (claims to be northern Arizona's most spectacular fireworks display).
Yuma—Fourth of July Celebration at Yuma County Fairgrounds.

August
Bullhead City—Hualapai Mountain Park Arts and Crafts at Hualapai Mountain Lodge.
Douglas—Arizona Junior Rodeo Association Rodeo.
Payson—World's Oldest Continuous Rodeo.

September
Mammoth—Chili-Salsa Cook-Off, red and green chili and salsa tasting.
Payson—State Championship Old-time Fiddlers Contest at Rumsey Park, fiddlers aged 6–86, cowboy poets, Irish step-dancers.
Sonoita—Labor Day Rodeo at Santa Cruz County Fairgrounds.
Williams—Labor Day PRCA Rodeo.

October
Bisbee—Gem and Mineral Show at Convention Center; Haunted Mine Tour at Copper Queen Mine.
Kingman—Kingman Auto and Airshow at Kingman Airport and Industrial Park; Mohave County Gem-stoner Gemfest.
Lake Havasu City—Advantage Boat

Calendar of Events *continued*

Regatta; Relics and Rods Run to the Sun at London Bridge Resort.

Mesa—Copperstate Regional EAA Fly In at Williams Gateway Airport (national and regional aerobatic stars).

Parker—Parker Indian Rodeo Association Junior Rodeo.

Phoenix—Boo! At the Zoo at Phoenix Zoo.

Scottsdale—Indian National Finals Rodeo at WestWorld.

Sedona—Sculpture Walk at Los Abrigados Resort.

Sierra Vista—Art in the Park at Veterans Memorial Park; International air show at Fort Huachuca, aerobatic performances.

Tucson—Desert Thunder Pro Rodeo at Tucson Rodeo Grounds.

Williams/Holbrook—Cruise the Route 66, car show and run.

Yuma—Yuma Regional Medical Center Western Dance at County Fairgrounds.

November

Chandler—NHRA World Series of Drag Racing at Firebird International Raceway.

Florence—Florence Junior Parada at Charles Whitlow Rodeo Arena (world's oldest continuous junior rodeo).

Fountain Hills—Parada de Los Cerros/ Parade of the Hills on Saguaro Blvd.; Thanksgiving Day parade.

Mesa—Arizona Mormon Temple Christmas Lighting, through end of December.

Parker—Parker Rodeo at Western Park; Holiday Lighted Boat Parade.

Prescott—Arizona's Largest Gingerbread Village at Prescott Resort, through the first of January.

Safford—Cowboy Christmas Arts and Crafts Show at National Guard Armory.

Scottsdale—Cox Communications Thunderbird Balloon Classic at West World, 130 hot air balloons; Arabian Horse Show at WestWorld; The Celebrity at Grayhawk; world-class golf, hosted by Clint Black; Mitsubishi Motors Invitational Pro Am; LPGA Tour event.

Sedona—Red Rock Fantasy of Lights at Los Abrigados Resort, through the middle of January.

Tucson—Holiday Scene Display at Old Pima County Courthouse.

Williams—Mountain Village Holiday, through January 1.

Winslow—Christmas Parade, 54th year of "Arizona's largest Christmas parade."

December

Ajo—Christmas Outdoor Lighting Contest and Community Christmas Concert.

Bullhead City—Christmas Parade of Lights at Lake Mohave.

Canyon Lake—Nautical Parade of Lights at Canyon Lake Marina.

Cottonwood—Christmas Parade; Chocolate Lovers Dessert Walk in Historic Old Town.

Florence—Courthouse Lighting at historic Victorian Courthouse.

Fountain Hills—Luminaria Lighting along Main Street.

Globe—Christmas Light Parade in historic downtown.

Holbrook—Parade of Lights at Historic Courthouse.

Kingman—Very Merry Parade of Lights.

Lake Havasu City—Boat Parade of Lights at Bridgewater Channel.

Phoenix—Pueblo Grande Indian Market at South Mountain Park Activity Center; Fiesta of Light Electric Parade on Central Avenue; Las Noche de las Luminarias at Desert Botanical Gardens; Zoo Lights at Phoenix Zoo, through January.

Prescott—AZ Christmas Parade and Courthouse Lighting Ceremony.

Show Low—Christmas Light Parade.

Springerville—Electric Light Parade.

Taylor—Winter Wunderland at Freeman Park.

Caliche

Caliche The dry Sonoran Desert environment produces a distinctive deposit called *caliche* (pronounced ka-LEE-chee) that can cover the soil for miles. In many areas the caliche is just under the surface of a thin layer of topsoil. It is formed by evaporation of water and leaves behind many minerals. In this case the soil particles are cemented together by calcium carbonate, or lime. The lime makes the ground appear to be covered with patches of snow. The caliche layer varies from a few inches to several feet thick. The texture can be brittle and crumbly, big hard lumps mixed with soil, or continuous like concrete. Caliche soils are often hard as rock, making root growth difficult or impossible for many plants. Caliche can form from natural drainage, the evaporation of rainwater, or in farmlands that have been irrigated for a long time. Caliche is not a geologic deposit.

Camel Experiment

Lieutenant Edward Beale led an expedition westward along the 35th parallel (the route of today's Interstate 40 across northern Arizona) in 1857 with two objectives: to build a wagon road to California, and to experiment with camels as a means of carrying mail and freight across the high desert. Along the way Lieutenant Beale wrote in his journal: "They [the camels] pack water for others four days under a hot sun and never need a drop. They subsist on greasewood and other worthless shrubs. . . . I look forward to the day when every mail route across the continent will be conducted . . . with this economical and noble brute."

Alas, the camels, brought from the Near East, proved unworkable. They panicked the horses and mules, smelled terrible, were feisty and irritable, and only foreign camel drivers could

Monument to camel driver Hi Jolly. Courtesy Southwest Studies, Scottsdale Community College

manage them. The experiment was called off and the camels released to roam in the desert, where their descendants were occasionally seen for several decades.

A Syrian camel driver named Hadji Ali (whom the Americans called "Hi Jolly") became a pioneer legend, remaining in Arizona Territory to become a prospector and an army scout. He died at Quartzsite, 19 miles east of Ehrenberg, in 1903. Visitors often come to view his grave, marked by a stone pyramid topped with a camel made of copper.

Camping (SEE ALSO FISH AND FISHING; FORESTS; LAKES; NATIONAL PARKS AND MONUMENTS; OUTDOOR RECREATION; STATE PARKS; TOURISM)

Whether you like to crawl into a sleeping bag on a grassy meadow or relax in a luxurious recreational vehicle, Arizona offers an amazing variety of camping experiences. Many out-of-state outdoor adventurers think of camping in terms of tall pines and mountain lakes, which Arizona has in abundance, but the state's desert wildernesses, canyons, and foothills also offer the camper unforgettable pleasures.

No serious camper should be without Jim Tallon's book, *Arizona's*

144 Best Campgrounds, a compilation of wonderful camping sites in every part of the state. Published in 1996 by Arizona Highways Books and edited by Wesley Holden, it literally pushes the reader out of his easy chair and onto the road to adventures far from city congestion. Tallon's criteria include scenic beauty, accessibility, nearby fishing and boating, and such mundane amenities as showers, toilets, and waste disposal. A few of Tallon's choices:

Northeast.

Wahweap Campground. This site is on the shore of Lake Powell, reachable on U.S. Route 89. Impounded by Glen Canyon Dam, the 180-mile-long lake offers facilities for all kinds of boats (including a favorite, houseboats), and excellent fishing. The scenery is gorgeous, the weather at 3,800 feet altitude is pleasant all year long, and the marina sells everything you might need.

North Central.

White Horse Lake Campground. A sparkling blue lake in a setting of tall pines, at 6,600 feet above sea level, makes this campsite irresistible. It's 20 miles southeast of Williams in Coconino County. Boating, fishing, a

Camping Facilities

	Days limit	Fee	Units	Water	Waste Disp.	Restrooms
Bonita Canyon	14	Yes	26	Yes	No	Yes
Buckskin Mountain	14	Yes	83	Yes	Yes	Yes
Canyon Point	14 (May-Sep)	Yes	117	Yes	Yes	Yes
Hawley Lake	None	Yes	99	Yes	No	Yes
Organ Pipe Cactus	14	Yes	200	Yes	Yes	Yes
Patagonia Lake	15	Yes	115	Yes	Yes	Yes
Wahweap	14	Yes	180	Yes	Yes	Yes
Whitehorse Lake	14 (May-Oct)	Yes	85	Yes	No	Yes
White Tank	14 (Nov-Apr)	Yes	40	Yes	No	Yes

well-equipped store, a base for hiking, and abundant wildlife are all here. Colorful Sycamore Canyon, often called Arizona's "Little Grand Canyon," is a natural wonder not far to the east of the camping area.

Mogollon Rim Country.
Canyon Point Campground. Three paved loop roads wind among towering ponderosa to 117 well-spaced-out camp sites. The facility is open May–September, and the 7,600-foot elevation on top of the Mogollon Rim assures comfortable summer temperatures. Facilities at this model campground include table-bench units, fire pits, safe water, waste disposal, rest rooms and showers. For fisher people, Woods Canyon, Willow Springs, and Black Canyon Lakes are a 15 minute drive. For those who forgot to bring "everything except the kitchen sink," the mountain community of Forest Lake Estates is just 2 miles down the road where there are a gas station, convenience store and steak house. In addition to countless back country roads and dramatic Rim Country vistas, expect to see elk and deer. Keep your camera handy! Canyon Point is a 2¹/₂-hour drive northeast of Phoenix via State Route 87 to Payson and State Route 260 eastward to the top of the Rim.

Colorado River Country.
Buckskin Mountain State Park. This campground is in the desert foothills of the Buckskin Mountains, 11 miles north of Parker on the Colorado River. It is well equipped

with all the amenities, even an arcade for children. Many species of waterfowl nest nearby, and the fish include largemouth and striped bass, and catfish. Boating enthusiasts flock here and there is outdoor fun for everyone.

South Central.
White Tank Regional Park. Not far west of Phoenix in the White Tank Mountains, this campground is reachable in less than an hour from the big city. This is a Sonoran Desert site, most enjoyable in fall, winter, and spring. Cactus wrens, Gambel's quail, and other lowland birds may interrupt the peace and quiet of this hideaway, and desert animals are often seen.

Looking Back

Dec. 21, 1967

The deepest snowfall, 91 inches, was recorded at Hawley Lake.

White Mountains.
Hawley Lake Campground. Dress warmly for your overnight stay at Hawley Lake. It sits at 8,500 feet above sea level, and it gets cold, even in summer. Fishing and boating in the 260-acre lake are the big attractions, but the magnificent forest and mountain scenery lure many people. Drive 7 miles east of McNary on State Route 260, then 8 miles south on State Route 473.

South Central.
Patagonia Lake State Park. Halfway between Nogales and Patagonia, off State Route 82, this charming campground is situated on a gentle slope above the lake. You're just a bit above 4,000 feet here, so the weather is temperate all year. There's a sandy beach and a variety of outdoor activity. Five miles to the east is the Patagonia-

Sonoita Creek Preserve, a wildlife sanctuary of the Nature Conservancy. Some 200 species of birds have been spotted there.

Southeast.

Bonita Canyon. This campground is in the Chiricahua National Monument, on the western reaches of the Chiricahua Mountains. It is 30 miles south of Interstate 10 via State Route 186, and offers some of the most spectacular scenery in the Southwest. The "Wonderland of Rocks" is aptly named. Hiking trails are abundant, and so is wildlife. Nearby **Rustler Park,** at 7,000 feet, is another good campground, but you can't get an RV into it, as you can at Bonita Canyon.

Southwest.

Organ Pipe Cactus National Monument. This is an ideal campground for a winter expedition, only 5 miles north of the Mexican border and a mile off State Route 85. This is Sonoran Desert scenery at its best, featuring the rare organ pipe cactus, the elephant 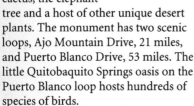 tree and a host of other unique desert plants. The monument has two scenic loops, Ajo Mountain Drive, 21 miles, and Puerto Blanco Drive, 53 miles. The little Quitobaquito Springs oasis on the Puerto Blanco loop hosts hundreds of species of birds.

Canyon de Chelly

One of Arizona's most popular tourist attractions is Canyon de Chelly (pronounced duh shay) near Chinle in Apache County. There are many prehistoric cliff dwellings in this national monument, which is composed of three deep gorges, 15 miles long: Canyon del Muerto, Canyon de Chelly, and Monument Canyon.

The site was occupied by the ancients for more than a thousand years before the Navajos came. The chasms have been carved out of sandstone, and its walls are higher than New York skyscrapers. In almost every niche is a prehistoric ruin, some small and others seemingly as large as castles.

Best known of the well-preserved cliff dwellings is White House, named for the white plaster, which has survived the centuries. There is a hiking trail into White House, the only ruins you can visit without a guide. All-day and half-day four-wheel-drive tours are also available.

Navajo legends are woven around Spider Rock, an 800-foot high monolith. This is the fabled home of Spider Woman. Navajo mothers tell their children that Spider Woman will come and carry them to her home atop the rocky tower if they misbehave.

The Capital on Wheels

The capital of Arizona Territory moved about so frequently during the mid- to late-1800s that map makers were hard pressed to keep up with it. It was first established in the early spring of 1864 at Fort Whipple, which had recently been established at Chino Valley, 15 miles north of present-day Prescott. Within three months, both the fort and the seat of government were moved south to Granite Creek and the town of Prescott soon sprang up there.

In 1867, Pima County legislators mustered enough political clout to have the capital moved to Tucson, where it remained until it was once again moved to Prescott in 1877. The

First Arizona Territory officers, 1864. Governor John Goodwin is seated, second from left. Courtesy Southwest Studies, Scottsdale Community College.

growing importance of the Salt River Valley, coupled with the difficulty of travel by many legislators to either Tucson or Prescott, led to the capital's final journey in 1889, this time to the more centrally located city of Phoenix.

There it has remained ever since, much to the relief of makers of maps.

Casa Grande
Casa Grande, *big house* in Spanish, is the name of a national monument and also of a major city of Pinal County. Casa Grande Ruins National Monument preserves a four-story adobe building and surrounding plaza and other structures. Occupied more than six centuries ago by a Hohokam Indian community, it may have served as an observatory and administrative center. Today it stands, still quite well preserved, near the city of Coolidge

and within a short drive of the city of Casa Grande. More than 200,000 people visit the monument each year.

The modern city of Casa Grande has a population of 23,175 and Coolidge about 8,000. Both are trading centers for surrounding farms and ranches.

Casinos
Since 1992 Indian tribal governments in Arizona have opened gaming casinos throughout the state. Others are in the planning stage. More than 30 gaming sites have been authorized. Those in operation include:

Apache Gold Casino, San Carlos, opened May 1994. San Carlos Apache Tribe.

Blue Water Casino, Parker, opened March 1995. Colorado River Indian Tribes.

Bucky's Casino, Prescott, opened November 1992. Yavapai-Prescott Indian Tribe.

Casino of the Sun, Tucson, opened March 1994. Pascua Yaqui Tribe of Arizona.

Cliff Castle Casino, Camp Verde, opened May 1995. Yavapai-Apache Nation.

Cocopah Casino, Somerton, opened November 1992. Cocopah Indian Tribe.

Desert Diamond Casino, Sells, opened October 1993. Tohono O'odham Nation.

Fort McDowell Gaming Center, near Fountain Hills, opened January 1993. Fort McDowell Mohave-Apaches.

Gila River Vee Quiva, Sacaton, opened June 1994 and **Gila River Wild Horse Pass**, Sacaton, opened May 1995. Gila River Indian Community.

Harrah's Ak-Chin Casino, south of Maricopa, opened December 1994. Ak-Chin Indian Community.

Hon Dah Casino, Whiteriver, opened December 1993. White Mountain Apache Tribe.

Mazatzal Casino, Payson, opened September 1993. Tonto-Apache Tribe.

Paradise Casino, Yuma, opened August 1996. Quechan Indian Tribe.

Spirit Mountain Casino, Needles, CA, opened April 1995. Fort Mohave Indian Tribe.

Central Arizona Project (SEE ALSO DAMS; RIVERS)

For half a century, beginning in the 1920s, Arizona leaders dreamed and labored for a way to bring Colorado River water to Phoenix and Tucson. In 1963, the U.S. Congress approved the massive engineering

Central Arizona Project canal at Picacho. Picacho Peak in background. Photo by James Tallon.

plan called the Central Arizona Project, which would make that dream come true.

Construction of the project began in 1968 north of Parker Dam. Through a series of pumping stations, Colorado River water was lifted and channeled through a tunnel in the Buckskin Mountains, from which it would flow through a 190-mile canal to Phoenix. From there, water would travel another 100-plus miles to the Tucson area.

Phoenix received its first water in 1986, and eventually the aqueduct brought Tucson its share. Some three-fourths of the project's cost is to be repaid by Arizona users and taxpayers.

Although the C.A.P., as it is commonly called, was originally planned as a means of bringing water to Arizona for agricultural use, the high cost of its water has made it too expensive for most farmers. Instead, present C.A.P. water is consumed primarily by urban dwellers.

Chambers of Commerce

The Arizona Department of Commerce, in its 1999 *Arizona Economic Development*

Directory, lists chambers of commerce and economic development organizations in the state. Those of larger cities and organizations are listed here.

Statewide.

American Indian Chamber of Commerce of Arizona, 3620 N. Sixth Ave., Suite 101W, Phoenix 85013

Arizona Association for Economic Development, 4620 E. Elwood St., Suite 13, Phoenix 85040

Arizona Chamber of Commerce, 1221 E. Osborn Road., Suite 100, Phoenix 85014

Arizona Hispanic Chamber of Commerce and Foundation, 2400 N. Central Ave., Suite 303, Phoenix 85004

Arizona Public Service Economic and Community Development Dept., 400 N. Fifth St., Phoenix 85072

Arizona Small Business Development Center Network, 2411 W. 14th St., Room 132, Tempe 85281

Arizona State University Economic Development Department, P.O. Box 871002, Tempe 85287

Northern Arizona University Bureau of Business and Economic Research, P.O. Box 15066, Flagstaff 86011

Salt River Project Economic Development, P.O. Box 52025, Phoenix 85072

U.S. Small Business Administration, 2828 N. Central Ave., Suite 800, Phoenix 85004

University of Arizona Office of Economic Development, P.O. Box 210066, Tucson 85721

Local.

Apache County Economic Security Corp., P.O. Box 767, St. Johns 85936

Bisbee Chamber of Commerce, 7 Main St., Bisbee 85603

Bullhead Area Chamber of Commerce, 1251 Hwy. 95, Bullhead City 86429

Greater Casa Grande Chamber of Commerce, 575 N. Marshall St., Casa Grande 85222

Chandler Chamber of Commerce, 218 N. Arizona Ave., Chandler 85224

Cochise County: Cochise County Office of Economic and Community Development, 1415 W. Melody Lane., Bldg. B, Bisbee 85603

Coolidge Chamber of Commerce, 320 W. Central Ave., Coolidge 85228

Cottonwood Chamber of Commerce, 1010 S. Main St., Cottonwood 86326

Douglas Chamber of Commerce, 1125 Pan American, Douglas 85607

Flagstaff Chamber of Commerce, 101 W. Route 66, Flagstaff 86001

Greater Florence Chamber of Commerce, 291 N. Bailey St., Florence 85232

Gila County Community Development, 714 S. Beeline Hwy, Payson 85541

Gila River Indian Community Econ. Devel. Dept., 315 W. Casa Blanca Road, Sacaton 85247

Gilbert Chamber of Commerce, 202 N. Gilbert Road, Gilbert 85299

Glendale Chamber of Commerce, 7105 N. 59th Ave., Glendale 85311

Greater Globe/Miami Chamber of Commerce, 1360 N. Broad St., Globe 85502

Graham County Chamber of Commerce, 1111 Thatcher Blvd., Safford 85546

Greenlee County Chamber of Commerce, P.O. Box 1237, RR Station, Clifton 85533

Holbrook Chamber of Commerce, 100 E. Arizona St., Holbrook 86025

Kingman Area Chamber of Commerce, 333 W. Andy Devine, Kingman 86402

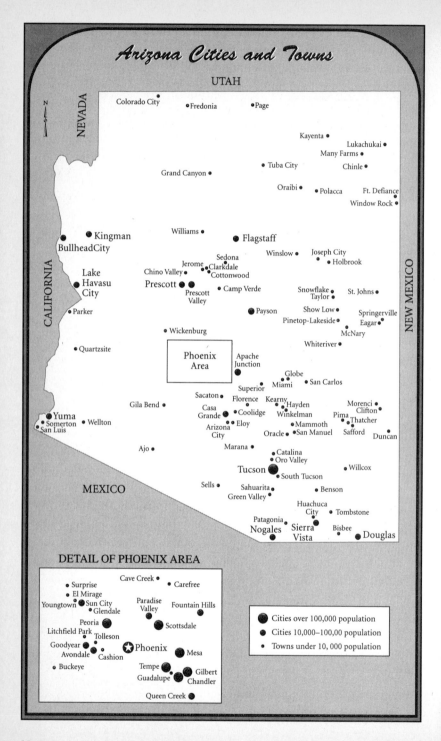

Arizona Cities and Towns

UTAH

NEVADA

CALIFORNIA

NEW MEXICO

MEXICO

Colorado City • Fredonia • Page

Kayenta •
Lukachukai •
Many Farms •
• Tuba City   Chinle •

Grand Canyon •

Oraibi •   • Polacca   Ft. Defiance
                     Window Rock •

• Kingman   Williams •   • Flagstaff
BullheadCity   Winslow • Joseph City
                                    • Holbrook
Lake   Sedona
Havasu   Jerome • Clarkdale
City   Chino Valley • • Cottonwood
• Parker   Prescott •   • Camp Verde   Snowflake • St. Johns •
           Prescott   Taylor •
           Valley   Show Low • Springerville •
• Quartzsite   • Payson   Pinetop-Lakeside • Eagar •
                                         McNary •
           • Wickenburg   Whiteriver •

              Phoenix   Apache
              Area   Junction •
                                Globe •
                             Miami • • San Carlos
                   Sacaton • Superior •
           Gila Bend •   Florence • Kearny • Morenci •
                       Casa   Hayden • Clifton •
• Yuma • Wellton   Grande • • Coolidge Winkelman Pima • Thatcher •
Somerton   • Eloy   • Mammoth Safford •
San Luis   Arizona   Oracle • • San Manuel   Duncan •
                   City
              Ajo •   Marana •
                          • Catalina
                          • Oro Valley
                   Tucson ●   • Willcox
                        ● South Tucson
           Sells • Sahuarita •   • Benson
                  Green Valley •
                          Huachuca
                          City • • Tombstone
                  Patagonia •   Bisbee •
                  Nogales • Sierra   ● Douglas
                          Vista

DETAIL OF PHOENIX AREA

• Surprise   Cave Creek •   • Carefree
• El Mirage
Youngtown • ● Sun City   Paradise
         • Glendale   Valley   Fountain Hills
Peoria ●
Litchfield Park   • Scottsdale
Goodyear • Tolleson
Avondale • ☆ Phoenix
       Cashion   • Mesa
• Buckeye
         Tempe ●
         Guadalupe • • Gilbert
              • Chandler
         Queen Creek •

● Cities over 100,000 population
● Cities 10,000–100,00 population
• Towns under 10, 000 population

Lake Havasu Chamber of Commerce, 314 London Bridge Road, Lake Havasu City 86403

Litchfield Park: Tri-City West Chamber of Commerce, 501 W. Van Buren St., Suite K, Avondale 85323

Marana Chamber of Commerce, P.O. Box 9, Marana 85653

Maricopa County: Western Maricopa Coalition, 9017 N. 57th Drive, Glendale 85302

Mesa Chamber of Commerce, 120 N. Center St., Mesa 85211

Mohave County Economic Development Authority, 3160 Shangri La Drive, Kingman 86401

Navajo County: Arizona North Eastern Economic Development, P.O. Box 487, Holbrook 86025

Navajo Nation Division of Community Development, P.O. Box 1896, Window Rock, AZ, 86515

Nogales/Santa Cruz County Chamber of Commerce, Kino Park, Nogales 85621

Oro Valley: Town of Oro Valley Economic Development, 11000 N. La Canada Drive, Oro Valley 85737

Page-Lake Powell Chamber of Commerce, 644 N. Navajo, Suite C, Page 86040

Parker Area Chamber of Commerce, 1217 California Ave., Parker 85344

Payson: Rim Country Regional Chamber of Commerce, P.O. Box 1380, Payson 85547

Peoria Chamber of Commerce, 8355 W. Peoria Ave., Peoria 85380

Greater Phoenix Chamber of Commerce, 201 N. Central Ave., Suite 2700, Phoenix 85073

Greater Phoenix Convention and Visitors Bureau, 400 E. Van Buren St., Suite 600, Phoenix 85004

Pima County: The Chamber of Northern Pima County, 200 W. Magee Road, Suite 120, Tucson 85704

Pinal County Development Board, 330 E. Butte, Florence 85232

Pinetop/Lakeside Chamber of Commerce, P.O. Box 4220, Pinetop 85935

Prescott Chamber of Commerce, 101 S. Cortez, Prescott 86302

Salt River Pima-Maricopa Indian Community, 10005 E. Osborn Road, Scottsdale 85256

Scottsdale Chamber of Commerce, 7343 Scottsdale Mall, Scottsdale 85251

Sedona-Oak Creek Canyon Chamber of Commerce, P.O. Box 478, Sedona 86339

Show Low Regional Chamber of Commerce, 951 E. Deuce of Clubs, Show Low 85902

Greater Sierra Vista Area Chamber of Commerce, 21 E. Wilcox Drive, Sierra Vista 85635

Superior Chamber of Commerce, P.O. Box 95, Superior 85273

Tempe Chamber of Commerce, 909 E. Apache Blvd., Tempe 85281

Tolleson Chamber of Commerce, 9555 W. Van Buren St., Tolleson 85353

Tombstone Chamber of Commerce, Fourth and Allen, Tombstone 85638

Metropolitan Tucson Convention and Visitors Center, 130 S. Scott Ave., Tucson 85701

Tucson Metropolitan Chamber of Commerce, 465 W. St. Mary's Road, Tucson 85702

Wickenburg Chamber of Commerce, 16 N. Frontier St., Wickenburg 85390

Willcox Chamber of Commerce, 1500 N. Circle l Road, Willcox 85643

Winslow Chamber of Commerce, 300 W. North Road, Winslow 86047

Yuma County Chamber of Commerce, 377 S. Main St., Suite 101, Yuma 85364

Chandler

Dr. Alexander J. Chandler, the first veterinary surgeon in Arizona Territory, bought 80 acres of land south of Mesa from the federal government in 1891. That was the beginning of the Chandler Ranch, which grew to 18,000 acres and was subdivided by Dr. Chandler in 1912. A year later the Hotel San Marcos was opened in the new town of Chandler. It was one of the finest in the Southwest and numbered among its early guests national political, entertainment, and industrial leaders.

Primarily an agricultural town until 1941, the nature of Chandler changed with the opening of Williams Army Air Base. Later known as Williams Air Force Base, it trained many thousands of American and allied jet fighter pilots until military operations were closed down in the mid-1990s. The base is now the home of Arizona State University's East Campus and several other educational and business entities.

Chandler's population has sky-rocketed with the establishment of high-tech industrial plants and other manufacturing operations in recent years. During the past two decades it has grown from 30,000 to an estimated 169,000. Chandler has an excellent performing arts center, museums, golf courses, retirement communities, and shopping malls. Its unique Ostrich Festival in March attracts upwards of 350,000 visitors.

Chiles

What do a summer in the Arizona desert and spicy chile peppers have in common? They're both *hot, hot, hot.* Arizona's favorite seasoning appears in many dishes, from soups to entrees to desserts. Chile peppers are also a common decorative item, such as a big bunch of dried chiles hanging beside the front door, strings of chile pepper lights around windows, or placemat and napkin motifs.

Chiles are the basic flavoring ingredient in Arizona-Sonoran cooking. The plants, native to the Western Hemisphere, have been cultivated for food and medicine since about 5200–3400 B.C., making them one of the oldest crops cultivated in the New World. They are not really peppers, as in salt and pepper. Christopher Columbus (who thought he had landed in India, remember?) named these fiery pods *pimiento*, which is Spanish for the black pepper that Europeans got from East India.

The scientific name for chiles is *Capsicum*, a genus in the nightshade family that includes tomatoes, potatoes, petunias, and tobacco. There are many varieties, including bell, ancho, jalapeño, cayenne, chiltepin, Thai, and habañero peppers. What makes a chile pungent, or hot, is a substance called capsaicin. The plant's genetics and the conditions in which it grows also determine how hot the chiles are.

A common way to measure chile potency is the Scoville Organoleptic Test. Bell peppers have no Scoville Heat Units (and no capsaicin). Jalapeños have 2,500–50,000 Scoville Units. Habañeros have the highest pungency level, with 200,000–577,000 Units! The *Guinness Book of World Records* calls the habañero "Red Savina" the hottest chile pepper in the world, at over 577,000 Scoville Units.

A red chile is not necessarily hotter than a yellow or green one. The smallest and thinnest peppers are the hottest ones, whatever their color. Those who eat chiles frequently become immune

When Tucson changed hands during the Civil War, from Union to Confederate and back again, residents had trouble switching loyalties. From What Is Arizona Really Like? *by Reg Manning.*

to the pain they can cause, but the first-time taster may find himself in severe distress. Don't try to put out the fire in your mouth with water— capsaicin is not water-soluble. Something with fat in it, like whole milk or a soft flour tortilla, will help douse the flames.

So why eat hot peppers if they cause such pain? When capsaicin stimulates nerves in your mouth, the brain releases substances that produce a mild euphoria, giving "chile-heads" a "hot pepper high." And which is it: "chile" or "chili"? Connoisseurs generally define "chili" as a dish, such as chili con carne, that uses chile peppers with meat; beans are optional. "Chile" refers to the pods themselves or the plants on which they grow.

Civil War in Arizona

Confederate Captain Sherod Hunter led his cavalry troop into Tucson on Feb. 28, 1862, and ran the Stars and Bars up a flagpole, to the cheers of the mostly pro-Southern populace. Not long thereafter, a much larger Union force known as the California Column, commanded by Col. James Carleton, crossed the Colorado River into Arizona and pressed eastward along the Gila River in an effort to drive the Confederates back into Texas.

At Stanwix Station, 80 miles east of Fort Yuma, a detachment of Hunter's troops engaged the Californians. In that skirmish a Union private, William Semmilrogge, became the first man wounded in Arizona Civil War action. On April 15, in what is usually termed the westernmost battle of the war, reconnaissance units from the opposing forces clashed at Picacho Peak, 40 miles north of Tucson. Three Californians were killed, and three of Hunter's men were captured. With the California Column only a few days away, Hunter wisely gave up Tucson and headed back to Texas, thus ending Civil War action in Arizona. There is now a state park at Picacho Peak.

Clifton

The county seat of Greenlee County, Clifton, is in southeastern Arizona near the New Mexico border. The San Francisco River, a tributary of the Gila, flows near the town and has been known to flood its streets on rare occasions. Copper was discovered in the area in 1865 and copper mining has been the economic foundation of Clifton and nearby Morenci since 1872, when the first mining operations began.

Phelps Dodge Corporation began excavating an open-pit mine, one of the largest in the nation, in the mid-1930s. In addition to copper, turquoise, azurite, and other semi-precious gemstones are found here.

Clifton's population is estimated at 3,000.

Climate (*SEE ALSO* THE FIVE C'S; GEOGRAPHY)

Arizona's climate is as diverse as its geography. The temperature may top 100°F in the southern deserts during the same month when it dips below freezing in the mountains. Some areas receive less than 3 inches of annual precipitation, while others average as much as 35 inches of rain and snow. Indeed, snowfall has been known to exceed 8 feet during some mountain winters.

Sunshiny days are the rule throughout the state. Phoenix and Tucson are sunny more than 300 days a year, and many other communities enjoy the same clear weather.

Arizona has, as a rule, two rainy seasons, in winter and mid-to-late summer. Winter rains are more steady, while summer often brings thunderstorms, spectacular lightning displays, and winds gusting up to 50 miles per hour. Throughout the state, humidity is usually very low. For this reason, temperatures over 100°F are more comfortable than 80s in areas of humid weather. The dry air of both mountains and deserts often results in temperature variations of 30°F or more in a single day.

Climate Zones. Arizona has three principal climate zones: **low desert,** essentially in the south central to southwestern third of the state, where temperatures range from an average

Looking Back

Jan. 7, 1971

The coldest day ever in Arizona was −40°F at Hawley Lake.

high of more than 100°F. in July to 60°F. in January, and precipitation is below 10 inches annually; **high desert and foothills,** including much of the northern third of the state and uplands in other areas, with average high temperatures in the low 90s in summer and 50s in winter; and **mountains,** including the San Francisco Peaks, White Mountains and Chiricahuas, with average high temperatures in the upper 70s in summer and 40s in winter. The "sky islands," mountains rising abruptly from the low desert, provide southern Arizona residents relief from summer heat and snow sports in winter.

Precipitation. The average annual precipitation in all of Arizona is about 13 inches. Yuma, on the Colorado River in the southwest corner of the state, averages some 3 inches, while McNary, in the White Mountains, averages 40 inches, with much of that in snowfall. Between those extremes, Flagstaff has 18 inches, Tucson has a little over 10 inches, and Phoenix 7.5 inches.

El Niño and La Niña. The Pacific Ocean phenomena of El Niño and La Niña, caused by a shift in the position of cold and warm ocean waters, are major determinants of Arizona's weather. El Niño ruled during the winter of 1997 through the summer of 1998 and brought higher than average levels of precipitation throughout the state. By 1999, La Niña was causing high pressure systems that steered moisture well north of the state, and Arizona's precipitation

(Continued on page 54)

Normal Temperature (F) and Precipitation (inches)

	Phoenix elev. 1,110 ft.	Flagstaff elev. 7,006 ft.	Tucson elev. 2,584 ft.
JANUARY			
Maximum	65.9	42.2	63.9
Minimum	41.2	15.2	38.6
Rainfall	0.67	2.04	0.87
Snowfall	0	20.5	0.3
FEBRUARY			
Maximum	70.7	45.3	67.8
Minimum	44.7	17.7	41.0
Rainfall	0.68	2.09	0.7
Snowfall	0	19.0	0.3
MARCH			
Maximum	75.5	49.2	72..8
Minimum	48.8	21.3	44.6
Rainfall	0.88	2.55	0.72
Snowfall	0	24.4	0.3
APRIL			
Maximum	84.5	57.8	81.2
Minimum	55.3	26.7	50.4
Rainfall	0.22	1.48	0.3
Snowfall	0	11.9	0.1
MAY			
Maximum	93.6	67.4	89.8
Minimum	63.9	33.3	58.0
Rainfall	0.12	0.72	0.18
Snowfall	0	1.9	0
JUNE			
Maximum	103.5	78.2	99.6
Minimum	72.9	41.4	67.9
Rainfall	0.13	0.4	0.2
Snowfall	0	0	0
JULY			
Maximum	105.9	81.9	99.4
Minimum	81.0	50.5	73.6
Rainfall	0.83	2.78	2.37
Snowfall	0	0	0
AUGUST			
Maximum	103.7	79.3	96.8
Minimum	79.2	48.9	72.1
Rainfall	0.96	2.75	2.19
Snowfall	0	0	0
SEPTEMBER			
Maximum	98.3	73.2	93.3
Minimum	72.8	41.2	67.5
Rainfall	0.86	2.03	1.67
Snowfall	0	0	0

	Phoenix elev. 1,110 ft.	Flagstaff elev. 7,006 ft.	Tucson elev. 2,584 ft.
OCTOBER			
Maximum	88.1	63.4	84.3
Minimum	60.8	31.0	56.6
Rainfall	0.65	1.61	1.06
Snowfall	0	2.5	0
NOVEMBER			
Maximum	74.9	51.1	72.7
Minimum	48.9	22.4	45.6
Rainfall	0.66	1.95	0.67
Snowfall	0	10.7	0
DECEMBER			
Maximum	66.2	43.3	64.3
Minimum	41.8	15.8	39.8
Rainfall	1.0	2.4	1.07
Snowfall	0	17.8	0.4
YEAR			
Maximum	85.9	61.0	82.2
Minimum	59.3	30.4	54.6
Normal number of days with maximum temperature above 90°	168.4	3.9	0
Normal number of days with minimum temperature below 32°	7.7	209.7	7.7
Possible sunshine, annual average	86%	78%	85%
Rainfall, annual average	7.66	22.8	12.0
Snowfall, annual average	0	108.8	1.4

(Continued from page 52)
charts were among the driest on record. Phoenix recorded more than 100 days without measurable rain and temperatures 10 degrees above normal during that period.

The Monsoon Season. Television weather analysts make much of the "monsoons" of mid- to late summer in the deserts. They announce that the "Monsoon Season" has begun when the average daily dew point exceeds 55°F for three days in a row. Unlike the torrential rains of south Asia, however, these are periods when rain clouds move up from Mexico or from the Pacific and raise the desert humidity to uncomfortable levels. This condition

Monsoon

The word "monsoon" brings to mind pictures of torrential tropical rains, but Arizonans have their own version. Summer rains, often following dust storms, make the Arizona variety of monsoon. Technically, the monsoon season begins in Arizona when the average daily dew point is 55 degrees or higher for three days in a row.

The arrival of moist air from the Gulf of California in early July sets off thunder showers, usually in the late afternoon. The monsoon season lasts about 55 days on average, and may produce as much as 9 inches of rain during that period. However, the average Arizona monsoon rainfall is about 3 inches. ✳

frequently results in late afternoon dust storms and sudden, pelting rains. Fierce winds associated with these storms often cause heavy damage. The high humidity renders evaporative coolers unable to lower temperatures inside homes and offices; thus refrigerated air conditioning is the cooling system of choice for most desert dwellers.

Air Quality. The more concentrated the population, the worse the air quality. The Phoenix area has the most serious problem, with hundreds of thousands of automobiles polluting the air at peak travel times. Mostly calm winds don't help, and a brown cloud is usually present over the Salt River Valley, especially during the winter months. Tucson suffers occasional periods of serious air pollution as well.

Phoenix has another problem: humidity. The many square miles of concrete, the many thousands of swimming pools and artificial lakes, and the many lawns and golf courses have measurably increased humidity and raised temperatures in Arizona's largest metropolitan area during recent decades.

Most cities and towns outside Maricopa and Pima counties have less troublesome air quality problems, with the result that automobile owners living there are not required by state law to have annual vehicle emission tests.

Cochise

Geronimo overshadows Chief Cochise in the minds of most Southwest history buffs, but Cochise will always be remembered as one of the towering figures of early Arizona tradition. Cochise, chief of the Chiricahua Apaches, was Geronimo's leader and mentor and was regarded as a wise and generally friendly chief until 1861, when a young army lieutenant named George Bascom violated a truce and captured him. Cochise escaped with three bullets in his body, and from that day until his death in 1874 he waged bloody war on white settlers in southeastern Arizona.

"The Bascom Affair," as the lieutenant's perfidy is known, signaled the beginning of 25 years of the Apache Wars.

Although he was hated and feared by his many victims, Cochise earned the respect of his contemporaries for his leadership abilities and military prowess. When he died, his fellow tribesmen buried his body in a secret place in the mountainous Cochise Stronghold and the location of his grave remains a mystery. His name is perpetuated in the naming of Cochise County in the southeast corner of the state.

Colossal Cave

Prehistoric people visited this cavern east of Tucson, but it was not rediscovered until 1879. It soon became a haven for robbers, and legend says there is money hidden there. The first public tours were offered in 1923.

Fantastic limestone formations abound in Colossal Cave, which is termed "dry" because its formations are no longer growing. No matter how hot or cold the weather on the surface, the cavern temperature is always 70°F. Its rooms have such imaginative names as Crystal Forest, Cathedral Room, Kingdom of the Elves, and Bandits' Escape Route.

Guided tours through this natural wonder are a half mile long and require about 45 minutes. Colossal Cave is high among the list of Tucson's most popular tourist attractions.

Congressional Representatives (*See Also* Elected Officials; Politics; State Government)

Future senator and presidential aspirant John McCain was honored by President Richard Nixon upon McCain's release from a North Vietnamese prison camp. Courtesy Southwest Studies, Scottsdale Community College.

Arizona Territorial Delegates

Delegate	Party	Dates Served
Charles D. Poston	Rep.	1864–65
John N. Goodwin	Rep.	1865–67
Coles Bashford	Ind.	1867–69
Richard C. McCormick	Unionist	1869–75
Hiram S. Stevens	Dem.	1875–79
John G. Campbell	Dem.	1879–81
Granville H. Oury	Dem.	1881–85
Curtis C Bean	Rep.	1885–87
Marcus A. Bean	Dem.	1887–95
Nathan O. Murphy	Rep.	1895–97
Marcus A. Bean	Dem.	1897–99
John F. Wilson	Dem.	1899–1901
Marcus A. Bean	Dem.	1901–03
John F. Wilson	Dem.	1903–05
Marcus A. Bean	Dem.	1905–09
Ralph H. Cameron	Rep.	1909-12

United States Senators

Senator	Party	Dates Served
Marcus A. Smith	Dem.	1912–21
Henry F. Ashurst	Dem.	1912–41
Ralph A. Cameron	Rep.	1921–27
Carl T. Hayden	Dem.	1927–69
Ernest W. McFarland	Dem.	1941–53
Barry M. Goldwater	Rep.	1953–65
Paul J. Fannin	Rep.	1965–77
Barry M. Goldwater	Rep.	1969–87
Dennis DeConcini	Dem.	1977–95
John McCain	Rep.	1987–
Jon Kyl	Rep.	1995–

United States Representatives

Representative	Party	Dates Served
Carl T. Hayden	Dem.	1912–27
Lewis W. Douglas	Dem.	1927–33
Isabella S. Greenway	Dem.	1933–37
John R. Murdock	Dem.	1937–53
Richard F. Harless	Dem.	1943–49
Harold A. Patten	Dem.	1949–55
John J. Rhodes	Rep.	1953–83
Stewart L. Udall	Dem.	1955–61
Morris K. Udall	Dem.	1961–91
George F. Senner, Jr.	Dem.	1963–67
Sam Steiger	Rep.	1967–77

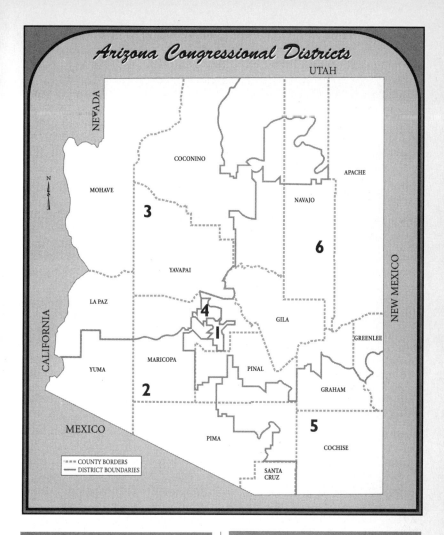

Arizona Congressional Districts

United States Representatives
continued

Representative	Party	Dates Served
John B. Conlan	Rep.	1972–77
Bob Stump	Rep.	1977–
Eldon Rudd	Rep.	1977–87
John McCain	Rep.	1983–87
Jim McNulty	Dem.	1983–85
Jim Kolbe	Rep.	1985–
John J. Rhodes III	Rep.	1987–93
Jon Kyl	Rep.	1987–95
Ed Pastor	Dem.	1991–

United States Representatives
continued

Representative	Party	Dates Served
Sam Coppersmith	Dem.	1993–95
Karan English	Dem.	1993–95
Matt Salmon	Rep.	1995–
John Shadegg	Rep.	1995–
J.D. Hayworth	Rep.	1995–

Coronado

(SEE ALSO HISTORY) Francisco Vasquez de Coronado was 25 years old when he arrived in New Spain (Mexico) in 1535. Four years later he was made governor of the province of Nueva Galicia in northwest Mexico. In 1540, after Fray Marcos de Niza had excited would-be conquistadores with tales of golden cities in what would become New Mexico, Coronado was chosen to lead an army of exploration and conquest into the unknown land.

His troops crossed southeastern Arizona and occupied some Zuni pueblos in New Mexico. Coronado sent a detachment of men westward, where they became the first Europeans to see the Hopi villages and the Grand Canyon. Coronado's army explored all the way to northern Kansas, found no gold, and returned to New Spain in 1542. He was received coolly, relieved of his governorship, and died in obscurity in 1554. Coronado's exploration of the Southwest is honored today in the Coronado National Memorial, west of Bisbee, and by the scenic 123-mile "Coronado Trail," U.S. Route 191 between Clifton and Springerville.

Cottonwood

Cottonwood, with a population of 8,845, is the largest of the Verde Valley cities of Yavapai County. Other cities along the Verde River near Cottonwood are Clarkdale and Camp Verde. Cottonwood traces its history back to 1874, when soldiers from Camp Verde were stationed in an adobe house on the site of the present city. Today it thrives on tourism, retirement facilities, farming and ranching, and is the commercial center of the area.

AZ if?!

The Arizona-Sonora Desert Museum in Tucson had a pair of peccaries (wild pigs, also known as javelinas) that were named Gregory Peccary and Olivia DeJavelina.

Counties

Arizona's 15 counties are remarkably varied in topography, climate, and the lifestyles of their residents. Greenlee in the east, has fewer than 10,000 residents; Maricopa in the south-central part of the state, is approaching 3 million. Apache is cowboy and Indian country, while Pima is known for its scientists, authors and cosmopolitan way of life. It may be wintry in Coconino on the same day they're basking in 90-degree sunshine in La Paz.

When Arizona Territory was created in 1863, it was divided into four counties: Yavapai, Pima, Yuma and Mohave. In 1865, the northern portion of Mohave was split off to form Pah-Ute Country, but a year later Congress gave the new state of Nevada the part of Pah-Ute west of the Colorado River. Thus Arizona lost the land on which Las Vegas later sprouted. Yavapai County was split several times over the years, forming Maricopa, Coconino, Navajo, Apache and parts of other counties; yet Yavapai remains larger than several eastern states.

Apache. In the far northeast corner of Arizona is Apache County, composed of two geographical regions: the scenic, high desert of the Navajo Indian Reservation in the north, and the forested

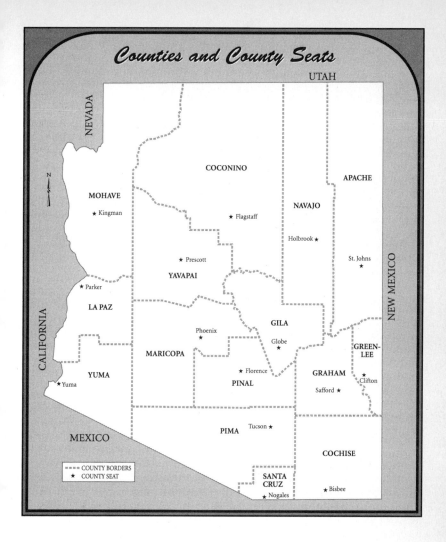

Counties and County Seats

UTAH

NEVADA

COCONINO

APACHE

MOHAVE
★ Kingman

NAVAJO

★ Flagstaff

Holbrook ★

★ Prescott

St. Johns
★

NEW MEXICO

YAVAPAI

★ Parker

LA PAZ

GILA

Phoenix
★

Globe
★

GREEN-
LEE

CALIFORNIA

MARICOPA

★ Florence

GRAHAM

Clifton
★

YUMA

PINAL

Safford ★

★ Yuma

Tucson ★

PIMA

MEXICO

COCHISE

COUNTY BORDERS
★ COUNTY SEAT

SANTA
CRUZ

★ Bisbee

★ Nogales

White Mountains in the south. Visitors come from around the world to see the Painted Desert, Petrified Forest, Canyon de Chelly, and other scenic attractions. Only 14 percent of the land is privately or corporately owned, with the Navajo and Fort Apache Indian Reservations, U.S. Forest Service, and state land making up most of the remainder. St. Johns is the county seat.

Cochise. Some of America's last frontier country lies in Cochise County, in Arizona's southeast corner. The Chiricahua Mountains, once a fortress for the Apache Chief Cochise and his warriors, lure increasing numbers of visitors to the remote beauty of the Wonderland of Rocks in Chiricahua National Monument and its forested recreation lands. Kartchner Caverns State Park near Benson is another tourist attraction, as is Tombstone, "The Town Too Tough

Counties, Their County Seats and Population

County	County Seat	July 1998	July 1999
Apache	St. Johns	68,734	68,562
Cochise	Bisbee	112,404	112,754
Coconino	Flagstaff	114,087	114,498
Gila	Globe	48,839	49,051
Graham	Safford	31,711	31,998
Greenlee	Clifton	9,323	9,018
La Paz	Parker	14,830	14,867
Maricopa	Phoenix	2,783,779	2,861,395
Mohave	Kingman	130,647	134,222
Navajo	Holbrook	96,838	98,327
Pima	Tucson	790,333	803,618
Pinal	Florence	140,947	152,301
Santa Cruz	Nogales	38,155	39,150
Yavapai	Prescott	148,748	152,957
Yuma	Yuma	131,903	135,614
Arizona		**4,667,277**	**4,778,332**

Source: U.S. Census Bureau

To Die," famed for its 1881 shootout at the OK Corral. Fort Huachuca, one of the U.S. Army's largest posts, is a major employment source. Ranching and tourism are also important to the economy. Bisbee is the county seat, but booming Sierra Vista, near Fort Huachuca, is by far the largest city.

Coconino. The largest Arizona county, Coconino, 18,575 square miles, also has the best-known natural wonders. The Grand Canyon lures more than 3 million visitors to the area each year. Oak Creek Canyon, Sunset Crater, Meteor Crater, the San Francisco Peaks (highest in Arizona), Wupatki National Monument and many other attractions are all within easy driving distance of Flagstaff, the county seat and largest city. Northern Arizona University, Lowell Observatory, and the Museum of Northern Arizona are all in Flagstaff. Native American reservation land comprises nearly half of Coconino's area. The Burlington Northern and Santa Fe Railroad main line, Interstate 40 and remnants of U.S. Route 66 also traverse the county.

Gila. Gila County was formed from parts of Coconino, Maricopa and Pinal in 1881. Globe, the county seat, was at one time a major copper producing center. Mining is still a component of the economy of Globe and its neighbor, Miami, but Gila County's economic strength now is moving towards tourism, recreation, ranching, and government. The Fort Apache and San Carlos Apache Indian Reservations make up more than a third of Gila's land area. The county's scenic attractions include Salt River Canyon (a "miniature Grand Canyon" you can drive through), the Mogollon Rim, Roosevelt Dam and Roosevelt Lake, and Tonto National Monument. Payson, in the northwest portion of the county, is now Gila's largest city.

Graham. Settled primarily by Mormon pioneers in the late 19th century, Graham County has long been a ranching and farming area. Its neighbors are Cochise on the south, Pinal on the west, Gila, Navajo and Apache on the north, and Greenlee County on the east. The Coronado National Forest and San Carlos Indian Reservation make up 16 percent of Graham's area. Mount Graham, which rises abruptly near the county seat, Safford, is a mecca for outdoor recreation lovers. Other points of interest include portions of the Aravaipa Canyon Wilderness and San Carlos Lake, created by Coolidge Dam.

Greenlee. Created in 1909 from eastern Graham County, Greenlee was Arizona's newest county until La Paz was carved out of Yuma County in 1983. Clifton, the county seat, and nearby Morenci are the largest communities. Copper mining was the economic engine that sustained Greenlee's people for decades and it still is a major source of employment. Cattle ranching and tourism are other key contributors to the economy. With fewer than 10,000 residents, Greenlee has the smallest population of Arizona's counties. The Coronado Trail, Apache National Forest, Blue River wilderness country and the Morenci open-pit mine are tourist attractions.

La Paz. Arizona's newest county was created from the northern half of Yuma County in 1983. Parker, on the Colorado River in the northern portion of La Paz County, is the county seat and largest town. Quartzsite, Ehrenberg, Hope, Wenden, Vicksburg, Brenda and Salome are other communities in the county. Parker is an agricultural center, and Quartzsite is noted for its annual rock and gem show, which draws tens of thousands of winter visitors to the town. La Paz County is named for the ghost town of La Paz, the former Yuma County seat and once a contestant for the Arizona territorial capital. Alamo State Park, Buckskin Mountain State Park, Parker Dam and Parker's river recreational facilities are prime tourist attractions.

Maricopa. More than half of Arizona's people live in Maricopa County, in the south-central portion of the state. Phoenix, the county seat and state capital, has a population estimated in 2000 at 1,300,000 and ranks as the eighth largest metropolitan center in the nation. Mesa, with more than 375,000 people, is the largest of 25 suburban cities. High tech manufacturing, government, education, tourism and agriculture are important aspects of the economy. Arizona State University, with its main campus in Tempe, is the largest of Arizona's three state universities. Scottsdale, with its world-class winter resort hotels and golf courses, is a tourist mecca. Popular attractions include the Mormon Temple in Mesa, antique shops in Glendale, water sports on the Salt River lakes, the Desert Botanical Garden, Phoenix Zoo, Maricopa County's many excellent museums and art galleries, and Phoenix's major league sports.

Mohave. One of Arizona's original four counties, Mohave was known for many decades for its mining and ranching activity. Both remain part of the economy, but today Mohave is best known for its tourism and Colorado River recreation. Lake Havasu City, with more than 40,000 residents, is the largest city. Nearby Bullhead City is also a major river resort. Kingman is the county seat. At 13,200 square miles, Mohave is second only to Coconino in land area. Some of Arizona's most famous tourist attractions are in Mohave County: Hoover Dam, Lake Mead National Recreational Area, Lake Havasu, and the lower portion of Grand Canyon National Park. Tourists come to see the London Bridge at Lake Havasu City, which was transported stone-by-stone from London and reassembled at its present site.

Navajo. A county of many contrasts, Navajo has high desert, pine forests, lofty mountains, vast empty spaces, Hopi villages, and the fast-growing White Mountain communities. Holbrook, the county seat, and Winslow were established as railroad towns in the late 19th century, when the Atlantic and Pacific (now Burlington Northern and Santa Fe Railroad) was built. In recent years the county's major population growth has been in the White Mountain cities of Show Low, Pinetop, and Lakeside. Parts of the Navajo, Hopi and Fort Apache reservations are here, as are portions of Monument Valley, the Painted Desert and Petrified Forest National Park. Ranching, tourism, coal mining and farming contribute to the economy.

Pima. This county's population, tourist attractions, and economic strength are largely concentrated in the Tucson metropolitan area, where 80 percent of Pima's people live. Tucson has an estimated 465,000 within the city limits and another 350,000 in outlying areas. Pima borders Mexico on the south, and its culture has long had an Hispanic flavor. The Tohono O'odham (formerly known as Papago) Nation covers nearly half of the county's land area. Tucson has much to offer its visitors: museums, sports and arts at the University of Arizona; San Xavier del Bac Mission; Saguaro National Park; Sabino Canyon Recreational Area; Old Tucson movie set; and Mount Lemmon winter sports area, to name a few. Other county attractions include Colossal Cave and Park, Kitt Peak National Observatory, Indian crafts at Sells, and Organ Pipe Cactus National Monument.

Pinal. Tucked between Arizona's two most populous counties, Maricopa and Pima, Pinal County often does not get the attention it deserves. Its best-known cities—Florence, Casa Grande, Coolidge and Superior—have recently been overtaken in population by Apache Junction in the northwest corner of the county. Pinal is an agricultural county, raising cotton, alfalfa, vegetables and other crops. Copper mining and ranching are also important. Within its boundaries are several notable tourist attractions: the 6-centuries-old Casa Grande Ruins National Monument of the Hohokam people; Boyce Thompson Arboretum State Park; Picacho Peak State Park; the Maricopa Ak-Chin Reservation; the Gila River Indian Reservation and Crafts Center; McFarland State Historic Park; Lost Dutchman State Park; and Pinal Pioneer Parkway. Florence is the county seat.

Santa Cruz. Santa Cruz, smallest of the 15 counties, occupies what was once the southeastern corner of Pima County. It borders on Sonora, Mexico, and well over half of its citizens are of Hispanic origin. Nogales, the county seat, is the American twin of Nogales, Sonora. Most tourists visiting Mexico from Arizona pass through Nogales on their way. Coronado National Forest covers much of the land area of the county. Favorite recreational areas include Pena Blanca Lake, Patagonia State Park, Ramsey Canyon and the Santa Cruz River valley. Tubac Presidio State Park marks the site of the first settlement of Europeans in Arizona. Tumacacori National Historic Park has the restored structure of Father Eusebio Kino's Tumacacori Mission.

Yavapai. Named for the Yavapai tribe, the county is located in north-central Arizona, between Coconino and Maricopa. It was the site of the first Arizona territorial capital, and Prescott is the county seat. Here we find Sharlot Hall Museum, constructed around the first Governor's Mansion, which was occupied by early territorial governors. Cattle ranching, mining and tourism are the leading economic producers. Mountainous Yavapai has several of Arizona's scenic attractions, including Montezuma Castle National Monument (cliff dwellings) and Tuzigoot National Monument, which preserves the ruins of an ancient Sinagua Indian community. Natural wonders include Sedona's red rocks and Prescott National Forest. And of course there is the dramatic drive across Mingus Mountain to "Ghost Town" Jerome, a mining camp that hangs precariously from the eastern slopes. It's difficult to give an elevation for Jerome, since its uppermost building is 1,500 feet above the lowest.

AZ if?!

Famed story teller Cap Hance loved to tell gullible Grand Canyon visitors about the time he skied across the canyon on top of frozen fog.

Yuma. Although primarily low land, Yuma County also has desert mountains and several popular water playgrounds. It is located in the southwest corner of Arizona. The county seat, Yuma, has about half of the county's population. One of the original four Arizona counties, Yuma has a rich history dating back to prehistoric times, the coming of the Spanish, river crossings by Mexican War and Civil War troops, the steamboat era, and the modern growth period. Yuma County has an Army proving ground, a Marine Corps air station, and gunnery ranges of the Air Force and Navy. Yuma

Cowboy-author Earle Forrest, ca. 1900.
Courtesy Southwest Studies, Scottsdale
Community College.

has Arizona Western College and a branch of Northern Arizona University. Agriculture, cattle feeding, the military, and tourism are economic pillars of the county.

Cowboys (SEE ALSO DUDE RANCHES; THE FIVE C'S; MOVIES; RANCHING; RODEOS)

To millions of people around the world, the name "Arizona" is synonymous with cowboys and Indians, and visitors to the state still clamor to get a sight of both. Although American Indians are in plentiful supply—in 20 tribal areas—cowboys are a bit more difficult to encounter. But they are here, working on cattle ranches large and small, showing off their riding and roping skills in rodeos, and bellying up to bars in rural towns throughout the state.

No other Arizona occupation has so much romance and tradition surrounding it as that of the cowhand. He works in the great outdoors, rides a horse all day, and shuns such impediments as suits and neckties, nit-picking bosses, rush hour traffic, house payments, and fears of layoffs. The hours are incredibly long, the weather often boiling or freezing, the threat of injury ever present, and the pay generally small, but most working cowboys wouldn't trade their lifestyle for any other.

Cowboys still rope and brand, as described in this brief excerpt from a colorful essay by William Blundell in the *Wall Street Journal* of June 10, 1981:

"The lariat whirls as the man on horseback separates a calf from the herd. Suddenly the loop snakes around one of the calf's rear legs and tightens. Wrapping a turn of rope around the saddle horn, the rider drags the hapless animal to his crew.

"The flanker whips the calf onto its back, and the medicine man inoculates the animal. Amid blood, dust, and bawling, the calf is dehorned with a coring tool, branded in an acrid cloud of smoke from burning hair and flesh, earmarked in the ranch's unique pattern (cowboys pay more attention to earmarks in identifying cattle than to brands) and castrated. It is all over in one minute."

Cowboy attire has changed little over the decades. A cowhand wears Levi's, high-heeled boots, a western shirt (not brilliantly colored) and broad-brimmed hat. He takes his hat off only to shower or sleep, and he refuses to remove it in restaurants, to the occasional annoyance of other patrons who consider that behavior grossly rude.

Although the golden age of the

cowboy was relatively brief, spanning little more than two decades in the 19th century, his impact continues far greater than his present numbers. Cowboy art fills museums and many western homes, cowboy poets convene annually in several Arizona towns, and the retailing of western attire to would-be cowboys is a multi-million dollar industry.

Arizona humorist Marshall Trimble often recites the following description of the cowboy at his frequent shows:

Cowboys is noisy fellers with bow-legs and brass stomachs that works from the hurricane deck of a U-necked cowpony and hates any kind of work that can't be done atop one.

They rides like Comanches, ropes like Mexicans, and shoots like Arizona Rangers.

They kin spit 10 feet into a stiff wind, whup their weight in wildcats, fight grizzlies bare knuckled, bite on the tail of live cougars, take on the whole Apache nation armed with one six-shooter, and ride anything that wears hair.

They lives in and loves the outdoors, hates fences and respects rivers. And they's independent, too. You just throw one of them into a river and he'll naturally float upstream. The only way to tame one of 'em is to cut off his head and bury it someplace where he can't find it.

Crime Rate (SEE ALSO

PRISONS) The rate of serious crimes reported in Arizona, according to a March, 1998 report from the Arizona Department of Public Safety, declined almost 14 percent from the previous

Winnie Ruth Judd

One of the most publicized crimes in Arizona annals was the murder of two young Phoenix women in 1931. Their former roommate, Winnie Ruth Judd, was accused of killing the pair, cutting up their bodies, and shipping them in trunks to Los Angeles. National press coverage of the murder and the trial was sensational, and Mrs. Judd was vilified as "the Trunk Murderess" and "the Tiger Woman."

She was found guilty and sentenced to hang, but state officials tried to avoid hanging because another convicted murderess, Eva Dugan, had been decapitated by the noose when she was executed a year earlier. Winnie Ruth was therefore found to be insane (although few believed that to be true) and placed in the Arizona State Hospital, from which she escaped numerous times before being pardoned by Governor Jack Williams four decades after her incarceration. ✳

annual report. Serious crimes are considered to be murder, rape, robbery, aggravated assault, burglary, larceny-theft, motor vehicle theft and arson.

Despite an almost 20 percent drop in the motor vehicle theft rate, Arizona continues to rank second nationally in that category. The Phoenix metropolitan area has experienced an almost 24 percent drop in motor vehicle theft, while the Tucson rate has remained essentially the same.

The violent crime rate in Arizona declined more than 11 percent, but the property crime rate climbed 14 percent. Arizona ranks 14th in the nation in violent crime, and third among the states and District of Columbia in property crimes.

Dams (_See also_ Central Arizona Project; Lakes; Rivers)

Arizona's population growth and economic well-being have come about in large part because of the dams that have provided a steady water supply, ample electric energy and outdoor recreation areas. Dams on two rivers in particular, the Colorado and the Salt, have played major roles in the state's development.

Agua Fria River. In 1993 the **New Waddell Dam** northwest of Phoenix was completed, raising the level of Lake Pleasant by 100 feet and increasing its surface area to 9,966 acres. The lake receives water from the Agua Fria River and from the Central Arizona Project canal. It serves as a storage reservoir for the CAP and provides water recreation for many thousands of users.

Colorado River. Located at Page, **Glen Canyon Dam** is just south of the Utah border northeast of Grand Canyon National Park. It stands 710 feet high and was completed in 1964. It impounds Lake Powell, one of the most popular water recreation facilities in the West. Glen Canyon Dam, like Hoover Dam downstream, is a major producer of electric power.

Perhaps the best known of all these structures is **Hoover Dam**, in the northwest corner of Mohave County, which impounds Lake Mead. Hoover Dam is 726 feet high, one of the highest in the world, and has water storage capacity of more than 28 million acre-feet. (An acre-foot is that amount of water necessary to cover an acre of land one-foot deep.) It was completed in 1936.

Further downstream from Hoover Dam are a series of dams—**Davis, Parker, Imperial** and **Laguna**—each of

Theodore Roosevelt Dam, bridge and Roosevelt Lake, after 77 feet was added to the height of the dam in 1996. Courtesy Salt River Project.

which has created a large lake. In total, these dams have so completely tamed the once-roaring Colorado River that it becomes a trickle of its once powerful self. Not far south of Yuma, in Mexico, the Colorado virtually disappears before reaching the Gulf of California.

Gila River. Once the Gila River flowed all across Arizona, from New Mexico to California, and was an important route for east-bound prehistoric people from Mesoamerica and early west-bound explorers headed to California gold fields. Since the completion of **Coolidge Dam** in south-western Gila County in 1928, the lower Gila to the Colorado River near Yuma has been dry much of the time. San Carlos Lake, created by Coolidge Dam, took nearly half a century to fill.

Salt River. While considered a tributary of the Gila River, the Salt is of major importance to the state because it supplies much of the water and power for several million people in south-central Arizona. It performs this essential service because of the chain of dams that have been built from south-western Gila County, downstream to the outskirts of Phoenix.

Most important of these is **Theodore Roosevelt Dam,** which impounds Roosevelt Lake. It was the key component of the Salt River Project, and America's first federally funded reclamation project. Construction of the dam was started in 1905 and completed in 1911. It was the world's largest masonry dam, 280 feet high and 184 feet thick at its base. In the past few years more than 70 feet was added to the top of the dam, increasing its storage capacity to 2.9 million acre feet.

Downstream from Roosevelt Dam are **Horse Mesa Dam,** which created Apache Lake; **Mormon Flat Dam,** which impounds Canyon Lake; and **Stewart Mountain Dam,** creator of Saguaro Lake. All these bodies of water are popular recreation lakes, and they store water from wet years for use in times of drought. Below the Salt's confluence with the Verde River is another dam in the project, the **Granite Reef Diversion Dam,** which diverts stored water into canals that serve the Phoenix metro area.

Verde River. Two dams on the Verde River, **Bartlett** and **Horseshoe,** also are part of the Salt River Project. The Verde River enters the Salt River just upstream from the Granite Reef Diversion Dam.

Disasters
Floods, fires, massacres of and by Indians, airplane crashes—even a meteorite invasion—Arizona has experienced all these and many other disasters. Among them:

Prehistoric. Some 50,000 years ago a giant meteorite plowed into the earth near present-day Winslow, destroying all life within a wide radius of the impact and leaving a crater 4,000 feet across and more than 800 feet deep. The winter of A.D. 1064–1065, a volcanic eruption near Flagstaff spewed deadly lava and ash on prehistoric dwellers for miles around. Its cone, now called Sunset Crater, is a national monument.

Yuma Missions Massacre. The first and only missions and presidios established on the Colorado River by Spain were attacked by Yuma Indians near the present city of Yuma on July 17, 1781. Enraged by the inhumane treatment meted out by Spanish soldiers, the Yumas killed every Spaniard in two mission communities, including the famed Father Francisco Garces.

Camp Grant Massacre. All America was outraged when it was revealed that 140 men from Tucson had raided an Apache camp outside Camp Grant in Graham County on the night of April 10, 1871, and murdered 83 Indian women and children.

Skeleton Cave. In December 1872, Union soldiers tracked a band of Yavapai Indians and trapped them in a cave near present-day Horse Mesa Dam. Bullets from the soldiers' guns ricocheted off the cave ceiling and killed 76 Yavapais.

Bisbee Massacre. Five masked

AZ if?!

Will Rogers, who spoke at the dedication of Coolidge Dam in 1930, was puzzled at the appearance of San Carlos Lake behind the dam. Because the lake was just beginning to fill, and was clogged with reeds, Rogers declared, "If this was my lake, I'd mow it!"

bandits held up the Goldwater-Castañeda store in Bisbee on Dec. 8, 1883, and killed four adults and an unborn baby in making their escape. The killers were all captured, and all but one were executed. The other, sentenced to life imprisonment, was snatched from the jail by vigilantes and hanged from a light post.

Pleasant Valley War. Zane Grey's epic novel, *To the Last Man,* told the story of the bitter feud between the Graham and Tewksbury families in Pleasant Valley. At least 50 men died before the final murder ended the killing in 1892.

Walnut Grove Dam Disaster. The collapse of Walnut Grove Dam on the Hassayampa River on Feb. 22, 1890, sent a wall of water down the river to Wickenburg and killed 50 people.

Mining Camp Fires. Virtually every mining town suffered devastating fires during the last half of the 19th century. Jerome and Tombstone were all but destroyed several times. One of the most memorable fires wiped out most of downtown Prescott on the night of July 14, 1900, including riotous Whiskey Row. Saloons and gambling houses set up business across the street in the courthouse square and were serving customers before the last flames were extinguished.

Epidemics. Tuberculosis claimed the lives of several thousand Arizonans in the early decades of the 20th century. Prescott alone had seven tuberculosis sanitariums operating at that time. The 1918 influenza epidemic devastated the young state, killing many hundreds of people and shutting down government operations, schools and churches.

Pioneer Hotel Fire. A 15-year old arsonist set fire to Tucson's most famous hotel, the Pioneer, just before midnight on Dec. 19, 1970, and 29 people, including several prominent Tucsonans, died in the inferno.

Grand Canyon Airplane Collision. The largest death toll in an American aircraft accident up to that time resulted from the 1956 collision of a United Airlines airplane with a Trans-World Airlines plane over the Grand Canyon. The death toll was 128 passengers and crew members.

Looking Back

1978 & 1980

The flooding of the Salt River in central Arizona caused millions in damage.

Douglas
Douglas is on the Mexican border in southeastern Arizona opposite its Sonora sister city, Agua Prieta. The city was founded in 1900 as a copper smelter center and named for James Douglas, president of Phelps Dodge Corporation. Smelting operations have now been closed down. Douglas' population is now estimated at 15,000. Ranching, tourism, retiree services, international trade, and farming contribute to Douglas' economy. Cochise College, opened in 1964, is the city's community college.

Dude Ranches
Whether you want to saddle up and work with the cowhands—driving, gathering and branding cattle—or play tennis, ride and relax in a ranch setting, Arizona's many dude ranches offer wonderful vacation opportunities. They are located all over the state, from the sunny Mexican border to the snowy high country. Wickenburg enjoys the title of "Dude Ranch Capital of

Dude ranch riders near Wickenburg. Photo by James Tallon.

the World," but other Arizona communities come close.

The Arizona Dude Ranch Association, P.O. Box 603, Cortaro 85652, has a wealth of information about its ranches and recreational amenities. Some are small, working ranches such as Price Canyon Ranch in the Chiricahua Mountains near Douglas. "We're not fancy," say its owners, "but you can experience what it was like here a hundred years ago." Others, such as Merv Griffin's Wickenburg Inn near Wickenburg, offer all the pleasures of a resort hotel.

The Arizona Dude Ranch Association members:

Circle Z Ranch, P.O. Box 194AZ, Patagonia 85624

Elkhorn Ranch, HCI Box 97, Tucson 85736

Flying E Ranch, 2801 W. Wickenburg Way, Wickenburg 85390-1087

Grapevine Canyon Ranch, P.O. Box 302, Pearce 85625

Horseshoe Ranch on Bloody Basin Road, HCR 34, Box 5005, Mayer 86333

Ironhorse Ranch, P.O. Box 536, Tombstone 85638

Kay El Bar Ranch, P.O. Box 2480, Wickenburg 85358

Lazy K Bar Ranch, 8401 N. Scenic Drive, Tucson 85743

Merv Griffin's Wickenburg Inn, 34801 N. Highway 89, Wickenburg 85390

Price Canyon Ranch, 10923 Price Canyon Road, P.O. Box 1065, Douglas 85608

Rancho de la Osa, P.O. Box 1, Sasabe 85633

Rancho de los Caballeros, 1551 S. Vulture Mine Road, Wickenburg 85390

Sprucedale Ranch, HC 61, Box 10, Alpine 85920

Tanque Verde Ranch, 14301 E. Speedway, Tucson 85748

The White Stallion Ranch, 9251 W. Twin Peaks Road, Tucson 85743

Economy (SEE ALSO AGRICULTURE; THE FIVE C'S; MINING; TOURISM)

Arizona's economy has several key segments, most important

of which are services (including tourism), trade and manufacturing. Mining and agriculture, once the keystones, remain significant. But services is the single largest economic sector, according to the Arizona Department of Commerce, employing some 620,000 people. Wholesale and retail trade provide more than 500,000 jobs. It is estimated that tourism accounts for $12 billion and employs more than 135,000 people. Another 225,000 are supported indirectly by tourism.

In 1998, manufacturing accounted for 216,641 jobs, or approximately 10.5 percent of the state's employment. It generated 14.9 percent of wages and salaries. Arizona has been especially successful in attracting high-technology industries, which have a total economic impact of $33 billion each year. Nearly 56 percent of all manufacturing in the state is in high-tech industries.

The construction sector, also very important to Arizona's economy, accounted for 141,593 jobs, or 6.89 percent, of the state's employment in 1998. Construction has experienced a substantial increase over the past several years. The market grew from $5.5 billion in 1994 to $11.2 billion in 1998.

Arizona's economy continues to be one of the nation's fastest growing. More than 400,000 private sector jobs were created between 1993-1997, making it the strongest five-year period of job growth in Arizona history.

Elected Officials (SEE ALSO CONGRESSIONAL REPRESENTATIVES; POLITICS; STATE GOVERNMENT)

Top 30 Private Sector Employers

1998 Rank	Company	Headquarters	Business in Arizona	Full-time Employees
1	Motorola	Schaumburg, IL	Electronics, computers	20,000
2	Intel	Santa Clara, CA	Semiconductors	9,275
3	Allied Signal	Morristown, NJ	Aircraft engines and parts	9,000
4	Wal-Mart Stores	Bentonville, AR	Discount stores	8,500
5	Bank One Arizona	Phoenix, AZ	Banking	8,391
6	American Express	New York, NY	Travel and financial services	8,200
7	America West Holdings	Tempe, AZ	Airline	7,826
8	Raytheon Missile Systems	Lexington, MA	Missile systems	7,700
9	Honeywell	Minneapolis, MN	Electronics, aviation systems	7,500
10	Pinnacle West Capital	Phoenix, AZ	Parent of Arizona Public Service Co.	6,940
11	US West Communications	Denver, CO	Telecommunications	6,500
12	Fry's Food Stores of Arizona	Phoenix, AZ	Supermarkets	6,429
13	Tosco Marketing	Phoenix, AZ	Convenience stores	6,078
14	Smith's Food & Drug Centers	Salt Lake City, UT	Supermarkets	6,000
15	Safeway	Pleasanton, CA	Supermarkets	5,941
16	Bashas'	Chandler, AZ	Supermarkets	5,513
17	Albertson's	Boise, ID	Supermarkets	5,500
18	Bank of America Arizona	Phoenix, AZ	Banking	5,400
19	Boeing Company	Seattle, WA	Aircraft	5,299
20	Kmart	Troy, MI	Discount stores	4,600
21	Walgreen	Deerfield, IL	Drugstores	4,300
22	AT&T	New York, NY	Telecommunications	4,300
23	Salt River Project	Tempe, AZ	Quasi-municipal utility	4,110
24	Southwest Airlines	Dallas, TX	Airline	4,057
25	Columbia/HCA Healthcare	Nashville, TN	Medical care, hospitals	3,805
26	Dayton Hudson	Minneapolis, MN	Target, Mervyns stores	3,624
27	TRW	Cleveland, OH	Automotive airbags	3,500
28	Home Depot	Atlanta, GA	Home-improvement retailer	3,400
29	Phelps Dodge	Phoenix, AZ	Mining, manufacturing	3,200
30	Marriott Int./ Host Marriott Hotels	Washington, DC	Hotels, food service	3,100

Source: *Arizona Republic*

Employment by Industry 1997

	Employment	% of Total
Agriculture	44,455	2.16
Manufacturing	216,641	10.53
Mining	14,000	0.45
Construction	141,593	6.89
Transportation, Communications, and Public Utilties	98,476	4.79
Wholesale Trade	109,438	5.32
Retail Trade	388,549	18.8
Finance, Insurance, and Real Estate	137,586	6.7
Services	615,538	29.93
Government	293,729	14.28
Non-Classifiable	3,210	0.16

Source: Arizona Department of Economic Security, 1997

Congressional Delegation

Senators.

John McCain (R), 241 Russell Senate Office Building, Washington, DC 20510

Jon Kyl (R), 724 Hart Senate Office Building, Washington, DC 20510

Representatives.

District 1. Matt Salmon (R), 115 Cannon House Office Bldg., Washington, DC 20515

District 2. Ed Pastor (D), 2465 Rayburn House Office Bldg., Washington, DC 20515

District 3. Bob Stump (R), 211 Cannon House Office Bldg., Washington, DC 20515

District 4. John Shadegg (R), 430 Cannon House Office Bldg., Washington, DC 20515

District 5. Jim Kolbe (R), 2266 Rayburn House Office Bldg., Washington, DC 20515

District 6. J. D. Hayworth (R), 1023 Longworth House Office Bldg., Washington, DC 20515

State Constitutional Officers

Governor Jane Dee Hull (R), 1700 W. Washington St., Phoenix 85007

Secretary of State Betsey Bayless (R), 1700 W. Washington St., Phoenix 85007

Attorney General Janet Napolitano (D), 1275 W. Washington St., Phoenix 85007

State Treasurer Carol Springer (R), 1700 W. Washington St., Phoenix, AZ 85007

Superintendent of Public Instruction Lisa Graham Keegan (R), 1535 W. Jefferson St., Phoenix 85007

State Mine Inspector Douglas Martin (R), 1700 W. Washington St., Phoenix 85007

Corporation Commissioners
Jim Irvin (R), Carl J. Kunasek (R), Tony West (R), 1200 W. Washington St., Phoenix 85007

44th Legislature, 1999-2000

Arizona State Senate.

1700 W. Washington St., Phoenix 85007

President, Brenda Burns

Aguirre, Linda (D), Dist. 23
Arzberger, Gus (D), Dist. 8
Bee, Keith A. (R), Dist. 9
Bennett, Ken (R), Dist. 1
Bowers, Russell "Rusty", Dist. 21
Brown, Jack A. (D), Dist. 4
Bundgaard, Scott (R), Dist. 19
Burns, Brenda (R), Dist. 17
Cirillo, Edward J. (R), Dist. 15
Cummiskey, Chris (D), Dist. 25
Cunningham George (D), Dist. 13
Day, Ann (R), Dist. 12

Governor Jane Dee Hull.

72

Five Women Hold Top Offices

Arizonans love to entrust their highest state offices to women. At no time has this been more true than the present, when women occupy the five most important elective posts in Arizona government.

In the general election of November 1998, Phoenix Republican Jane Dee Hull won an easy victory in the gubernatorial race. A former member of the state legislature, she had also served as Secretary of State.

In the other four major races, Betsey Bayless was retained as Secretary of State; Janet Napolitano, former U.S. attorney, was elected Attorney General; Carole Springer won the race for State Treasurer; and Lisa Graham Keegan was retained as Superintendent of Public Instruction. ✷

Freestone, Tom (R), Dist. 30
Gnant, Randall (R), Dist. 28
Grace, Sue (R), Dist. 24
Guenther, Herb (D), Dist. 5
Hamilton, Darden (R), Dist. 16
Hartley, Mary (D), Dist. 20
Huppenthal, John (R), Dist. 6
Jackson, Jack C. (D), Dist. 3
Lopez, Joe Eddie (D), Dist. 22
Mitchell, Harry (D), Dist. 27
Petersen, David A. (R), Dist. 29
Richardson, Elaine (D), Dist. 11
Rios, Pete (D), Dist. 7
Smith, Tom (R), Dist. 26
Solomon, Ruth (D), Dist. 14
Soltero, Victor (D). Dist. 10
Spitzer, Mark (R), Dist. 18
Wettaw, John (R), Dist. 2

House of Representatives.
1700 W. Washington St., Phoenix 85007
Speaker, Jeff Groscost
Allen, Carolyn S. (R), Dist 28
Anderson, Mark (R), Dist. 29
Avelar, Carlos (D), Dist. 23
Binder, Linda (R), Dist. 1
Blewster, Barbara (R), Dist. 1
Brimhall, Debra (R), Dist. 4
Brotherton, Bill (D), Dist. 20
Burns, Robert (R), Dist. 17
Cardamone, Carmine (D), Dist. 11
Carpenter, Ted (R), Dist. 19
Carruthers, Jim (R), Dist. 5

Cheuvront, Ken (D), Dist. 25
Clark, Harry D. (D), Dist. 7
Cooley, Dean (R), Dist 21
Daniels, Lori S. (R), Dist. 6
Dunbar, Kathleen (R), Dist. 13
Flake, Jake (R), Dist. 4
Foster, Kathi (D), Dist. 20
Gardner, Michael (R), Dist. 27
Gardner, Wayne (R), Dist 29
Gerard, Susan (R), Dist. 18
Gleason, Lowell "Mike" (R), Dist. 15
Gonzales, Sally Ann (D), Dist. 10
Gordon, Tom (R), Dist. 3
Gray, Linda (R), Dist. 16
Griffin, Gail (R), Dist. 8
Groscost, Jeff (R), Dist. 30
Hart, Joe (R), Dist. 2
Hatch-Miller, Jeff (R), Dist. 26
Horne, Tom (R), Dist. 24
Horton, Herschella (D), Dist. 14
Huffman, Steve (R), Dist. 12
Jarrett, Marilyn (R), Dist. 21
Johnson, Karen (R), Dist. 30
Knaperek, Laura (R), Dist. 27
Kyle, Richard (R), Dist. 6
Landrum, Leah (D), Dist. 23
Laughter, Sylvia (D), Dist. 3
Leff, Barbara (R), Dist. 24
Loredo, John (D), Dist. 22
Maiorana, Mark (D), Dist. 8
Marsh, Wes (R), Dist. 28
May, Steve (R), Dist. 26
McGibbon, Bill (R), Dist. 9
McGrath, Jean (R), Dist. 17

McLendon, Robert J. (D), Dist. 5
Miranda, Richard (D), Dist. 22
Nichols, Andy (D), Dist. 13
Norris, Debora (D), Dist. 11
Overton, Jerry (R), Dist. 15
Pickens, Marion Lee (D), Dist. 14
Preble, Lou-Ann (R), Dist. 9
Rios, Rebecca (D), Dist. 7
Schottel, Dan (R), Dist. 12
Valadez, Ramon (D), Dist. 10
Verkamp, John (R), Dist. 2
Voss, Roberta
(R), Dist. 19
Weason, Christine
(D), Dist. 25
Weiers, Jim (R),
Dist 16
Wong, Barry (R),
Dist. 18

Arizona Supreme Court.

1501 W. Washington St., Phoenix 85007
Chief Justice Thomas A. Zlaket
Vice Chief Justice Charles E. Jones
Justice Stanley G. Feldman
Justice Frederick J. Martone
Justice Ruth McGregor

Endangered and Threatened Species

(SEE ALSO BIRDS; FISH AND FISHING; MAMMALS; PLANTS; REPTILES; AMPHIBIANS) Arizona has 35 species of plants and animals identified by the federal government as endangered and 16 whose existence is considered threatened.

Endangered Species.

Mammals:. Sanborn's long-nosed bat; Mount Graham red squirrel; jaguar; jaguarundi; Hualapai Mexican vole; Sonoran pronghorn; ocelot.

Snails: Kanab ambersnail. **Birds:** Yuma clapper rail; masked bobwhite (quail); southwestern willow flycatcher; northern uplomado falcon; cactus ferruginous pygmy-owl. **Fish:** Gila trout; razorback sucker; bonytail chub; Virgin River chub; desert pupfish; Gila topminnow; woundfin; humpback chub; Yaqui chub; Colorado squawfish. **Amphibian:** Sonora tiger salamander. **Plants:** Arizona agave; Brady pincushion cactus; Peebles Navajo cactus; Canelo Hills ladies-tresses; Kearney's blue-star; Arizona cliff-rose; Sentry milk-vetch; Pima pineapple cactus; Huachuca water umbel; Arizona hedgehog cactus; Nichol's Turk's head cactus.

AZ if?!

Bisbee's *Brewery Gulch Gazette* for many years used the slogan: "The sun shines on Brewery Gulch 330 days a year, but there is moonshine every night."

Threatened Species.

Birds: Mexican spotted owl; bald eagle. **Fish:** Yaqui catfish; Sonora chub; loach minnow; spikedace; Little Colorado spinedace; beautiful shiner; Apache trout. **Reptile:** Desert tortoise. **Plants:** San Francisco Peaks groundsel; Navajo sedge; Cochise pincushion cactus; Jones cycladenia; Welsh's milkweed; Siler pincushion cactus.

Eleven other species of plants and animals are being considered as candidates for protection as endangered or threatened.

Candidate Species.

Mammal: Black-tailed prairie dog. **Bird:** Mountain plover. **Amphibian:** Chiricahua leopard frog. **Plants:** Goodings onion; Blumer's dock; Kaibab pincushion cactus; Holmgren milk-vetch; Acuna cactus; Fickelsen pincushion cactus;

Palo Verde Nuclear Generating Station west of Phoenix. Photo by James Tallon.

Arizona bugbane; Lemmon fleabane.

Energy (*SEE ALSO* CENTRAL ARIZONA PROJECT; DAMS; SALT RIVER PROJECT) Electric power, produced by coal-fired, diesel, gas and hydroelectric plants; solar power; and one giant nuclear plant, is the lifeblood of Arizona living. Natural gas is another important element in the energy equation.

Arizona Public Service Company provides electricity to more customers and a broader area of the state than any other energy producer. Salt River Project serves Maricopa County (as does Arizona Public Service) and parts of Pinal and Gila counties.

Tucson Electric Power Company provides electricity for Tucson and surrounding areas of southern Arizona. Several smaller power companies serve rural areas around the state.

America's largest nuclear facility is Palo Verde Nuclear Generating Station, 45 miles west of Phoenix.

Palo Verde is operated by Arizona Public Service Company, which owns 29.1 percent of the plant. Co-owners are Salt River Project, Southern California Edison, Public Service Company of New Mexico, El Paso Electric Company, Los Angeles Department of Water and Power, and the Southern California Public Power Authority. This triple-unit facility is the energy cornerstone of the Southwest, and generates electricity to serve some four million people. In 1998 it became the first American power plant to generate more than 30 billion kilowatt-hours of electricity in a single year.

Salt River Project now serves more than 700,000 electric customers. It is actually two companies: the Salt River Project Agricultural Improvement and Power District, and the Salt River Valley Water Users Association. The former is a political subdivision of the state, and the latter is a private corporation.

Arizona Public Service, which has 39 generating units totaling about 8,000 megawatts, is the principal subsidiary of Pinnacle West Capital Corporation. Pin West, as it is commonly called, is a $7 billion company based in Phoenix. APS serves not only Arizona but has customers in California as well.

Tucson Electric Power Company is the principal subsidiary of Unisource Energy Corporation. TEP serves some 325,000 customers within an area of 1,155 square miles of southern Arizona, and in 1998 it ranked among the top 2 percent of American electric utilities in reliability of service.

Because much of Arizona enjoys more than 300 sunny days each year, the state has been a leader in the development of solar energy production and use. All of the state's electric utilities are working to make sun power provide more of Arizona's energy needs. An example is the new 14-acre, 99-home community in Tucson's historic Armory Park area, which will have solar material on every rooftop to supply electricity, hot water and space heating.

Southwest Gas Company serves more than a million natural gas customers in Arizona, Nevada, and California. Its Central Arizona Division is headquartered in Phoenix and its Southern Arizona Division offices are in Tucson. Smaller corporate and municipal gas distributors serve other parts of the state.

AZ if?!

Don't sneer at a man wearing a cowboy hat while eating in an Arizona restaurant. Cowboys never take their hats off, except maybe in the shower, and maybe not even then.

Entertainers

Many nationally known entertainers have come from, or been associated with, Arizona. A complete list would be difficult to make, but some of them include:

Movies, TV and Radio Personalities. Many of the earliest celebrities from Arizona were cowboy actors and singers. **Tom Mix** (1880–1940), movie cowboy, died in a car accident near Florence, and a memorial marks the spot there. A hometown boy, movie cowboy and singer, **Rex Allen** (1920–99) was born and raised in Willcox. His birthplace still celebrates Rex Allen Days. Kingman has a street named after its favorite son, movie star **Andy Devine** (1905–77).

Later stars include **Steve Allen** (1921–) author, musician, and radio and television personality. He attended Arizona State College, the present-day ASU, and had a radio show on KOY. ASU's School of Broadcast Journalism is named for newscaster **Walter Cronkite** (1916–). Dancer **Ann Miller** (1919–) now makes her home in Sedona. **Dick Van Dyke** (1925–), movie and TV star, lives in Carefree, as does TV personality **Hugh Downs** (1921–).

Former baseball player and TV personality **Joe Garagiola, Sr.** (1926–), lives in the Phoenix area and broadcasts some baseball games for the Arizona Diamondbacks. **Al Michaels** (1944–), sportscaster for ABC, is an ASU alumnus. Popular radio personality **Paul Harvey** (1918–) has a home in Phoenix.

Comedian **Garry Shandling** (1949–) is an alumnus of the University of Arizona, as are actors **Greg Kinnear** (1963–) and **Craig T. Nelson** (1946–). Television personality and author **Geraldo Rivera** (1943–) graduated from the U of A before he went to law school. **Joan Ganz Cooney** (1929–), creator of the PBS television show *Sesame Street,* is another U of A alumna.

ASU and Scottsdale's Saguaro High School are alma maters for **David Spade** (1965–), TV and movie comedian. **Mare Winningham** (1959–), TV and movie actor, was born in Phoenix, and actor **Sean Young** (1959–) has her own production company in Arizona. Television stars **Jaime Lyn Bauer** (1949–) and **Lynda Carter** (1951–) grew up in Phoenix. And director and producer **Steven Spielberg** (1947–) attended Arcadia High School in Phoenix.

Musicians.

Country singers **Marty Robbins** (1925–82) and **Waylon Jennings** (1937–) have Arizona roots. Writer of *Ghost Riders in the Sky* and other western songs, **Stan Jones** (1914–63) came from Douglas. Singer **Glen Campbell** (1936–) now lives in Paradise Valley. **Stevie Nicks** (1948–), formerly of Fleetwood Mac, was raised in Scottsdale. Singer **Linda Ronstadt**'s (1946–) roots in Tucson go back several generations. Popular Las Vegas entertainer **Wayne Newton** (1942–) grew up in Phoenix and got his start as a child on a local TV show. And singer **Alice Cooper** (1948–) graduated from Phoenix' North High School and owns a popular restaurant near the Bank One Ballpark, called Alice CoopersTown.

Native Arizonan **R. Carlos Nakai** (1946–), is a Grammy-nominated flutist who uses his Navajo and Ute heritage and his classical music training to create scores for film and television. Nakai has produced many solo albums and collaborated with Arizona musicians such as **William Eaton** (1946–) and **Will Clipman** (1945–). **Robert Tree Cody** (1928–), of Maricopa and Dakota heritage, is another well-known flutist.

Several bands come from Arizona. These include **Gin Blossoms**, **Megadeth Arizona**, and **The Refreshments**.

Ethnic Distribution

Caucasians, including Hispanics, dominate the Arizona population with 89 percent of the total. The fastest growing ethnic sub-group is that of Hispanics, which now comprise about 21 percent of the state's people. In second place are American Indians, members of Arizona's 21 tribes, with 6 percent. African Americans make up 3.4 percent, and Asians or Pacific Islanders 1.7 percent.

Ethnic Breakdown

	1990	1994
White	3,288,290	3,623,222
% of total population	89.4	88.9
African American	115,575	138,609
% of total population	3.1	3.4
Native American	215,826	238,475
% of total population	5.9	5.9
Asian or Pacific Islander	59,012	75,782
% of total population	1.6	1.8
Hispanic origin (of any race, total)	695,789	823,587
% of total population	18.9	20.2

Source: *1997–1998 Arizona Yearbook*

Fairs and Festivals

(*SEE ALSO* CALENDAR OF EVENTS) These are some of the many celebrations held each month throughout Arizona:

January

Carefree—Fine Arts and Wine Festival on Ho Hum and Easy Streets.

Litchfield Park—West Valley Native American Invitational Fine Arts Festival at West Valley Fine Arts Center.

Phoenix—Dr. Martin Luther King Jr. Cultural Festival at Margaret T. Hance Park.

Tucson—Southern Arizona Square and Round Dance Festival; First People's Worlds Fair and Pow Wow; Thunder in the Desert at Rillito Raceway Park.

Willcox—Wings Over Willcox Sandhill Crane Celebration.

Yuma—Lettuce Days at Main Street Plaza, celebrating the winter lettuce capital of the world; Old Town Jubilee at Main Street Plaza.

February

Apache Junction—Lost Dutchman Days (gold panning, pro rodeos); Arizona's Renaissance Festival, weekends through March.

Benson—Territorial Days at City Park.

Casa Grande— O'odham Tash (Pow Wow, all-Indian rodeo).

Flagstaff—Winterfest at Arizona Snowbowl (winter games, sled dog races, snow sculpture).

Fountain Hills—Great Fair (arts and crafts fair, hot air balloons).

Goodyear— Goodyear Rodeo Days at Estrella Mountain Regional Park.

Mesa—AZ Scottish Highland Games at Mesa Community College.

Phoenix—Chinese Week at Patriot's Square; New Year's Banquet; Matsuri: A Festival of Japan at Heritage Square.

Tubac—Festival of the Arts.

Wellton—Pioneer Day Parade and Fiesta at Westside and Butterfield Parks.

Wickenburg—Gold Rush Days (rodeo, gold panning, mining contest).

Yuma—Yuma Crossing Days at Yuma Crossing State Historic Park.

March

Ajo— O'odham Day Celebration at Organ Pipe Cactus National Monument.

Black Canyon City—White Cane Day Parade and Fiesta Days.

Buckeye—Pioneer Days at City Park.

Casa Grande—Pinal County Fair at Pinal County Fairgrounds.

Cave Creek—Magic Bird's Cave Creek Sonoran Spring Festival.

Chandler—Ostrich Festival (ostrich races, carnival).

Coolidge—Cotton Days at San Carlos Park (cotton bale rolling contest).

Florence—Founders Day festivities.

Marana—Founders Day Celebration at Marana Park (all-Indian market and fair).

Mesa—Chicago Fest at the corner of Main and Macdonald Streets.

Parker—La Paz County Fair at Manataba Park.

Phoenix—St. Patrick's Day Parade and Irish Family Faire; Heard Museum Guild Indian Fair and Market.

San Carlos—Indian Festival at St. Charles School (Apache Crown Dancers).

Scottsdale—National Festival of the West at Rawhide; chuck wagon cook-off, mounted action shooting championships, stick horse races.

Sedona—International Film Festival (international independent cinema).

Superior—Welcome Back Buzzards at Boyce Thompson Arboretum (local flock of turkey vultures return to the eucalyptus grove).

Tempe—Tempe Spring Festival of the Arts on Mill Avenue.

Tombstone—Territorial Days (1880 fire cart championship races).

Tucson—Fourth Avenue Spring Street Fair; St. Patrick's Day Parade and Irish Festival.

Yuma—County Fair at Yuma County Fairgrounds.

April

Cave Creek/Carefree—Fiesta Days.

Chandler—San Tan Arts Festival at Chandler-Gilbert Community College.

Deer Valley—Lions Airlift and Deer Valley Days at Deer Valley Airport (Confederate Air Force fliers).

Kearny—Pioneer Days Festival at Pioneer Park.

Miami—Mining Country Boom Town Spree (old-fashioned mining competitions, a bed race through town).

Peoria—Pioneer Days.

Phoenix—Arizona Asian Festival at Patriot's Park; Maricopa County Fair at Arizona State Fairgrounds.

Pima—Heritage Days.

Tolleson—Whoopee Daze at Sports Complex.

Tsalle—Navajo Community College Pow Wow at Navajo Community College.

Tucson—Pima County Fair at Pima County Fairgrounds.

Looking Back

July 4, 1876

New England immigrants raise a flag on a pine tree, giving Flagstaff its name.

May

Ajo—Cinco de Mayo (celebrating Mexico's defeat of the French in the 19th century).

Bisbee—Mile High Chili Cook-Off.

Cottonwood—Sizzlin' Salsa Sunday/Cinco de Mayo Celebration in Historic Old Town; Verde Valley Fair.

Globe—Cinco de Mayo Fiesta downtown (mariachi bands, piñata breaking).

Lake Havasu City—Cinco de Mayo Regatta at Thompson Bay.

Mesa—Cinco de Mayo Fiestas at Pioneer Park.

Page—Cowboy Days and Indian Nights (Native American Pow Wow).

Pine—Mountain Arts and Crafts Festival at the Community Center.

Prescott—Cinco de Mayo Celebration at Granite Creek Park.

Rock Springs—Sweet Onion Festival at Rock Springs Café.

Tombstone—Wyatt Earp Days (gunfights, saloon girls, public hanging).

Tucson—Cinco de Mayo at Kennedy Park (folklorico dancers).

Williams—Rendezvous Days

(re-enacts reunion of Mountain Men, black powder shoot).

Yarnell—Yarnell Daze.

Yuma—Cinco de Mayo Parade and Celebration in Historic Downtown; Colorado River Festival (float the Colorado River).

June

Goodyear—Cool Corn and Melon Celebration at Duncan's Sunfresh Farms.

Holbrook—Old West Celebration and Bucket of Blood Races at the Old Courthouse Lawn; Native American Dances at Historic Courthouse Square (various authentic dances in which public can participate through August 15).

Mayer—Mayer Daze at the Recreation Center.

Phoenix—Firecracker Sports Festival at the Rose Mofford Softball Complex (state's longest-running softball tournament); Juneteenth Celebration at East Lake Park; African-American Independence Day celebration.

Prescott—Folk Arts Fair at Sharlot Hall Museum.

Queen Creek—Peach and Potato Festival at Schnepf Farms.

Saint Johns—Fiesta de San Juan Baptista (annual event since 1875).

San Carlos—Apache Independence Day on the San Carlos Apache Reservation.

Strawberry—Strawberry Festival.

Tucson—Juneteenth Festival at Kennedy Park Fiesta Area.

July

Alpine—Worm Race at the Rodeo Grounds and Worm Parade down Main Street (community activities featuring Worm King and Queen).

Bisbee—Fourth of July Celebration (includes a mining contest).

Camp Verde—Cornfest (corn eating and corniest joke contests, hog calling).

Flagstaff—Fair of Life Festival of Arts and Crafts Extraordinaire at Wheeler Park.

Jerome—July Fourth (Indian dances, watermelon and firemen's contests).

Oatman—Sidewalk Egg Frying Challenge; and other "eggciting" events.

Patagonia—July Fourth Celebration (includes Cowchip Tossing Contest).

Peach Springs—Hualapai Youth Pow Wow.

Pinetop/Lakeside—White Mountain Native American Art Festival and Indian Market.

Prescott—Frontier Days and World's Oldest Rodeo.

St. Johns—Pioneer Days (held since 1879).

Seligman—Seligman Days.

Snowflake—Pioneer Day Celebration.

Window Rock—Fourth of July Celebration, PRCA Rodeo and Pow Wow.

August

Eagar—Eagar Daze at Ramsey Park (logging competition).

Prescott—Arizona Cowboy Poets Gathering at Sharlot Hall Museum

---

Miss Americas

Two Miss Arizona winners have gone on to become Miss America in the annual pageant at Atlantic City, New Jersey. The first, Jacque Mercer of Litchfield Park, reigned in 1949. The second, Vonda Kay Van Dyke of Phoenix, was Miss America in 1965. ✻

(cowboy yodeling, traditional and contemporary cowboy poetry recitation).

Sierra Vista—Southwest Wings Birding Festival at Windemere Hotel in the Hummingbird Capital of the United States.

Tombstone—Vigilante Day (shoot-outs, hangings, saloon girls).

Willcox—Peach Mania Festival at Apple Annie's Orchard.

September
Ajo—Fiesta de Septiembre at Bud Walker Park.

Bisbee—Brewery Gulch Days.

Chino Valley—Chino Valley Days at Memory Park; First Territorial Capital Days.

Cottonwood—Verde River Days at Dead Horse Ranch State Park.

Douglas—Cochise County Fair at County Fairgrounds.

Duncan—Greenlee County Fair at the Fairgrounds.

Elgin—Harvesting of the Vine Festival (dancing, wine tasting, music).

Flagstaff—Coconino County Fair at Fort Tuthill County Fairgrounds.

Globe—Gila County Fair.

Holbrook—Navajo County Fair and Rodeo at Navajo County Fairgrounds.

Kingman—Mohave County Fair at Mohave County Fairgrounds.

Oatman—Gold Camp Days (burro biscuit tossing contest).

Parker—National Indian Days (Pow Wow).

Pine—Mountain Arts and Crafts Festival at the Community Center.

Pinetop/Lakeside—Fall Festival.

Prescott—Yavapai County Fair.

Prescott Valley—Gold Fever Day at Fain Park (fishing, gold panning).

St. Johns—Apache County Fair.

Salome—Dick Wick Day

sponsored by the Lion's Club.

Sedona—Jazz on the Rocks Benefit Festival at Verde Valley School Amphitheater (internationally known jazz festival).

Sierra Vista—Oktoberfest at Veterans Memorial Park.

Sonoita—Santa Cruz County Fair at Fairgrounds (3-day roping event).

Superior—Bye-Bye Buzzards at Boyce Thompson Arboretum (seasonal departure of resident flock of turkey vultures).

Tucson—Oktoberfest at Mount Lemmon Ski Valley; Great Southwest Oktoberfest at Kino Sports Complex.

Whiteriver—White Mountain Apache Tribal Fair and Rodeo.

Williams—American Indian Heritage Festival at Visitor's Center.

Window Rock—Navajo Nation Fair; Pow Wow, rodeo, fry bread contest.

Winslow—West's Best Rodeo and Bull Sunday.

October
Ajo—Fall Festival.

Ash Fork—Oktoberfest at Centennial Park.

Avondale—Billy Moore Days at Coldwater Park (founders day celebration).

Benson—Butterfield Overland Stage Days.

Camp Verde—Fort Verde Days; Oktoberfest in the Southwest on Main Street.

Cave Creek—Halloween West Fest.

Clarkdale—October Square Fest at Clark Memorial Hall (square and round dancing).

Congress—Old Congress Days.

Coolidge—Calvin Coolidge Days.

Dewey—Young's Farm Pumpkin Festival.

Eagar/Springerville—Indian

Summer Round-Up at Round Valley Dome.

Elfrida—Harvest Festival at Van-Meter Park.

Flagstaff—Oktoberfest at Wheeler Park.

Glendale—Fire Prevention Parade and Firefighter's Muster at Murphy Park.

Globe/Miami—Apache Jii Day (all-Indian celebration; Bustle and Boots Square Dance Festival at Gila County Fairgrounds).

Goodyear—Pumpkin Festival at Duncan's Sunfresh Farms.

Kearny—Fall Street Fair.

Kingman—Andy Devine Days and PRCA Rodeo at Mohave County Fairgrounds.

Lake Havasu City—London Bridge Square Dance Jamboree under the Bridge and London Bridge Days.

Oatman—Jezebel Day (saloon girl performing group, gunfights).

Page—Air Affaire (hot air balloons, Navy Leap Frog Parachute Team).

Patagonia—Fall Festival in Town Park.

Peoria—Mid-West Fest at Peoria Sports Complex (iguana beauty pageant).

Phoenix—Arizona Classic Jazz Festival at Crowne Plaza Hotel; Arizona State Fair at State Fairgrounds; Dia de los Muertos Festival at Heard Museum.

Pinetop/Lakeside—Oktoberfest.

Prescott—Folk Music Festival at Sharlot Hall Museum.

Safford—Graham County Fair.

Sedona—Fiesta Del Tlaquepaque (piñatas, mariachis, folklorico groups, Flamenco and classical guitarists).

Tempe—Mill Avenue Masquerade Adventure at Hayden Square; Way Out West Oktoberfest on Hayden Square.

Tombstone—Helldorado Days (shootouts, Indian dancers, period fashion show).

Tucson—Oktoberfest at Mount Lemmon Ski Valley; Tucson Heritage Experience Festival at El Presidio Park (multi-ethnic fair).

Willcox—Rex Allen Days at Keiller Park; PRCA rodeo, General Willcox International Turtle Race.

Yuma—Dia de los Muertos celebration.

November

Ahwatukee—Foothills Festival of Lights (horse-drawn hayrides, through January).

Bisbee—Festival of Lights.

Bullhead City—Hardyville Days (founders day celebration, Old West activities).

Chandler—Tumbleweed Tree Lighting Ceremony and Parade of Lights at A. J. Chandler Park.

Cottonwood—Zeke Taylor Open Pit Barbecue.

Flagstaff—Independent Film Festival.

Fountain Hills—Fountain Festival of Arts and Crafts.

Glendale—Glendale Glitters Spectacular at Murphy Park, through end of December.

Lake Havasu City—Havasu Gem and Mineral Festival at Nautical Inn Conference Center; Festival of Lights at English Village and London Bridge.

San Carlos—Veterans' Memorial Fair, Pageant and Rodeo.

Surprise—Grand Old West Fest.

Wickenburg—Bluegrass Festival and Fiddle Championship at Constellation Park.

December

Flagstaff—Holiday of Lights Festival at Little America Hotel, through January.

Page—Festival of Lights Boat Parade (view from Wahweap Lodge and Marina).

Peoria—Holiday Tree Fest in Washington Park.

Phoenix—Victorian Holiday Celebration and Craft Fair.

Pinetop/Lakeside—Tree Lighting and Woodland Holiday Lighting Festival at Woodland Lake Covered Bridge.

Prescott Valley—Holiday Festival of Lights.

Sedona—Festival of Lights at Tlaquepaque.

Tempe—Fall Festival of the Arts on Mill Avenue; Fiesta Bowl Block Party on Mill Avenue New Year's Eve.

Tubac—Fiesta Navidad.

Tucson—Fourth Avenue Street Fair.

Tumacacori—La Fiesta de Tumacacori.

Wickenburg—Cowboy Christmas and Cowboy Poets Gathering at Desert Caballeros Western Museum.

Willcox—Christmas Apple Festival.

Window Rock—Christmas Arts and Crafts Fair.

Famous Arizonans of the Past (SEE ALSO COCHISE; GERONIMO; POSTON, CHARLES)

Mary Bernard Aguirre (1844–1906) writer, teacher

Nellie Trent Bush (1888–1963) first woman licensed riverboat pilot; founder of Parker, Arizona; women's suffrage leader

Christopher Houston "Kit" Carson (1809–68) Army scout and outdoorsman

Nellie Cashman (1844–1925) gold prospector, businesswoman, philanthropist

Cochise (1812–74) Chiricahua Apache chief

General George Crook (1828–90) led U.S. Army in Apache Wars

Andrew Ellicott Douglass (1867–1962) astronomer, inventor of dendrochronology (tree ring dating)

Wyatt S. Earp (1848–1929) frontier lawman

Eulalia Elias (1786–1865) cattle rancher

Estevan (?–1539) North African who explored Arizona for Spain

John C. Fremont (1813–90) explorer, Civil War general, Arizona governor

Geronimo (1829–1909) Chiricahua Apache warrior

Sharlot M. Hall (1870–1943) poet, author, historian

Maie Bartlett Heard (1868–1951) co-founder of Heard Museum

John Henry "Doc" Holliday (1851–87) dentist, gambler, frontier gun fighter

Josephine Brawley Hughes (1839–1926) teacher, journalist, women's activist

Father Eusebio Kino (1645–1711) missionary

Lozen (1840s–90s) Chiricahua Apache warrior, medicine woman

General Nelson A. Miles (1839–1925) man to whom Geronimo surrendered, ending Apache Wars

Carlos Montezuma (given name Wassaja) (1865–1923) physician, early American Indian activist

Frances Lillian Willard Munds (1866–1948) state Senator, women's activist

Nampeyo (1860–1942) started the revival of high-quality, polychrome Hopi pottery

Fray Marcos de Niza (1495–1558) Spanish missionary and explorer

Charles D. Poston (1825–1902)

entrepreneur, territorial delegate to Congress, "Father of Arizona"

Ida Redbird (1892–1971) instrumental in revival of Maricopa tribe's pottery industry

Sarah Herring Sorin (1861–1914) attorney, teacher

Carmen Soto Vasquez (1861–1934) impresario, theatrical producer

Fish and Fishing

Williams Creek National Fish Hatchery raises the golden Apache trout, Arizona's state fish and a protected species. Mountain lakes have rainbow and brown trout and bass, among others. In the lakes at lower elevations are bass, crappie, sunfish, catfish, and trout, to name a few. The endangered desert pupfish lives in Quitobaquito Spring at Organ Pipe Cactus National Monument and in Ayer Lake at Boyce Thompson Arboretum.

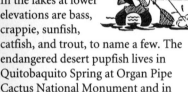

Some interesting fish you can find in Arizona include:

Apache Trout *(Oncorhynchus gilae apache):* This bright golden yellow trout with black freckles is Arizona's state fish and is found only in the state. It's a small fish that eats invertebrates and tinier fish. The largest one ever caught weighed 5 lb., 3 oz. One of only two trout native to Arizona (the other is the Gila trout), the Apache used to be abundant in the state's high-country eastern rivers. Today it is only found in a small area on the Fort Apache Indian Reservation. Although it was listed as "endangered" in 1969, its status was upgraded to "threatened" in 1974 due to conservation efforts. On public land, if you catch one, you must release it.

Fishing in Arizona's lakes, rivers and mountain creeks is popular the year around. The Game and Fish Department (2221 W. Greenway Road, Phoenix 85023, telephone 602-942-3000) lists these "best fishing" locations:

Arctic grayling: Lee Valley Reservoir.

Bluegill (sunfish): Apache, Roper, Saguaro, Pleasant, Arivaca, Powell and Bartlett lakes.

Carp: Havasu, Mohave, Mead, Powell, Roosevelt, San Carlos, Bartlett, Pleasant, Saguaro, Canyon and Apache Lakes.

Crappie: Roosevelt, Bartlett, Pleasant and San Carlos Lakes.

Flathead catfish: Colorado River at Yuma, Roosevelt and Bartlett Lakes, Verde River at Camp Verde and below Horseshoe Lake, San Carlos Lake and Gila River at Safford.

Largemouth bass: Alamo, Bartlett, Roosevelt, Apache, Canyon, Saguaro, San Carlos, Havasu, Mead, Powell, Pleasant and Mittry Lakes.

Northern pike: Upper Lake Mary, Stoneman Lake and Long Lake.

Pupfish (Genus *Cyprinodon*) These fish are tiny (only 1 to 2 inches long), but they can live in water that is hotter and saltier than can any other fish. They can also withstand extreme changes in temperature. In the winter, they burrow into the mud at the bottom of the pond and go dormant. Their silver skin has dark bands of color on the sides. When ready to breed, in the spring and early summer, males turn iridescent blue. They eat brown and green algae. When desert pools dry up in late summer, most pupfish die, but a few survive and can live for about one year. The desert pupfish *(Cyprinodon macularius macularius)* and Quitobaquito pupfish

(Continued on page 86)

Arizona Fish Records

Species	Angler	Weight lbs.	oz.	Length (inches)	Place	Year
Inland Waters, Hook and Line						
Bass, Largemouth	Randall E. White, Mesa	16	7.68	28.0	Canyon Lake	1997
Bass, Smallmouth	Dennis K. Barnhill, Mesa	7	0.96	22.75	Roosevelt Lake	1988
Bass, Striped	David Jackson, Phoenix	23	8.32	39.25	Alamo Lake	1997
Bass, White	David Amburgey, Peoria	4	11.7	19.5	Upper Lake Pleasant	1972
Bass, Yellow	Glenn D. Davis III, Flagstaff	1	15.8	11.25	Upper Lake Mary	1995
Bluegill	Ernest Garcia, Safford	3	5.0	13.0	Pond, San Carlos Res.	1965
Buffalo, Bigmouth	Leon Stewart, Payson	36	6.0	38.5	Roosevelt Lake	1995
Buffalo, Black	David Hoenshell, Mesa	35	6.72	40.5	Canyon Lake	1995
Bullhead, Black	Wallace Nakagawa, Willcox	2	4.6	15.3	Parker Canyon Lake	1993
Bullhead, Yellow	Patricia Simmon, Phoenix	4	8.1	17.75	Mormon Lake	1989
Carp	Jonathan Gardner, Phoenix	37	0.0	40.0	Bartlett Lake	1987
Catfish, Blue	Richard Lujan, Tucson	31	0.0	40.0	Randolph Park, Tucson	1970
Catfish, Channel	Chuck Berndt, Sierra Vista	32	4.0	38.75	Parker Canyon Lake	1987
Catfish, Flathead	Clayton Randall, Pine	71	0.0	52.0	Roosevelt Lake	1998
Crappie, Black	John Shadrick, Mammoth	4	10.0	n/a	San Carlos Lake	1959
Crappie, White	Robert Schnell, Glendale	3	5.28	16.75	Lake Pleasant	1982
Grayling, Arctic	Glenn D. Davis III, Flagstaff	1	9.76	14.65	Lee Valley Lake	1995
Mullet	Sylvia Van Etten, Yuma	1	1.3	15.75	Salinity Canal, Yuma	1981
Northern Pike	Adolph W. Zeugner, Jr.	24	3.0	47.5	Upper Lake Mary	1991
Roundtail Chub	Richard Walton, Chandler	3	14.9	18.5	Lower Salt River	1984
Sucker, Desert	Edith Toney, Mesa	2	10.75	18.0	Verda River	1992
Sucker, Sonora	Jay Nochta, Phoenix	5	6.4	20.25	Canal Park Lake	1996
Sunfish, Green	Paul Bennett, Sierra Vista	1	9.0	11.0	Parker Canyon Lake	1996
Sunfish, Hybrid	Mikey Alan Porter, Tucson	2	2.22	12.5	Patagonia Lake	1998
Sunfish, Redear	Jay Adkins, Prescott	3	9.0	14.5	Goldwater Lake, Prescott	1993
Tilapia	Tim Pudney, Mesa	5	8.0	18.5	Saguaro Lake	1996
Trout, Apache	Lyle Hemphill, Lakeside	5	15.5	24.0	Hurricane Lake	1993
Trout, Brook	Marshall Gregg, Whiteriver	4	15.2	20.5	Sunrise Lake	1995
Trout, Brown	Burke Hudnall, Snowflake	16	7.0	29.5	Horseshoe Cienaga Lake	1985
Trout, Cutthroat	Eric James Walter, Tucson	6	5.0	22.3	Luna Lake	1976
Trout, Rainbow	Eddie Sorenson, Tucson	11	1.0	29.0	Nelson Reservoir	1979
Walleye	Bruce Mohning, Lakeside	12	12.0	29.63	Show Low Lake	1989
White Amur (Trip)	David Glover, Wittman	40	3.68	40	Encanto Park	1998
Yellow Perch	Art Ellico, Kingman	1	10.0	13.5	Stoneman Lake	1984
(Tie)	Curt Bryant, Flagstaff	1	10.0	13.5	Stoneman Lake	1984
Inland Waters, Non-Hook and Line (Archery)						
Buffalo, Bigmouth	Michael T. Young, Mesa	39	8.0	41.5	Saguaro Lake	1990
Buffalo, Black	Ronald Nuss, Jr., Mesa	25	7.2	36.0	Apache Lake	1997
Buffalo, Smallmouth	David Hester, Chandler	38	8.0	36.0	Canyon Lake	1997
Carp	David J. Duckwiler, Tucson	33	8.0	42.0	Roosevelt Lake	1991
Sonora Sucker	Ronald Nuss, Jr., Mesa	4	15.52	23.5	Lower Salt River	1997
Tilapia	Dell Owens, Phoenix	4	1.0	18.0	Alamo Lake	1984
Colorado River Waters, Hook and Line						
Bass, Largemouth	Date Uden, Yuma	16	14.0	28.25	Colorado River, Yuma	1996
Bass, Smallmouth	Gene Albers, Fontana, CA	5	2.72	21.5	CO River, Parker	1997
Bass, Striped	Jeff Smith, Henderson, NV	67	1.0	47.5	CO River, Willow Beach	1997
Bass, White	Norman Mize, Chula Vista, CA	5	5.0	19.6	Imperial Reservoir	1972

Species	Angler	Weight lbs.	oz.	Length (inches)	Place	Year
Colorado River Waters, Hook and Line *continued*						
Bluegill	Ben Mellott, Kingman	2	11.5	11.75	Bradley Bay, Lake Mead	1989
Bullhead, Yellow	Douglas R. Pinotti, Mesa	2	8.8	15.5	CO River/Bullhead City	1986
Carp	Gary Ramsfield, Lake Havasu City	42	0.0	43.0	Lake Havasu	1979
Catfish, Channel	Wendo Tull, Barstow, CA	35	4.0	38.0	Topock Marsh	1952
Catfish, Flathead	Walter Wilson, Bard, CA	74	0.0	51.5	CO River/ Laguna Dam	1998
Crappie, Black	Julie Grammer, Makanda, IL	2	12.0	16.0	Havasu Spgs, Lake Havasu	1996
Goldfish	Jack E. Bogel, Parker	5	13.0	18.38	CO River/Castle Rock	1997
Mullet	Buddy E. Fike, Glendale	9	8.0	25.5	CO River/Gila Rvr confl	1976
Pacific Tenpounder	Charles Reel, Jr. Yuma		12.6	15.75	Near Pilot Knob	1981
Sucker, Razorback	Freeman Summers, Lake Havasu City	9	13.0	29.0	CO River/Lake Havasu	1978
Sunfish, Green	Jose Orozco, Poston	1	5.28	11.5	Lake Havasu	1997
Sunfish, Redear	Corey Milbrandt, Cathedral City, CA	2	14.0	14.0	Lake Havasu	1995
Tilapia	Tom Bruce Wilson, Winterhaven, CA	5	6.0	17.75	CO River/ Yuma	1991
Trout, Brook	Moe Beck, Glendale	5	4.0	19.0	Lee's Ferry	1982
Trout, Brown	Chuck Holland, Phoenix	17	0.0	32.0	Last Chance Bay, Lake. Powell	1971
Trout, Cutthroat	Jeff Vincent, Mohave Mesa	9	8.0	30.5	S. of Davis Dam	1979
Trout, Rainbow	John Reid, Las Vegas, NV	21	5.5	n/a	Willow Beach	1966
Walleye	Bud Clifford, Phoenix	8	1.0	29.0	Lake Powell	1977
Warmouth	Patrick Ferguson, Yuma		12.0	10.0	Senator Lake	1974
Colorado River Waters, Non-Hook and Line (Archery)						
Carp	Gil Blum, Wittmann	23	4.0	37.5	CO River/Imperial Dam	1995
Mullet	Dell Owens, Phoenix	3	13.0	21.0	CO River/Yuma	1991
Tilapia	Kenny Marler, Yuma	7	11.0	19.38	CO River/Imperial Dam	1996

Source: Arizona Game and Fish Department

(Continued from page 84)
(Cyprinodon macularius eremus) are endangered and protected by federal law.

Smallmouth bass: Powell, Roosevelt, Apache and Black River.

Striped bass: Havasu, Mohave, Mead and Powell.

Trout: In most mountain lakes, Black River, Blue Ridge Reservoir, Colorado River in the Grand Canyon, Oak Creek near Sedona, Salt River near Phoenix and Tonto Creek.

Walleye: Canyon, Apache, Show Low, Long, Mary and Saguaro Lakes.

White bass: Lake Pleasant.

Yellow bass: Saguaro, Canyon and Apache Lakes.

Fishing licenses are required. Arizona resident general fishing license, warm water species only, $12; nonresident, $38. Trout stamps are an additional $10. Combination hunting and fishing license, resident, $34; nonresident, $100.

The Five C's
From territorial times to the recent past, Arizona's economy was based on its "Five C's"— Copper, Cattle, Cotton, Citrus and Climate.

Mining was the first lure that drew

adventurers here. Lust for gold brought hordes of treasure seekers to central Arizona's Bradshaw Mountains and to several strikes along the Colorado River. Tombstone's boom was based on silver. But the precious metals soon were exhausted and it became evident that Arizona's long-term mining prosperity depended on copper. Huge deposits were discovered at Jerome, Bisbee, Bagdad, Globe, Morenci and several locations near Tucson. For many years, Arizona has been the nation's leading producer of copper, and the industry continues to survive, despite the depressed price of copper.

Cattle ranching provided employment for many thousands of Arizonans in the late 19th century and the first half of the 20th. Vast areas were encompassed in such great ranches as the Sierra Bonita in southeast Arizona and the CO-Bar in the northern portion of the territory. For years, sheep made an important economic impact, but today they have almost disappeared from the scene. Cattle ranching too has declined in relative importance, but cowboys, roundups and rodeos will be a colorful part of Arizona life for decades to come.

Cotton has also passed its peak in the state's economic picture. Once cotton fields covered large areas of central and southern Arizona and made a mighty contribution to the economy. Gradually the cotton farms of the Salt River Valley have been replaced by residential tracts. The advent of synthetic fibers was a blow to the market. But cotton farming, made possible by irrigation, is still important, particularly in Maricopa and Pinal Counties south of Phoenix to Eloy, and other hot-weather portions of the state.

Citrus groves once covered much of the Salt River Valley, and Arizona

Daylight Saving? No

When most other Americans turn their clocks forward in April and thus lose an hour of sleep, Arizonans ignore Daylight Saving Time. Most of the state's people live in sunny desert cities where summer temperatures routinely climb past 100°F. They decided many years ago that they did not need an extra hour of sunlight during the hot months.

Visitors should therefore remember that Arizona (with the exception of the Navajo Reservation) is on the same clock setting as the Pacific coast in summer. For six months beginning in October, Arizona is on the same time as other Rocky Mountain states, Mountain Standard Time. ✳

oranges, grapefruit and lemons were exported all over the nation. Today some of the groves in Mesa, in the East Valley, remain as a reminder of the citrus boom. Most of the trees around Phoenix and its environs have been removed to make room for housing developments. Today there are more citrus trees in the Yuma area, along the Colorado River, than in Phoenix, but residents in the Salt River Valley who are lucky enough to have one or more orange and grapefruit trees in their yards are grateful.

Climate brought many hundreds of thousands of new residents to Arizona over the years and made possible the very lucrative tourism industry. In the early years of the 20th century, more people came to Arizona because of respiratory ailments than for any other reason. The warm, dry climate benefited many sufferers from tuberculosis and asthma. During the last 30 years, increasing numbers of "snowbirds" have flocked to the state from northern cold country to enjoy Arizona's warm winters. Today, affluent guests at the luxury resort hotels of Scottsdale, Phoenix, Tucson, and other sun-drenched cities, as well as tens of thousands of RVers in campgrounds and remote desert sites, swell Arizona's population from October to May.

Flagstaff

Flagstaff is the queen city of northern Arizona. Not only does it have much to offer the visitor in scenery, education, the arts and recreation, but it is the hub city for exploration of all northern Arizona tourist attractions. It is the home of Northern Arizona University, the Snowbowl winter sports facility, excellent hotels and restaurants, Lowell Observatory, the Museum of Northern Arizona, Riordan State Historic Park and much more.

Within two hours' driving distance are the Grand Canyon, Oak Creek Canyon, Sedona, Sunset Crater, the Walnut Canyon cliff dwellings, Wupatki and Tuzigoot ruins, Meteor Crater, Montezuma Castle and Montezuma Well, Mount Humphreys and Jerome State Historic Park.

Situated at an altitude of 7,000 feet, Flagstaff is surrounded by one of North America's most extensive pine forests. Its 60,000-plus residents enjoy snow in winter, and very little hot weather in summer. Flagstaff traces its origins to July 4, 1876, when New England settlers arrived and nailed a flag to the top of a pine tree to celebrate the nation's centennial. During its colorful history it has been a railroad town (Santa Fe), a forestry town, a cow town, a college town, and a tourist mecca. Flagstaff offers visitors Amtrak rail travel, a convenient municipal airport, and the junction of two major freeways, Interstate 40 and Interstate 17.

Florence

Florence, the county seat of Pinal County, was founded in 1866 as a stage stop and copper mining trade center. Many adobe homes from the territorial period are still standing, including the home of Levi Ruggles, the first settler.

The Arizona Territorial Prison was moved here from Yuma after the turn of the century and became a major source of employment. Farming and ranching are other economic supports of the city. Its population is estimated at almost 15,000.

McFarland State Historic Park, an adobe brick building which housed the town's early courthouse, jail and hospital, attracts many visitors, as does the Victorian courthouse (1891).

Food

(SEE ALSO CHILES) Arizonans love many kinds of food, and, like Americans everywhere, eat plenty of pizza, fried chicken and hamburgers. Southwest cooking, however, conjures up images of cowboy steaks and chuckwagon beans, barbecues and chili cook-offs. It seems everyone in Arizona has a family recipe for *chili con carne,* with a patented "secret ingredient." While *carne* means "meat" in Spanish, in cattle country carne can mean only one thing—beef, Podnuh.

Throughout the Southwest one can find *carne asada, carne machaca* and *carne seca.* However, the influence of the state's Native American and

Looking Back

Dec. 30, 1853

The Gadsden Treaty was signed with Mexico, annexing southern Arizona.

Mexican heritage shows most in foods considered "home-cooking." While other states also savor American Indian and Mexican dishes, Arizona-Sonoran cuisine features distinctive tastes, ingredients and names.

For example, most people know about salsa, the tomato-based sauce used for dipping. In Arizona, cumin and cilantro are popular ingredients, and salsas can be made from many 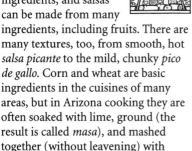 ingredients, including fruits. There are many textures, too, from smooth, hot *salsa picante* to the mild, chunky *pico de gallo*. Corn and wheat are basic ingredients in the cuisines of many areas, but in Arizona cooking they are often soaked with lime, ground (the result is called *masa*), and mashed together (without leavening) with water or fat and patted out into thin, flat, round *tortillas* (in Spanish, "small cakes"). The following foods are made with tortillas:

Burritos—Place cooked meat, cheese, onions, refried beans, etc. onto a flour tortilla and wrap them in it, folding up the bottom edge so it won't leak.

Cheese Crisp or **Corn Crisp**—Melt cheese over a flour tortilla (cheese crisp) or a corn tortilla (corn crisp). You may also add guacamole or strips of green chiles.

Chimichangas—Make a burrito, deep-fry it, and top with enchilada sauce. Some also add sour cream, cheese and guacamole.

Enchiladas—Wrap corn tortillas around meat, cheese or other ingredients, cover with a chile-based sauce and more cheese, and bake.

Flautas—Roll corn tortillas around beef or pork, then deep-fry and top with guacamole (paste made from avocados, chiles and onions).

Tacos—Form corn tortillas into a U shape and fry until crisp. Inside place meat, cheese, fish, etc., along with vegetables such as lettuce and tomato, and add a chile sauce to the top. These are a little bit like Middle Eastern pita sandwiches, but crispy.

Tostadas—Fry corn tortillas flat until crisp and spread *frijoles refritos* (refried beans) and other things on top. In Tex-Mex cooking, these may be called "chalupas."

Corn masa is used to make these favorite foods:

Sonoran Enchiladas—Cover a thick cake of corn masa with red chile and cheese, fry it flat and serve it open-faced with red chile sauce.

Tamales—Press corn masa around meat, seafood, beans, cheese or fresh corn and wrap in a corn husk. Steam until tender, remove the husk, then serve plain or covered with a red or green chile sauce.

Indian Fry Bread is found throughout North America, and no Native American meal, pow wow or fair in Arizona would be complete without it. In fact, fry bread was named Arizona's favorite food in a 1995 *Arizona Republic* survey. It can also be covered with meat, beans and cheese and served flat; this is sometimes called a "Navajo taco."

The most common beans used in Arizona cooking are pinto beans, but black beans are popular, too. Other favorite foods are soups and stews. Mutton-based soups and stews are found most in areas where they raise sheep, and corn is the basis for many recipes. *Pozole* is a corn and meat stew. *Sopa de albóndigas* (meatball soup) and *sopa de tortillas* (tortilla soup) are local favorites. Sonoran *menudo* (tripe stew) is prized by aficionados for its white color (unlike Texas menudo, which is red) and is considered by many to be the best cure for a hangover.

What is Arizona's most popular mixed drink? Why a margarita, of course, particularly if it's made with high-quality Mexican tequila. You can have yours straight up with a coating of salt around the glass, the traditional way, or blended with ice and fruit. *Cerveza* (beer) is also a popular thirst quencher. Non-alcoholic drinks include *horchata*—rice water and cinnamon.

For dessert you might have *sopapillas* (small deep-fried pillows of sweet dough) or fry bread, sprinkled with honey, cinnamon or powdered sugar. *Almendrado* is an almond treat especially popular in Tucson. And don't forget prickly pear cactus fruit candies, jelly or pie. Candies and jelly can also be made from the fruits of the saguaro cactus. Prickly pear cactus fruits are good when pureed over ice cream or in salad dressing.

Football
From high school through the National Football League, football draws huge crowds in Arizona. Almost every town in the state has its lighted football field, and Sun Devil Stadium in Tempe, largest of the football arenas, seats more than 73,000.

On the professional level, the Arizona Cardinals of the NFL host the best teams in the league on autumn Sundays. Since moving to Arizona from St. Louis, the Cardinals have had only marginal success. But Jake Plummer, rated by many as the next great pro quarterback, leads a team that promises to be a contender. The Cardinals play in Sun Devil Stadium. In January of 1996, Arizona played

host to professional football's Super Bowl for the first time.

The Arizona Rattlers in the Arena Football League have been a winner since the team's recent inception. Coached by former Arizona State University and Dallas Cowboys quarterback Danny White, the Rattlers have a national championship under their belts and are contending for more. The Rattlers play in Phoenix's America West Arena.

On the collegiate level, Arizona State University and the University of Arizona play in the prestigious Pacific Ten Conference. Twice ASU has won the conference title and gone on to the Rose Bowl. The Fiesta Bowl, one of the nation's major New Year's Day classics, is played in Sun Devil Stadium. The University of Arizona, which draws nearly 60,000 fans to Arizona Stadium in Tucson, has dominated its century-old series with Arizona State in recent years. Northern Arizona University plays its home games in the Walkup Skydome in Flagstaff and has been successful in the Big Sky Conference.

Forests
One of the nation's largest unbroken stands of Ponderosa pine and Douglas fir forest covers much of Arizona's high country. From the Kaibab National Forest north of the Grand Canyon to the Coronado National Forest in southeastern Arizona, wooded lands are the rule. Nearly a fourth of the state's area is forested.

National Forest preserves offer recreational treasures—lakes, camp-grounds, scenic beauty, winter sports, relief from summer heat—in addition to regulated ranching operations and lumbering. Cattle and sheep ranching is still conducted on National Forest lands, but not as extensively as a century ago, when the open range and lack of regulation made it a more profitable business. Once timber cutting and processing was a major anchor of the state's economy, but the industry has lost much of its importance in recent decades, partly because of stringent government regulation on timber harvesting.

Sawmills in some forest areas process logs into lumber, and there are a number of specialized wood product plants. A sawmill at McNary in the White Mountains was once one of the largest in the Southwest, but it is no longer in operation.

The National Forests in Arizona:

Apache-Sitgreaves National Forest. Easternmost of Arizona's national forests, it is located in Greenlee, Apache, Navajo, and Coconino counties. Information may be obtained from the headquarters office at P.O. Box 640, Springerville 85938.

Coronado National Forest. This forest in southeastern Arizona is divided into 10 sections in Graham, Pima, Santa Cruz, and Cochise counties. Information is available by writing to the forest headquarters, 300 W. Congress St., Tucson 85701.

Coconino National Forest. The forest extends from a point north of Flagstaff to the Tonto Rim on the south. Headquarters address: 2323 E. Greenlaw Lane, Flagstaff 86004.

Kaibab National Forest. Northernmost of the national forests in the state, its headquarters is at 800 S. Sixth St., Williams 86046.

Prescott National Forest. Prescott is in the center of this smallest of the Arizona national forests, in Yavapai County. Headquarters address: 503 E. Gurley St., Prescott 86301.

Tonto National Forest. This forest in central Arizona covers an area in Yavapai, Maricopa, Gila, and Pinal counties. Headquarters address: 2324 E. McDowell Road, Phoenix 85066.

Fountain Hills
Aquatic sports lovers driving from Mesa north

World's highest fountain, 560 feet, Fountain Hills. Photo by James Tallon.

UTAH

NEVADA

GRAND CANYON COUNTRY

INDIAN COUNTRY

N

Flagstaff
•

Kingman
•

Prescott
•

CENTRAL TERRITORY

HIGH COUNTRY

NEW MEXICO

CALIFORNIA

ARIZONA'S WEST COAST

Phoenix
✪
VALLEY OF THE SUN

Yuma
•

OLD WEST COUNTRY

Tucson
•

MEXICO

Nogales
•

to Sahuaro Lake keep an eye out for Fountain Hills and the spouting of its famous fountain, which can be seen for many miles. It spews water 560 feet into the air and is certified by the *Guinness Book of World Records* as the tallest fountain in the world. Fountain Hills is a residential community of nearly 20,000 people. Started by an industrialist and developer, Robert McCulloch, it is a relative newcomer to the central

Arizona family of cities; it was incorporated in 1989.

Gadsden Purchase

Only five years after Mexico had ceded nearly a third of its territory to the United States in 1848, Mexican dictator Antonio Lopez de Santa Anna agreed to sell an additional 29,670 square miles, most of it comprising the area south of the Gila River in Arizona. Commissioner James

Gadsden and Mexican officials signed the treaty on Dec. 30, 1853, setting a price of $15 million on the land, through which the U.S. hoped to build a portion of a transcontinental railway. Gadsden had hoped to acquire a much larger piece of northern Mexico including an outlet on the Gulf of California, but Santa Anna would not agree to part with more.

Ratification of the treaty was hotly debated in the U.S. Senate for months, with many northern senators opposed because they believed it would strengthen the southern states in the sectional strife that was already heating up. The Senate finally approved the purchase on April 25, 1854, but lowered the price to $10 million.

Tucson and other southern Arizona cities are in the purchase area.

Geography
A key word in describing Arizona's geography is "diversity." The state's highest point, Mount Humphreys in Coconino County, soars 12,670 feet above sea level. That's 12,600 feet above the lowest point, along the Colorado River in Yuma County. A rule of thumb is that the temperature drops 3.5 degrees for each thousand feet of ascending elevation. That is why, over the year, Arizona frequently has some of America's hottest and coldest days. Temperatures may range from 120°F+ to −30°F. Precipitation has enormous variations too: from less than 3 inches of rain in many desert areas to more than 40 inches (including snow melt) in the mountains.

Arizona is 393 miles long and 338 miles wide, with some 500 square miles of water.

Life zones. Across its 113,900 square miles of area, Arizona has several well-defined life zones. The Merriam system, cited in James D. Kavanagh's *The Nature of Arizona,* is based on the type of plants found between various elevations. It identifies these zones in Arizona:

Lower Sonoran. From 0 to 4,500 feet. Arizona's deserts are essentially dry, (except for "sky islands" which rise abruptly from the desert floor in many locations.) Cacti and other drought-resistant plants, such as ironwood, mesquite, and paloverde, thrive here. Animal species include the coyote, kangaroo rat, jack-rabbit, big horn sheep, reptiles, and many species of birds.

Upper Sonoran. 4,500–6,500 feet. Grasslands and scrub oak and juniper wooded areas are abundant, with tall pines at the upper elevations. Trees include piñon pines, chaparral, oaks, junipers, and Ponderosa pines. Deer, javelina, pronghorn antelopes, and reptiles are plentiful.

From *What Is Arizona Really Like?* by Reg Manning.

93

Transition. 6,500–8,000 feet. Ponderosa pine forests dominate in this zone. Many forest grasses and flowers thrive. Animal species include mountain lions, some bears, squirrels, deer and elk. Jays, turkeys and hummingbirds are among the hundreds of winged residents.

Canadian. 8,000–9,000 feet. Douglas fir and Ponderosa pine forests cover much of the land and grow to 90 feet and higher. Spruce and aspen are abundant. Animal species include elk, deer, squirrels, juncos and jays.

Hudsonian. 9,500–11,500 feet. Stunted trees and windswept terrain meet the eye, and even the summers are cold at night. Spruce, fir and bristlecone pine survive. The short growing season limits plant and animal life.

Alpine. 11,500–12,670 feet: This zone is above the tree line and supports few plants or animals.

Geographic features.

Deserts. The Sonoran Desert, which occupies most of southwestern and south-central Arizona, is the largest of four deserts that are found in the state. The eastern portion of the Mohave Desert is in northwestern Arizona; the Great Basin Desert is in the northeast; and the Chihuahuan Desert is in the far southeast corner of the state.

The Colorado Plateau. This area in the northeastern portion includes some of Arizona's most spectacular scenery. The Grand Canyon is by far the most famous, but Canyon de Chelly, the Painted Desert, Petrified Forest and Monument Valley attract many thousands of visitors. The Colorado Plateau is high country, with level terrain pierced by deep canyons.

Ponderosa Pine Country. The largest unbroken stand of Ponderosa pine in America is found in north-central and east-central Arizona. High mountains, lakes and green valleys invite the vacationer. Lumbering was for many years a mainstay of the economy, but its importance has diminished in recent years.

Mogollon Rim. A mighty upheaval of the earth's crust during the Mesozoic Age created this vertical wall of rock some 2,000 feet high in east-central Arizona. Rim communities such as Heber and Show Low are at an altitude of nearly 6,500 feet, while Payson and Young, below the Rim, are at 5,000 feet.

San Francisco Peaks. North of Flagstaff in Coconino County are the remnants of what was once a volcano rising more than 15,000 feet above sea level. Three peaks, including Mount

Humphreys, remain. Nearby Sunset Crater erupted only recently in geologic terms (about A.D.1065), and its cinders still lie beneath its cone as though they had been deposited yesterday.

Colorado River Country. From the far northeast portion of the state to the far southwest, more than 700 miles, the Colorado River is a dominant geographic feature.

The Little Colorado River flows into it in the northeast; the Bill Williams River in the west; and the Gila River, with its main tributaries, the Salt and Verde, in the southwest. A series of dams on the Colorado River, including the lofty Hoover Dam, have created huge lakes that provide recreation for millions of people each year.

Geronimo

Geronimo, perhaps the most famous of all American Indians in Arizona, led a band of some 75 Chiricahua Apache warriors in devastating raids on ranches and mining camps in south-eastern Arizona during the 1870s and early 1880s. For several years, a fourth of the U.S. Army and thousands of Mexican troops tried in vain to capture

Geronimo, famed Chiricahua Apache leader. Courtesy Southwest Studies, Scottsdale Community College.

him. It was not until he surrendered in 1886 that Arizona's Indian wars came to an end. Up to this time, settlement suffered because people in the United States thought that it was not safe to come to Arizona.

Chloride, a restored ghost town in western Arizona. Photo by James Tallon.

Geronimo and his followers were sent to Florida and then to Fort Sill, Oklahoma, and were not permitted to return to their homeland. Geronimo died at Fort Sill in 1909.

Ghost Towns (SEE ALSO JEROME)

There is no better way to experience Arizona's yesteryears than to stand among the silent, decaying buildings of a deserted mining camp and visualize the energy and vitality of those who labored here a century or more ago. Arizona has more than a hundred of these ghost towns. Some, like La Paz, Charleston, Swansea and Copper Hill, are now deserted. Others, such as Chloride and Stanton, still have a few residents. Some, including Jerome, Tombstone and Bisbee are "ghosts" only in the sense that their mines have closed, but the towns survive, even thrive, with a fraction of their former population.

Some ghost towns a visitor to Arizona would enjoy seeing:

Chloride. By 1900, Chloride (founded in 1864) had a population of some 2,000, drawn to the Mohave County silver and gold mining camp by the hope of quick riches. When the mines

95

closed the population declined sharply, but it still has 350 residents, mostly retirees. Chloride is a ghost town well worth visiting, and its people have preserved a portion of its Old West heritage. On its main street are a general store, post office and several shops. The cemetery west of town draws many visitors. Chloride is 15 miles northwest of Kingman, just 4 miles east of U.S. Highway 93.

Fairbank. Established in 1882 as a supply depot for the Tombstone mines, Fairbank was a busy railroad town in territorial days. It won fame as the site of a 1900 train robbery engineered by former lawmen Burt Alvord and Billy Stiles. Several territorial buildings still stand at Fairbank, which is now the headquarters for the San Pedro River Conservation Area.

Jerome. Billed as "the billion dollar copper camp" in its heyday, Jerome was once Arizona's third-largest city with more than 15,000 residents. But the mines closed, and by 1955 there were fewer than a thousand people remaining. Today it survives as a tourist attraction, art colony and retirement community. Jerome, perched precariously on the steep slopes of Cleopatra Hill, has carefully preserved scores of its 19th-century buildings, thus presenting visitors with an easily accessible ghost town experience.

La Paz. In sharp contrast to Jerome and Oatman is La Paz, the Colorado River mining town that once aspired to be the capital of Arizona Territory. It was the site of the Goldwater brothers' first Arizona store and it served as the county seat of Yuma County until 1871. Located 7 miles north of Ehrenberg, it is now completely deserted. Only the foundations of adobe buildings remain as a reminder of its past glory.

Oatman. Getting up close to history is easy in Oatman, via historic Route 66 in northwestern Arizona. Although its population plummeted from 10,000 to fewer than a hundred after gold mining operations stopped and Interstate 40 bypassed it, Oatman has made a comeback by showing off its century-old past to tourists. They come to see the Oatman Hotel, a two-story adobe where Clark Gable and Carole Lombard honeymooned after their wedding in nearby Kingman; to pet the wild burros that roam the streets; and to wander along board sidewalks and visit the picturesque Victorian structures.

Ghost town authority Philip Varney also rates these among principal sites: **Swansea,** not far east of Parker; **Ruby,** northwest of Nogales in Santa Cruz County; **Vulture,** near Wickenburg; and **Sasco,** northwest of Tucson. Varney's book, *Arizona Ghost Towns and Mining Camps,* published by *Arizona Highways,* has detailed information about virtually all of the state's ghost towns.

Gila Trail The Gila River has
its headwaters in southwestern New Mexico and flows across the entire

---

Looking Back

1846

Mormon Battalion makes wagon road across southern Arizona during Mexican War.

width of Arizona to its confluence with the Colorado River at Yuma. Indigenous peoples lived along the stream and used it as a convenient highway for thousands of years before the white man came.

In the mid-1820s, bands of Americans trapped beavers all along the river route, and in 1846, during the Mexican War, Stephen Kearny and Philip St. George Cooke used the Gila Trail as a passageway for their military forces en route to California. Cooke and his Mormon Battalion mapped the first wagon road across Arizona as they traveled.

The Butterfield Overland Mail stagecoaches used the Gila Trail for much of their route in the late 1850s and Col. James Carleton led his Union Army, known as the California Column, eastward along the river on their way to the Pima villages and Tucson in 1862. Today the Union Pacific (formerly Southern Pacific) Railroad and Interstate 8 parallel the Gila River bed.

Gilbert

Only a decade ago, Gilbert counted its population at 59,138. As the 20th century came to a close that figure had climbed past 100,000, with no slowing in sight. Located just south of Mesa in eastern Maricopa County, Gilbert has become one of the fastest growing cities in the nation.

Gilbert is principally a residential community, and construction has been a primary economic pillar for several years. But farming in the region, at one time the only major occupation, is still important. The city struggles to build enough infrastructure, schools, public buildings, parks and commercial facilities to cope with the tide of newcomers.

Today, Gilbert offers a family oriented lifestyle that has made it one of the state's most sought-after locations. The town was incorporated in 1920.

AZ if?!

Jerome boosters knew how to turn bad news into good news. When its jail slid several hundred feet down a steep mountainside in 1925, the residents coined a new promotional slogan: "Jerome— a Town on the Move."

Glendale

Brethren Church members from the Midwest settled Glendale in 1892 as a haven from the boisterous lawlessness of Arizona Territory, banning liquor sales and gambling from their new town. For half a century Glendale, 9 miles northwest of downtown Phoenix, was a quiet farming community of fewer than 5,000 people, but it now has a population exceeding 200,000 and ranks as Arizona's fourth-largest city.

Glendale is known as the home of the American Graduate School of International Management, which trains business executives for service all over the world. Arizona State University's West Campus serves Glendale and other westside cities. Glendale Community College is another institution of higher learning. Honeywell and other high tech manufacturing firms are major employers, as is nearby Luke Air Force Base.

The city's many antique shops lend credence to Glendale's claim as "Arizona's Antique Shopping Capital."

Its *Gaslight Antique Walk* each December attracts many thousands of visitors. The American Graduate School sponsors *WorldPort* in March, featuring music and food of many nations. The *Glendale Jazz and Blues Festival* and the annual *Juried Fine Arts Show*, both in April, are other annual events.

Globe

Globe is the county seat of Gila County. The discovery of a silver lode in 1875 led to the establishment of a mining camp here. Copper was found in the same area, and it has proved to be the major economic pillar of the city. Miami, Globe's sister city, is 5 miles to the west. The population of Globe is estimated at a little over 8,000 and Miami at 2,500. At an altitude of 3,500 feet, both communities enjoy a cooler climate than that of the Salt River Valley and attract many tourists and retirees.

Gold

The lure of gold has for many centuries sent men rushing into unmapped wildernesses, risking life and limb to make that one big strike. Coronado's 1540 exploration of the Southwest, which opened up a vast new area for settlement, was triggered by gold lust. The 1849 gold rush to California sent many thousands of adventurers trekking across Arizona and made Yuma Crossing (of the Colorado River) well known for the first time.

Discoveries of gold in the early 1860s at La Paz on the Colorado, and on the desert near modern Wickenburg, brought more throngs to Arizona Territory.

Senator Barry Goldwater, at the microphone of his ham radio rig. Courtesy Southwest Studies, Scottsdale Community College.

And the Walker party's 1863 strike on Lynx Creek in the Bradshaw Mountains attracted so many settlers to the area that the first territorial capital was established at nearby Prescott.

The veins of gold were soon exhausted, however, and Arizona eventually found that copper was the metal which would sustain its economy for many decades to come.

Goldwater, Barry

(*SEE ALSO* MAGAZINES) Senator Barry Goldwater, who died in 1998 at age 89, was the most famous Arizonan of the 20th century. He led the conservative resurgence in American politics in the 1950s and 1960s and was the Republican candidate for president of the United States in 1964. Although he lost the election to Lyndon B. Johnson, he remained a well-known figure on the national and world stage until his death. Goldwater achieved remarkable success in many fields of endeavor. He was a photographer of international note, the best-known ham radio operator in America, a World War II pilot who rose to the rank of major general in the Air Force Reserve, the author of several best-selling books (*The Conscience of a Conservative* sold more than four million copies), and a lecturer in demand all over America.

Golf Blessed with excellent year-around golfing weather, southern and central Arizona has developed golf as one of its major industries. At last count, Greater Phoenix alone had 165 courses, the majority open to public play, and more are being added. Every city in the area has one or more municipal course; each resort hotel has excellent golfing facilities; country clubs are built around fairways; retirement communities demand golf facilities; and developers find it necessary to include a course or two in each residential addition. The sale of golfing equipment and attire makes up a significant percentage of retail trade.

But golf is not restricted to the desert cities. Flagstaff, Sedona, Williams, Pinetop, Prescott, Payson and several other communities have excellent courses to which desert dwellers and vactioners flee during hot summer months.

Tucson, Phoenix and Scottsdale host tournaments on the annual tours of the Professional Golf Association, the Ladies PGA, and the Seniors. The Tradition, played on a spectacular course among desert foothills north of Scottsdale, is one of the coveted major events on the Seniors tour.

The Tucson Open and Phoenix Open (played in Scottsdale), held in early spring, attract some of the biggest crowds on the professional tours. Tucson and Phoenix both host the top women professionals in their tournaments. More than 20 leading pros competing in tournaments throughout the year are Arizona based, including Tom Lehman, who won the 2000 Phoenix Open.

Many of the biggest names in the professional ranks played their collegiate golf at Arizona State University or the University of Arizona.

Annika Sorenstam of Sweden, who attended the U of A, is a frequent winner on the LPGA circuit. Former U of A stars Jim Furyk and Robert Gamez make headlines, as do Phil Mickelson, Billy Mayfair and Joanne Carner of ASU.

Karsten Solheim, donor of the Solheim Cup and developer of the famed Ping golf club line, was a Phoenix engineer who played golf and believed he could design better equipment than was then in use. His firm now is one of the major manufacturers in the field. Arizona State University's Karsten Golf Course is named in his honor.

Many visitors ask how a state as arid as Arizona finds enough water to supply the imposing roster of golf courses now in operation. The Phoenix area relies heavily on Salt River Project canals and waste water effluent to keep its fairways green. Tucson's underground water resources and treated effluent supply that area, and others rely on some combination of water supplies.

The availability of fine golfing facilities is essential to the attraction of tourists. Arizona has some of the nation's best courses, and they are enjoyed all year long by both visitors and residents.

Governors of the State (SEE ALSO ELECTED OFFICIALS; HUNT, GEORGE W. P.; POLITICS; STATE GOVERNMENT)

Grand Canyon Arizona is blessed with scores of world-renowned scenic wonders, but none approaches the Grand Canyon in awesome

Grand Canyon. Photo by Marshall Trimble.

immensity and breathtaking beauty. Known as one of the Seven Natural Wonders of the World, it attracts visitors from every continent of the globe each year.

A dozen miles wide and more than a mile deep, the Canyon was carved from the Colorado Plateau over eons of time by the Colorado River. The South Rim is easily accessible to visitors, 81 miles northwest of Flagstaff on U.S. 180, or 58 miles due north of Williams via State Route 64 and U.S. 180.

Most tourists see the Canyon from the South Rim, at 6,876 feet above sea level, where Grand Canyon National Park headquarters and Grand Canyon Village are situated. The North Rim, at 8,200 feet, is more difficult to reach and still relatively pristine, but there are excellent accommodations there. Facilities at the North Rim are closed during the winter months.

Whatever the season, the South Rim offers spectacular views of the gorge and within it the colorful mountains of rock which rise abruptly from the river's course. The pines and oaks of Kaibab National Forest, on both north and south sides of the Canyon, add to the beauty of the setting. Warm days and cool nights are the rule in summer; snowstorms bring a majestic white blanket in winter; and spring greenery and fall colors impart their own unique charms.

Many visitors spend just a few hours gazing into the canyon, unfortunately, before heading for the gift shops and restaurants. But only an extended stay, seeing this masterpiece of nature in its many moods of clouds and sunshine, can give a visitor full appreciation of its wonder.

Prehistoric inhabitants of this area built cliff dwellings in the gorge and hunted the animals that abounded here. The first Europeans to see the canyon were members of Coronado's party who came in 1540–41. The daring Colorado River exploration of John Wesley Powell in 1869 gave Americans their first accurate picture of the river and its giant chasm. But it was not until the Santa Fe Railroad built a spur line from Williams to the Grand Canyon and erected the El Tovar Hotel at the South Rim in 1905, that tourists in great numbers spread the Canyon story around the world. The El Tovar, fashioned in rustic style with logs and native stone, is still a favorite accommodation there.

Grand Canyon National Park was established by Teddy Roosevelt in 1908, assuring that the Canyon would be safe from private exploitation for all time to come. More than 3 million people enjoy it each year, and commercial ventures, other than authorized concessionaires, must stay outside the park.

Many thousands of visitors enjoy hiking into the Canyon via the Bright Angel Trail or riding mules to Phantom Ranch at the water's edge. More adventurous ones take part in river trips, going down the Colorado River in inflatable rafts or wooden dories that run the rapids and set hearts to pounding. Helicopter and fixed-wing planes also offer spectacular views of the gorge from above.

Arizona's automobile license plates have long been inscribed with the slogan, "Grand Canyon State." The Canyon is the state's great asset and its pride and joy.

Green Valley
Located in the Santa Cruz Valley 25 miles south of Tucson, Green Valley is an age-restricted retirement community of 20,000 year-round residents. The population increases significantly during winter months. Another 5,000 people live in family oriented subdivisions nearby. At an altitude of 3,000 feet, Green Valley enjoys comfortable weather all year.

Like other large retirement communities across Arizona, Green Valley has a multitude of amenities for retirees, including golf, swimming, and other recreational and social activities.

Grey, Zane
Zane Grey's love affair with Arizona began in 1906, when he and his bride honeymooned at the Grand Canyon. During a quarter century of Arizona residency, he built homes in Oak Creek Canyon, at the Grand Canyon, and in the remote forest east of Payson, beneath the Mogollon Rim.

Grey wrote 30 novels with Arizona settings and did more to romanticize Arizona's frontier lifestyle in the eyes of millions of readers than any other author. He hunted and fished the Arizona wilderness for decades, and bemoaned the increasing urbanization of the country he loved so well.

He was born Pearl Zane Gray and became a dentist, but he had wanted to write from early childhood. His Grand Canyon honeymoon convinced him that he should give up dentistry and try to make a living writing novels about the "wild west." To make his name more intriguing, he dropped the "Pearl" and started spelling his last name with an "e." His first novel, *The Last of the Plainsmen,* got a cold reception at Harper's. The editor wrote him, "I do not see anything in this to convince me you can write either narrative or fiction."

But Grey did not give up. He finally found a publisher for the book, and his second novel, *Riders of the Purple Sage,* became one of the best sellers of all time. He was 40 when it came out in

1912. Many of his Arizona-based books were later made into movies.

In 1930, after an embarrassing argument with the Arizona Game and Fish Commission over his request to hunt bear out of season, he left Arizona and never set foot in the state again. "The glory and beauty of Arizona is being sacrificed to the lumbermen and sheep and cattle raisers," he declared in his published explanation.

Guadalupe Hidalgo Treaty

When the American army under Gen. Winfield Scott occupied Mexico City on Sept. 14, 1847, the Mexican government had no choice but to end the Mexican War on enemy terms. Peace came on Feb. 2, 1848, with the signing of the Treaty of Guadalupe Hidalgo, in which Mexico ceded more than half a million square miles of its territory to the United States. Included in this vast acquisition were the future states of California, Utah, Nevada, Arizona north of the Gila River, almost all of New Mexico, and parts of Colorado and Wyoming. The U.S. Senate ratified the treaty on July 4, 1848. As compensation, the U.S. agreed to pay Mexico $15 million and to assume more than $3 million in claims that American citizens had against Mexico.

Gunfighters of the Old West (SEE ALSO HISTORY)

In old western movies it was easy to tell the bad guys from the good. The bad guys wore black hats, the good guys wore white ones. But it was not all that clear in real life on the Arizona frontier.

Wyatt Earp, one of the giants of western gunfighting lore, was a hero

Wyatt Earp, famed lawman and gunfighter. Courtesy Southwest Studies, Scottsdale Community College.

to many for his exploits as a lawman in Tombstone and other wild towns. But many historians believe that he sometimes used his badge as a means of stealing from others, and for getting even with his enemies. After the OK Corral shootout, Tombstone Sheriff Johnny Behan arrested Wyatt for murder, and Ike Clanton filed murder charges against him the next day. Earp was found not guilty in court, but his name was never really cleared in the minds of many Arizona citizens after that.

Behan himself was an example of a bad guy operating under the guise of upholding the law. As a sheriff, he was known to look the other way while his friends stole cattle, and several times he was accused of lining his own pockets from the public treasury. Moreover, he was a womanizer of the worst kind.

Burt Alvord was another turncoat.

He had been a lawman in Willcox, in southeastern Arizona Territory, but found that he could enrich himself much more easily by masterminding train robberies. He recruited three accomplices who robbed a Southern Pacific train of $30,000 in September of 1899. Some six months later, the gang tried to rob the train depot in Fairbank, but the men were met with a hail of gunfire that left one of them dead and another wounded. Alvord lit out for Mexico.

There were others who were rotten through and through and would not have worn a badge if their lives depended on it. Fleming Parker was one of that breed. He and a companion robbed a train near Peach Springs in northwestern Arizona Territory in 1897, but Parker was captured and jailed. His sidekick, a man named Wilson, was killed during the robbery by a Wells Fargo detective.

Parker and two other prisoners broke out of the Yavapai County jail, killing a pursuer in the process. Yavapai County Sheriff George Ruffner, a famed lawman, trailed Parker for many days, and the outlaw was finally captured in northeastern Arizona. Parker was tried, found guilty, and on the night before his hanging in Prescott he won a place in Arizona lore by passing up his traditional choice of a last meal in favor of an hour with his favorite Whiskey Row prostitute. It was said he died with a smile on his face.

Black Jack Ketchum was another thoroughly evil outlaw. One day in 1899 he entered a store at Camp Verde and casually killed the storeowner and his clerk. Then he tried to shoot three men who approached the store, but succeeded in wounding only one of them. Ketchum often killed men whom he disliked, and was known across Arizona Territory for his cold-blooded disregard for life. His philosophy, which he expounded after his capture, was summed up in these words: "My advice to the boys . . . is not to steal horses or sheep, but either rob a train or a bank when you have got to be an outlaw. Every man who comes in your way, kill him. Spare him no mercy, for he will show you none."

As he awaited the hangman in 1901, he uttered another memorable line: "Why don't they hurry? I'd like to eat dinner in hell!"

One of the really good guys was Jim Roberts, a deputy sheriff in Jerome and other mountain towns. Roberts was a shy man who hated the adulation and publicity he received in 1887 for shooting five Graham men in the famed Graham-Tewksbury feud in the Pleasant Valley War. He wore shoes instead of boots, carried his pistol in a pocket instead of a holster, and often rode a mule instead of a horse.

At age 71, after a long and notable career in law enforcement, he accepted a sort of retirement job as a deputy sheriff at Clarkdale, in the Verde Valley. A year later he happened upon a robbery at a Clarkdale bank. He shot and killed one of the robbers who was driving the getaway car and captured the other.

Even in retirement, it seemed, Jim Roberts could not escape the spotlight of fame.

Burt Mossman certainly belongs on any listing of Arizona's good guys. It was he who was appointed captain of the Arizona Rangers in 1901, at a time when the territory's scarlet reputation for lawlessness threatened to delay its admission to statehood. Mossman had won the admiration of Territorial Governor Nathan Murphy for his successes in capturing cattle rustlers on the vast Hashknife Ranch and soon proved he was just as good at jailing desperados of many kinds. The Rangers put 125 of the worst Arizona outlaws behind bars during Mossman's captaincy, and were forced to kill only one lawbreaker in the process.

A cowboy from age 15, Mossman was happy to resign from the Rangers and return to ranching. But before he returned to civilian life, he wanted to capture Agustin Chacon, who bragged that he had killed 37 Mexicans and 15 Americans during his forays into Arizona from his home in Sonora.

Mossman went into Sonora, posed as an outlaw to gain Chacon's trust, and eventually brought the killer back to Arizona, where he was soon dangling at the end of a hangman's rope.

Looking Back

Oct. 26, 1881

The Earps and the Clantons battle in "Gunfight at the OK Corral," in Tombstone.

Reenactments of the Old West.

Blazin' M Ranch, P.O. Box 160, Cottonwood 86326, (800) WEST-643.

Goldfield Ghost Town & Mine Tours, 4650 N. Mammoth Mine Road, Goldfield 85219, (480) 983-0333.

Immortal Gunfighters of Chloride, Second and Tennessee, Chloride 86431, (520) 565-2204.

Old Tucson Studios, 201 S. Kinney Road, Tucson 85735, (520) 883-0100.

Rawhide 1880s Western Town, 23023 N. Scottsdale Road, Scottsdale 85255, (480) 502-1880.

Rockin' R Ranch, 6136 E. Baseline, Mesa 85206, (480) 832-1539.

Tombstone Visitors Center, P.O. Box 995, Tombstone 85638, (520) 457-3929.

Health Care
Arizona has several world-renowned health care facilities. You can find several fine Level I trauma centers in Phoenix and Tucson. And many hospitals have state-of-the-art neonatal intensive care units, coronary care units, and maternity care centers.

There are also many types of medical schools. One can earn the degree of Medical Doctor through the University of Arizona's College of Medicine in Tucson. Also available is the Doctor of Osteopathy through Midwestern University's Arizona College of Osteopathic Medicine in Glendale. And one can become a naturopathic physician at Southwest College of Naturopathic Medicine & Health Sciences in Tempe. There are, however, no colleges of dentistry, chiropractic, or homeopathy in Arizona.

Some of the internationally known medical facilities and programs are:

Barrow Neurological Institute. Located on the campus of St. Joseph's Hospital and Medical Center in Phoenix, Barrow Neurological Institute (BNI) provides neuroscience research and medical care to patients who come from all over the world. Dr. Robert F. Spetzler, M.D. directs the Institute and is its premier neurosurgeon. Physicians and scientists treat and study diseases and conditions of the brain, spine and peripheral nerves, including epilepsy, stroke, cancer, head injury, spinal cord injury and neurological diseases. For example, the Muhammad Ali Parkinson Research Center is a National Parkinson Foundation Center of Excellence.

Mayo Clinic Hospital. Arizona's newest hospital, and the first designed and built outside of Minnesota by the world famous Mayo Clinic of Rochester, opened in October 1998 in Phoenix. Patients diagnosed at Mayo Clinic's Scottsdale facility can be treated here if hospitalization becomes necessary. Among other services, they have Maricopa County's only liver and first bone marrow transplant programs.

Program in Integrative Medicine at University of Arizona. Integrative medicine incorporates many types of health-oriented therapies, including what are considered "alternative medical" systems, to add a more complete approach to the art and science of medical practice. The University is progressive in adding the study of these healing methods to their College of Medicine. The program is headed by Dr. Andrew Weil, M.D., nationally known author of many books, including *Natural Health, Natural Medicine* and *Spontaneous Healing.*

University Medical Center. In addition to serving as a teaching hospital for the University of Arizona College of Medicine, *U.S. News and World Report*'s 1995 guide to "America's Best Hospitals" listed UMC as among the best for treatment of cancer and rheumatology (arthritis). The Arizona Cancer Center's research programs have lead to better methods of diagnosing, treating, and preventing many cancers. Research at the Arizona Arthritis Center has resulted in similar advances in that field. Arizona's first heart transplant was done at UMC in 1979, and the hospital now offers transplantation of bone marrow, heart, heart-lung, pancreas, liver and kidney.

Center for Multiple Birth at Good Samaritan Regional Medical Center. The word has gone out around the country, and beyond, that Phoenix is the place to come for women expecting three or more babies. No other medical facility has delivered more multiples Their research has also led to these pregnancies lasting longer and producing larger, healthier babies. Good Samaritan works in conjunction with Phoenix Perinatal Associates and Phoenix Children's Hospital to achieve the best possible outcomes.

Hospitals.

Arizona Heart Hospital, 1930 E. Thomas Road, Phoenix 85016

Arizona Heart Institute, 2632 N. 20th St., Phoenix 85006

Arizona State Hospital, 2500 E. Van Buren, Phoenix 85008

Arrowhead Community Hospital & Medical Center, 18701 N. 67th Ave., Glendale 85308

Aspen Hill Behavioral Health, 305 W. Forest Ave., Flagstaff 86001

Benson Hospital, 475 S. Ocotillo Ave., Benson 85602

Boswell, Walter O., Memorial Hospital, 10401 W. Thunderbird Blvd., Sun City 85351

Carondolet Holy Cross Hospital and Health Center, 1171 W. Target Range Road, Nogales 85621

Carondolet St. Joseph's Hospital and Health Center, 350 N. Wilmot Road, Tucson 85711

Carondolet St. Mary's Hospital, 1601 W. St. Mary's Road, Tucson 85745

Casa Grande Regional Medical Center, 1800 E. Florence Blvd., Casa Grande 85222

Chandler Regional Hospital, 475 S. Dobson Road, Chandler 85224

Charter Behavioral Health System—East Valley, 2190 N. Grace Blvd., Chandler 85224

Chinle Comprehensive Health Care Facility, P.O. Drawer PH, Chinle 86503

Cobre Valley Community Hospital, 5850 S. Hospital Drive, Globe 85501

Community Hospital Medical Center, 6501 N. 19th Ave., Phoenix 85015

Copper Queen Community Hospital, 101 Cole Ave., Bisbee 85603

Del E. Webb Memorial Hospital, 14502 W. Meeker Blvd., Sun City West 85375

Desert Samaritan Medical Center, 1400 S. Dobson Road, Mesa 85202

El Dorado Hospital and Medical Center, 1400 N.Wilmot Road, Tucson 85712

Flagstaff Medical Center1200 N. Beaver St., Flagstaff 86001

Good Samaritan Regional Medical Center1111 E. McDowell Road, Phoenix 85006

Havasu Regional Medical Center, 101 Civic Center Lane, Lake Havasu City 86403

HealthSouth Meridian Point Rehabilitation Center, 11250 N. 92nd St., Scottsdale 85260

HealthSouth Rehabilitation Hospital of Southern Arizona, 1921 W. Hospital Drive, Tucson 85704

HealthSouth Rehabilitation Institute of Tucson, 2650 N. Wyatt Drive, Tucson 85712

HealthSouth Valley of the Sun Rehabilitation Hospital, 13460 N. 67th Ave., Glendale 85304

Hu Hu Kam Memorial Hospital, Seed Farm Road and Career Center Road, Sacaton 85247

Kingman Regional Medical Center, 3269 Stockton Hill Road, Kingman 86401

Kino Community Hospital, 2800 E. Ajo Way, Tucson 85713

La Paz Regional Hospital, 1200 Mohave Road, Parker 85344

Lincoln, John C., Hospital—Deer Valley, 19829 N. 27th Ave., Phoenix 85027

Lincoln, John C., Hospital—North Mountain, 250 E. Dunlap Ave., Phoenix 85020

Maricopa Integrated Health System, 2601 E. Roosevelt St., Phoenix 85008

Maryvale Hospital Medical Center, 5102 W. Campbell Ave., Phoenix 85031

Mayo Clinic Hospital, 5777 E. Mayo Blvd., Phoenix 85054

Mayo Clinic Scottsdale, 13400 E. Shea Blvd., Scottsdale 85259

Mesa General Hospital Medical Center, 515 N. Mesa Drive, Mesa 85201

Mesa Lutheran Hospital, 525 W. Brown Road, Mesa 85201

Mohave Valley Hospital & Medical Center, 1225 Hancock Road, Bullhead City 86442

Mount Graham Community Hospital, Inc. 1600 S. 20th Ave., Safford 85546

Navajo Area Indian Health Service, P. O. Box 9020, Window Rock 86515

Navapache Regional Medical Center, 2200 E. Show Low Lake Road, Show Low 85901

Northern Arizona Veterans Affairs Health System, 500 N. US Highway 89, Prescott 86313

Northern Cochise Community Hospital, 901 W. Rex Allen Drive, Willcox 85643

Northwest Medical Center, 6200 La Cholla Blvd., Tucson 85741

Page Hospital, 501 N. Navajo Drive, Page 86040

Palo Verde Mental Health Services, 2695 N. Craycroft, Tucson 85712

Paradise Valley Hospital, 3929 E. Bell Road, Phoenix 85032

Payson Regional Medical Center, 807 S. Ponderosa, Payson 85541

Phoenix Baptist Hospital & Medical Center, 2000 W. Bethany Home Road, Phoenix 85015

Phoenix Children's Hospital, 1111 E. McDowell Road, Phoenix 85006

Phoenix Memorial Hospital, 1201 S. Seventh Ave., Phoenix 85007

Raymond W. Bliss Army Hospital, Fort Huachuca 85613

Sage Memorial Hospital, P. O. Box 457, Ganado 86505

St. Joseph's Hospital & Medical Center, 350 W. Thomas Road, Phoenix 85013

St. Luke's Behavioral Health Center—St. Luke's Medical Center, 1800 E. Van Buren, Phoenix 85006

Scottsdale Healthcare Osborn, 7400 E. Osborn Road, Scottsdale 85251

Scottsdale Healthcare Shea, 9003 E. Shea Blvd., Scottsdale 85260

Sedona Medical Center, 3700 W. Highway 89A, Sedona 86336

Select Specialty Hospital, Inc., 350 W. Thomas Road, Phoenix 85013

Sierra Vista Regional Health Center, 300 El Camino Real SE, Sierra Vista 85635

Southeast Arizona Medical Center, 2174 W. Oak Ave., Douglas 85607

Southern Arizona Veterans Affairs Health Care System, 3601 S. Sixth Ave., Tucson 85723

Tempe St. Luke's Hospital, 1500 S. Mill Ave, Tempe 85281

Thunderbird Samaritan Medical Center, 5555 W. Thunderbird Road, Glendale 85306

Tuba City Indian Medical Center, 167 N. Main St., Tuba City 86045

Tucson Area Indian Health Service, 7900 S. J. Stock Road, Tucson 85746

Tucson General Hospital, 3838 N. Campbell Ave., Tucson 85719

Tucson Heart Hospital, 4888 N. Stone Ave., Tucson 85704

Tucson Medical Center, 5301 E. Grant Road, Tucson 85712

U.S. Air Force Base Hospital, 7219 N. Litchfield Road, Luke Air Force Base 85309

U.S. Air Force Hospital, 4175 S. Alamo Ave., Davis-Monthan Air Force Base 85707

U.S. Public Health Service Indian Hospital—Fort Defiance, P. O. Box 249, Fort Defiance 86504

U.S. Public Health Service Indian Hospital—Fort Yuma, P. O. Box 1368, Yuma 85364

U.S. Public Health Service Indian Hospital—Keams Canyon, 1 Main St., Keams Canyon 86034

U.S. Public Health Service Indian Hospital—Parker, Rural Route 1, P.O. Box 12, Parker 85344

U.S. Public Health Service Indian Hospital—San Carlos, P.O. Box 208, San Carlos 85550

U.S. Public Health Service Indian Hospital—Sells, Highway 86 and Topowa Road, Sells 85634

U.S. Public Health Service Indian Hospital—Whiteriver, State Route 73, Milepost 342, Whiteriver 85941

U.S. Public Health Service—Phoenix Indian Medical Center, 4212 N. 16th St., Phoenix 85016

University Medical Center, 1501 N. Campbell Ave., Tucson 85724

Valley Lutheran Hospital, 6644 E. Baywood Ave., Mesa 85206

Vencor Hospital, 355 N. Wilmot Road, Tucson 85711

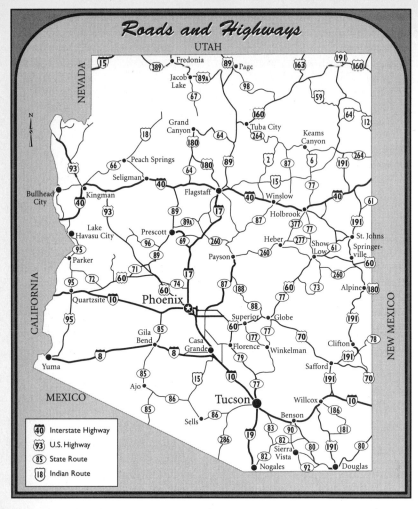

Roads and Highways

Vencor Hospital—Phoenix, 40 E. Indianola Ave., Phoenix 85012

Verde Valley Medical Center, 269 S. Candy Lane, Cottonwood 86326

Veteran's Affairs Medical Center, Carl T. Hayden, 650 E. Indian School Road, Phoenix 85012

Westcenter, 2105 E. Allen Road, Tucson 85719

Western Arizona Regional Medical Center, 2735 Silver Creek Road, Bullhead City 86442

White Mountain Regional Medical Center, 118 S. Mountain Ave., Springerville 85938

Wickenburg Regional Medical Center, 520 Rose Lane, Wickenburg 85390

Winslow Memorial Hospital, 1501 Williamson Ave., Winslow 86047

Yavapai Regional Medical Center, 1003 Willow Creek Road, Prescott 86301

Yuma Regional Medical Center, 2400 S. Ave. A, Yuma 85364

Highways (SEE ALSO SPEED LIMITS)

In the late 1920s, the federal highway known as Route 66 came into being, bringing many thousands of vacationers and immigrants into Arizona from the Midwest and California. It crossed the northern portion of the state, approximately along the route now followed by Interstate 40: from New Mexico to Holbrook, Flagstaff and Kingman to Needles, California.

Other major interstate freeways cross the state from east to west. Interstate 10 enters southern Arizona west of Lordsburg, New Mexico, and goes to Tucson and Phoenix, entering California near Blythe. Interstate 8 goes from Casa Grande to Yuma and on to San Diego. The north–south freeways are Interstate 17, from Phoenix to Flagstaff, and Interstate 19, from Tucson to Nogales and Mexico.

All but the most remote communities of Arizona are now served by good paved highways.

(See mileage chart on pages 110–111.)

History—A Brief Overview (SEE ALSO AMERICAN INDIANS; CORONADO; GADSDEN PURCHASE; GUADALUPE HIDALGO TREATY; GUNFIGHTERS; MILITARY POSTS; PIONEERS AND SETTLERS; STATEHOOD BATTLE)

Prehistoric. Most archaeologists believe that people first migrated to the American Southwest across the Bering Strait Land Bridge (perhaps some by boat) from Asia at least 20,000 years ago, some say 40,000, and made their way south over the centuries. Human remains and artifacts place prehistoric hunters in Arizona 11,500 years ago, and it is likely that humans lived here even earlier.

The Patayan, Anasazi, Mogollon and Hohokam cultures were in Arizona before the arrival of the Spanish. The three most prominent were the Anasazi, who lived on the Colorado Plateau; the Mogollon, in the eastern mountain belt; and the Hohokam, on the southern deserts. These later three had advanced cultures before the beginning of the Christian era.

Many cliff dwellings, pueblos and the amazing multi-story Casa Grande ruins (near Coolidge in Pinal County) have survived and are visited by thousands each year. It is believed that Old Oraibi, a village on the Hopi mesas, has been continuously occupied since about A.D. 1000, which would make it the oldest town in the United States.

In the mid-1300s, for reasons that archaeologists are only now beginning to realize, the complex Hohokam culture began to collapse. By the time the first Spanish arrived there were only small, scattered villages of Pima and Papago in southern Arizona where the Hohokam had once flourished. Cocopah, Yuma and Mohave lived along the lower Colorado River; Havasupai and Hualapai in and around the Grand Canyon; Utes and Paiutes in the far north; some Yavapai in the Prescott and Camp Verde areas; and the Hopi in their mesa-top villages in northeastern Arizona. It is uncertain whether or not Coronado met any Navajo or Apache. The Expedition passed through that country and met many people using various names. Navajo and Apache people may have been among them, but not by those names.

(Continued on page 112)

Mileage Between Cities

Driving Mileage Between Principal Points

	Ajo	Ash Fork	Benson	Bisbee	Blythe, CA	Casa Grande	Clifton	Coolidge	Cottonwood	Douglas	Flagstaff	Florence	Fredonia	Gila Bend	Glendale	Grand Canyon	Havasu City	Holbrook	Hoover Dam	Kingman
Ajo	0	262	175	225	200	99	290	120	216	249	258	125	453	42	116	337	245	301	369	296
Ash Fork	262	0	307	357	210	196	349	208	82	381	49	212	246	220	155	76	155	140	167	94
Benson	175	307	0	49	310	115	115	112	261	74	301	113	498	172	169	382	362	286	415	342
Bisbee	225	357	49	0	360	164	164	161	311	24	351	163	547	221	218	431	412	335	464	391
Blythe, CA	200	210	310	360	0	199	352	211	202	384	248	216	439	158	153	285	97	339	232	158
Casa Grande	99	196	115	164	199	0	198	21	150	188	190	34	387	57	58	271	249	207	304	231
Clifton	290	349	115	164	352	198	0	179	303	156	302	166	498	259	208	383	401	213	457	383
Coolidge	120	208	112	161	211	21	179	0	157	185	197	13	394	80	65	278	256	204	311	238
Cottonwood	216	82	261	311	202	150	303	157	0	335	48	166	243	173	103	129	236	139	248	175
Douglas	249	381	74	24	384	188	156	185	335	0	376	187	573	242	244	457	43	335	488	415
Flagstaff	258	49	301	351	248	190	302	197	48	376	0	206	197	209	144	81	204	91	216	143
Florence	125	212	113	163	216	34	166	13	166	187	206	0	404	93	73	286	267	191	319	246
Fredonia	453	246	498	547	439	387	498	394	243	273	197	404	0	404	340	197	361	288	417	339
Gila Bend	42	220	172	221	158	57	259	80	178	242	209	93	404	0	74	288	203	256	320	247
Glendale	16	155	169	218	153	58	208	65	103	244	144	73	340	74	0	225	193	231	246	172
Grand Canyon	337	76	382	431	285	271	383	278	129	457	81	286	197	288	225	0	231	172	243	170
Havasu City	245	155	362	412	97	249	401	256	236	437	204	267	361	203	193	23	0	296	135	61
Holbrook	301	140	286	335	339	207	213	204	139	335	91	191	288	256	231	172	296	0	308	234
Hoover Dam	369	167	415	464	232	304	457	311	248	488	216	319	417	320	246	243	135	398	0	73
Kingman	296	94	342	391	158	231	383	238	175	415	143	246	233	247	172	170	61	234	73	0
Las Vegas, NV	399	197	445	495	191	334	487	341	278	519	246	349	204	350	276	273	165	338	30	103
Mesa	125	167	153	202	170	32	188	41	121	226	161	49	357	83	247	241	221	175	270	197
Miami	180	232	157	206	235	82	117	61	175	207	194	48	377	148	89	275	286	142	339	266
Needles, CA	286	158	403	453	113	292	451	300	239	477	207	308	404	245	234	234	41	298	88	64
Nogales	194	326	73	89	329	134	198	139	279	112	320	133	517	167	188	401	361	304	434	360
Page	392	185	437	487	384	328	438	334	183	511	136	342	104	343	280	137	340	215	326	279
Parker	207	194	324	373	59	212	365	220	195	39	243	229	439	169	154	269	38	334	173	100
Payson	203	140	228	380	248	117	190	119	72	282	91	127	288	161	102	172	299	98	307	234
Phoenix	110	152	156	205	155	45	207	51	106	229	146	61	342	68	13	226	206	191	259	186
Prescott	212	50	257	307	160	146	299	153	41	331	87	262	286	163	100	126	192	174	217	144
Safford	257	316	82	131	319	165	43	144	250	123	250	133	447	233	173	349	370	212	423	350
St. Johns	329	198	283	332	374	220	155	201	196	321	149	188	340	288	228	230	353	58	365	292
Sedona	222	77	275	325	220	164	297	171	19	349	28	180	224	180	117	108	232	120	244	171
Show Low	284	187	238	287	329	175	169	156	163	287	139	143	336	242	183	220	343	48	355	282
Sierra Vista	210	342	35	33	345	150	150	46	296	57	336	149	534	203	204	417	396	320	448	376
Springerville	330	230	284	303	375	221	123	202	218	289	181	189	373	289	229	262	385	90	382	309
Tempe	120	161	156	205	164	45	188	47	115	229	155	55	352	78	18	236	215	181	268	195
Tombstone	201	333	26	24	336	141	141	137	288	48	327	140	524	194	194	408	388	311	441	367
Tuba City	335	128	380	430	321	269	381	281	127	455	79	285	138	278	223	79	283	162	295	222
Tucson	131	263	45	94	266	70	159	67	217	118	257	70	453	124	124	338	317	241	370	297
Wickenburg	168	111	214	263	115	103	256	114	101	287	150	122	347	119	44	186	148	251	201	128
Willcox	211	344	36	86	346	151	82	148	297	74	337	151	534	205	205	398	398	261	451	378
Williams	273	17	333	383	227	203	334	229	80	407	32	238	229	231	176	59	172	123	184	111
Winslow	294	107	318	368	306	210	246	208	105	368	58	208	255	252	193	139	262	33	274	201
Yuma	158	268	284	334	106	174	381	192	259	358	307	205	504	116	192	316	156	374	290	216

Mileage Between Cities *continued*

Las Vegas, NV	Mesa	Miami	Needles, CA	Nogales	Page	Parker	Payson	Phoenix	Prescott	Safford	St. Johns	Sedona	Show Low	Sierra Vista	Springerville	Tempe	Tombstone	Tuba City	Tucson	Wickenburg	Willcox	Williams	Winslow	Yuma
399	125	180	286	194	392	207	203	110	212	257	329	222	284	210	330	120	201	335	131	168	211	273	294	158
197	107	232	130	326	105	194	140	152	50	316	190	77	107	312	230	161	333	120	260	111	311	17	107	260
445	153	157	403	73	437	324	228	156	257	82	283	275	238	35	284	156	26	380	45	214	36	333	318	284
495	202	206	453	89	487	373	280	205	307	131	332	325	287	33	303	205	24	430	94	263	86	383	368	334
191	170	235	113	329	384	59	248	155	160	319	374	220	329	345	375	164	336	321	266	11	346	227	306	106
334	32	82	292	134	328	212	117	45	146	165	220	164	175	150	221	45	141	269	70	103	151	203	201	174
487	183	117	451	198	438	365	190	207	299	43	155	297	169	150	123	188	141	381	159	256	82	334	246	381
341	41	61	300	139	334	220	119	51	153	144	201	171	156	146	202	47	137	281	67	114	148	229	208	192
278	121	175	239	279	183	195	72	106	41	250	196	19	163	296	218	115	288	127	17	101	297	80	105	259
519	226	207	477	112	511	397	282	229	331	123	321	349	287	57	289	229	48	455	118	287	74	407	368	358
246	161	194	207	320	136	243	91	146	87	250	149	28	139	336	181	155	327	79	257	150	337	32	58	307
349	49	48	308	133	342	229	127	61	162	133	188	180	143	149	189	55	140	285	70	122	151	238	208	205
204	357	377	404	517	104	439	288	342	286	447	340	224	336	534	278	352	524	138	53	347	534	229	255	504
350	83	148	25	187	343	169	161	68	163	233	288	180	242	203	289	78	194	278	124	119	205	231	252	116
276	24	89	234	188	280	154	102	13	100	173	228	117	183	204	229	18	194	223	124	44	205	176	193	192
273	241	275	234	401	137	269	172	226	126	349	230	108	220	417	262	236	408	79	338	186	398	59	139	316
165	221	286	41	381	340	38	299	206	192	370	353	232	343	396	385	215	388	283	317	148	398	172	262	156
338	175	142	298	304	215	334	48	191	174	212	58	120	48	320	90	181	311	162	241	251	261	123	33	374
30	270	339	88	43	326	173	307	259	217	423	365	244	355	448	382	268	441	295	370	201	451	184	274	290
103	197	266	64	360	279	100	234	186	144	350	292	171	282	376	309	195	367	222	297	128	378	111	201	216
0	300	369	100	464	296	203	337	290	247	453	395	274	385	480	427	298	471	325	400	231	481	214	304	320
300	0	65	263	169	297	183	78	15	117	149	204	135	159	185	205	6	176	240	106	73	186	193	169	199
369	65	0	328	176	334	248	83	80	182	84	139	193	94	192	140	72	183	277	112	138	134	228	175	264
100	263	328	0	422	343	80	298	248	208	412	356	235	346	438	388	257	429	286	356	189	439	175	265	197
464	169	176	422	0	456	342	247	175	276	154	301	295	256	65	302	175	71	399	63	233	107	352	337	303
296	297	334	343	456	0	379	227	282	228	440	263	164	275	471	295	329	463	77	393	279	474	169	194	446
203	183	248	80	342	379	0	261	169	154	332	387	214	342	358	388	177	349	316	279	110	360	211	295	117
337	76	83	298	247	227	261	0	93	99	159	135	86	90	266	136	84	266	170	183	151	208	123	91	277
290	15	80	248	175	282	169	93	0	102	164	219	119	174	189	220	9	181	225	11	58	192	170	184	184
247	117	182	208	276	228	154	99	102	0	267	238	60	228	291	281	111	283	161	213	61	294	6	147	218
453	149	84	412	154	440	332	159	164	267	0	198	264	164	116	16	155	107	329	130	222	49	282	245	348
395	204	139	356	301	263	387	135	219	238	198	0	177	45	317	32	210	308	222	238	277	247	181	91	403
274	135	193	235	294	164	214	86	119	60	264	177	0	175	310	220	129	301	107	230	120	311	60	86	288
385	159	94	346	256	275	342	90	174	228	164	45	175	0	272	46	165	263	218	193	232	213	171	81	348
480	185	192	438	65	471	358	266	189	291	116	317	310	272	0	288	191	33	415	79	249	71	368	353	319
427	205	140	388	302	295	388	136	220	281	166	32	220	46	288	0	211	279	254	239	273	215	213	123	404
298	6	72	257	175	291	177	84	9	111	155	210	129	165	191	211	0	182	234	112	63	192	179	175	193
471	176	183	429	71	463	349	266	181	283	107	308	301	263	33	279	182	0	406	70	239	62	351	344	310
325	240	277	286	399	77	316	170	225	161	329	222	107	218	415	254	234	406	0	336	222	417	111	129	380
400	106	112	356	63	393	279	183	111	213	130	238	230	193	79	239	112	70	336	0	169	81	281	274	240
231	73	138	189	233	279	110	151	58	61	222	277	120	232	249	273	63	239	222	169	0	250	128	208	174
481	186	134	439	107	474	360	20	192	294	49	247	311	213	71	215	192	62	417	81	250	0	362	294	320
214	193	228	175	352	169	211	123	170	67	282	181	60	171	368	213	179	351	111	281	128	362	0	90	285
304	169	175	265	337	194	295	91	184	147	245	91	86	81	353	123	175	344	129	274	208	194	90	0	365
320	199	264	197	303	446	117	277	184	218	348	403	288	348	319	404	193	310	380	240	174	320	285	365	0

(Continued from page 109)

Spanish Exploration. Rumors of golden cities in the Arizona-New Mexico area prompted the viceroy of New Spain (Mexico) to send Fray Marcos de Niza, a missionary adventurer, to explore the unknown land to the north in 1539. With him was a Moorish slave, Esteban, who had trekked across Texas and northern Mexico with members of the Cabeza de Vaca party in 1535 and might possibly (although unlikely) have touched on southeastern Arizona soil.

Esteban went in advance of Fray Marcos in 1539 and thus is believed to be the first non-Indian to enter Arizona. While de Niza surveyed the areas he was passing through, Esteban forged ahead. When runners brought word that Esteban had been killed near the Zuni villages, de Niza fled back to Mexico with wild tales of seeing cities of gold. Francisco Vasquez de Coronado quickly organized an army of exploration which reached southeastern Arizona in 1540 and went on to the New Mexico pueblos and eventually to northern Kansas without finding the gold for which they hungered.

Spain claimed the new territory, and several other explorations were made before Father Eusebio Kino came to northern Sonora and Arizona in 1687. He established a chain of missions, the most famous and most beautiful of which is San Xavier del Bac, a few miles south of Tucson. It is still a magnet for worshipers and tourists today. He also introduced advanced agriculture and brought the first cattle to Arizona. Father Kino's statue has a place of honor in the national capitol in Washington, D.C. At Tubac, between Tucson and the present border with Mexico, the Spanish established Arizona's first presidio (military headquarters) in 1752. It was moved to Tucson in 1775.

Mexico declared its independence from Spain in 1821, and took over supervision of the Arizona settlements. But the settlements were too far from Mexico City to warrant much interest, and Arizona (along with much of the rest of the American Southwest) was ceded to the United States at the close of the Mexican War in 1848.

Territorial years. Arizona comprised the western half of New Mexico Territory when the latter was formed in 1850. Four years later, the United States bought the Gadsden Purchase land, lying between the Gila River and the present Mexican border, for 10 million dollars. In 1863, President Lincoln signed legislation creating the Territory of Arizona, which had its first seat of government near today's Prescott. The first census, conducted in 1864, showed that 4,573 people (exclusive of Indians, who were not counted) lived in the territory.

The Baron of Arizona

James Addison Reavis, a former streetcar motorman in St. Louis, arrived in Tucson in 1882 and announced that he held title to the Peralta grant, an old Spanish land grant encompassing much of central Arizona and some of western New Mexico—235 miles wide and 75 miles deep. The United States had agreed in the Treaty of Guadalupe Hidalgo to honor all such grants if they could be legally documented. Reavis produced the documents, which he had painstakingly forged over several years of preparation for his con game. So convincing was he that the railroads and many other major property owners in the "grant" paid Reavis nearly half a million dollars for quit claim deeds to clear their land titles. For several years Reavis lived like a king and was nicknamed "the baron of Arizona." But his victims hired experts to prove that Reavis' documents were forgeries, and at last it was shown that they were written with a steel pen and that the print on some of them was of fairly recent design. The "baron" was tried in a federal court in 1895 and was found guilty of fraud. But he conned the judge into letting him off with a sentence of only two years in prison and a $5,000 fine. He died penniless in Colorado in 1914. ✳

Phoenix was born in 1870, and its satellite communities of Tempe and Mesa followed soon thereafter. The migration of Mormon settlers swelled Arizona's population during the 1880s and 1890s, and many mining towns sprang up during this period. One of those towns, rowdy Tombstone, became one of the largest in the territory almost overnight in the early 1880s. But Tucson remained Arizona's largest city throughout the territorial period.

The original four counties (Yuma, Mohave, Yavapai, and Pima) were divided time and again, and today there are 15. Development of the territory was slowed by the long-raging wars against the fierce Apaches, but Geronimo's surrender in 1886 ended that threat to migrating pioneers. In 1911 Roosevelt Dam was completed, followed by more dams in the Salt River system which created storage lakes that made irrigated farming in the Salt River Valley more stable and profitable. A year later, on Feb. 14, 1912, President Taft signed a proclamation admitting Arizona as the 48th state of the Union.

Statehood. Admission to the Union had been delayed because the new Arizona Constitution provided for recall of judges by popular vote, a provision President Taft would not accept. The people voted in 1911 to remove the offending recall measure, but as soon as statehood was granted, they voted it back in again. George W.P. Hunt of Globe was elected the first state governor, and he was re-elected six times.

In 1917, striking miners with membership in the International Workmen of the World were rounded up in Bisbee, herded into freight cars, and shipped out of the state. The nation's first municipal airport was opened in 1919 in Tucson. Coolidge Dam on the Gila River was dedicated in 1928 by President Coolidge and Will Rogers.

In 1934, Governor Benjamin B. Moeur sent the Arizona National Guard to stop construction of Parker Dam on the Colorado River because he believed it would enable California to steal Arizona's share of the river water. President Roosevelt dedicated Boulder Dam, later renamed Hoover Dam, in

1936. In the mid-1930s, affordable evaporative air cooling units made summer living in the desert areas more comfortable and started a population boom. Another such boom came at the close of World War II when servicemen who had been stationed in Arizona returned to live here.

Arizona's economic base underwent radical change in the 1950s when high-tech manufacturing and tourism first surpassed mining and agriculture in importance.

Construction of the Central Arizona Project, a huge irrigation plan, began in 1974 and was completed in 1985.

Arizona's population soared in the 1980s, with most of the growth centered in Maricopa and Pima counties. The U.S. Census of 1990 showed that the state had 3.7 million residents. As a result, Arizona added another Congressional district, its sixth.

Arizona Chronology.

A.D. 1–1450—Anasazi, Mogollon, and Hohokam cultures thrive in Arizona. Their cultural collapse still puzzles anthropologists.

1539—Fray Marcos de Niza and Moorish slave Esteban explore southeastern Arizona, Esteban is killed by Indians. Marcos returns to Mexico saying he found cities of gold in what is now New Mexico.

1540—Francisco Vasquez de Coronado leads an army of exploration into Arizona in search of gold, remains in New Mexico for more than two years, explores as far east as Kansas, finds no gold.

1690s–early 1700s—Father Eusebio

Francisco Kino brings Christianity to the Indians of northern Sonora and southern Arizona, builds chain of missions, most famous of which is San Xavier del Bac, just south of Tucson.

1752—Spanish establish fort at Tubac in southern Arizona to protect settlers. Garrison moved to Tucson in 1775. Tucson dates its existence from 1775.

1846—Lieutenant Colonel Philip St. George Cooke builds first wagon road across Arizona, leads his Mormon Battalion more than a thousand miles to San Diego during the Mexican War.

1848—Treaty of Guadalupe Hidalgo forces Mexico to give up most of American Southwest, including Arizona, to the United States after Mexican War.

1850—Congress passes bill creating New Mexico Territory. Western half is now Arizona.

1852—First steamboat on the Colorado River, the *Uncle Sam*, reaches Yuma from Gulf of California.

1854—Gadsden Purchase ratified; United States buys land between Gila River and present southern boundary of Arizona from Mexico. It includes Tucson and Tubac.

1857—Lieutenant Edward Beale experiments will camels to carry passengers and freight across northern Arizona. His route along 35th parallel is now Interstate 40 and Santa Fe Railroad.

1858—First Butterfield Overland

Looking Back

Feb. 24, 1863

President Lincoln signed a bill creating the Territory of Arizona.

President William Howard Taft signs the Arizona statehood bill, Feb. 14, 1912. Courtesy Southwest Studies, Scottsdale Community College.

stagecoaches make trip across southern Arizona.

1861—Arizona claimed as Confederate Territory by Col. John Baylor. Confederate Congress makes Arizona and New Mexico separate territories.

1862—Confederate troops occupy Tucson. A scouting party of Confederates, and a detachment from the Union Army California Column, meet at Picacho Peak, 40 miles north of Tucson, in what is called the farthest west battle of the Civil War. Three soldiers killed.

1863—U.S. Congress creates separate Arizona Territory, sends governor and other officials to set up territorial capital at Camp Whipple, 17 miles north of Prescott.

1864—Camp Whipple and the capital are moved to present site of Prescott. First territorial census counts 4,573 residents—excluding Indians—in Arizona.

1867—Capital moved to Tucson.

1869—Major John Wesley Powell leads an exploration of Colorado River, through Grand Canyon to Gulf of California.

1870—Phoenix is born. Citizens mark out town site, sell lots.

1877—Capital moved back to Prescott.

1880—First railroad train, Southern Pacific, reaches Tucson.

1881—Atlantic and Pacific Railroad reaches northern Arizona. Shootout at the OK Corral in Tombstone.

1885—"Thieving Thirteenth" Legislature votes funds for university at Tucson and normal school (now Arizona State University) at Tempe. Normal opens 1886, the university in 1891.

1886—Geronimo surrenders, ending Indian wars.

1889—Capital moved permanently to Phoenix.

1895—James Reavis, "The Baron of

Arizona," found guilty of forging land titles to huge area of Arizona land.

1898—Arizona's Rough Riders leave for combat in Cuba.

1899—Normal school (now Northern Arizona University) opens in Flagstaff.

1903—Roosevelt Dam, key to Salt River Project irrigation, authorized by U.S. Department of Interior.

1906—Congressional plan to admit Arizona to Union as part of New Mexico is soundly defeated by Arizona voters.

1910—President Taft signs enabling act to bring Arizona into Union.

1911—Roosevelt Dam completed, launching new area of growth for central Arizona.

1912—President Taft signs proclamation making Arizona the 48th state. Plank highway built across sand dunes near Yuma on way to San Diego.

1917—Striking IWW miners deported from Bisbee, attracts national attention.

1919—Grand Canyon becomes national park. Nation's first municipal airport opens in Tucson.

1925—*Arizona Highways* magazine begins publication.

1926—First scheduled air service in Arizona.

1928—Coolidge Dam dedicated by former President Coolidge and Will Rogers.

1930—Planet Pluto discovered at Flagstaff's Lowell Observatory.

1934—Governor B.B. Moeur sends National Guard to stop construction on Parker Dam north of Yuma; says California stealing water.

1935—Air conditioning, first evaporative and later refrigerated, makes summer living in Arizona desert areas comfortable, leads to population boom.

1936—President Roosevelt dedicates Boulder Dam, later renamed Hoover Dam.

1941—World War II leads to feverish construction of air bases and other military installations all over Arizona.

1946—American Institute of Foreign Trade opens doors near Glendale. Population booms when servicemen who were stationed in Arizona return to live in the state.

1952—Barry Goldwater stuns political world, defeats Ernest W. McFarland, Senate Majority Leader, in November U.S. Senate election; Jerome's "billion dollar copper camp" closes, it becomes a ghost town.

1964—Barry Goldwater wins Republican presidential nomination, loses to Lyndon Johnson.

1968—Senator Carl Hayden retires after 57 years in Congress.

1970—Fire in Tucson's venerable Pioneer Hotel kills 29.

1974—Construction started on Central Arizona Project, mammoth reclamation project.

1975—State capitol addition completed.

1978—Governor Wesley Bolin dies in office; is succeeded by Bruce Babbitt.

1979—Devastating flooding of Salt River in central Arizona.

1981—Sandra Day O'Connor becomes first female justice of the U.S. Supreme Court.

1982—La Paz County, formed from northern Yuma County, is Arizona's 15th county.

1985—Central Arizona Project dedicated, sending Colorado River water to Arizona cities and farms.

1988—Governor Evan Mecham impeached, convicted; Rose Mofford succeeds him.

1991—Population within Phoenix city limits tops 1 million; state has 3.7 million. Arizona has six Congressional districts.

1995—State university system enrollment reaches 100,000 for first time; community colleges enroll 153,000.

1997—Governor Fife Symington charged with fraud, is convicted; Jane Dee Hull succeeds him.

1998—Women elected to all five major state offices.

1999—Senator John McCain announces candidacy for president.

Hockey

There were those who declared that ice hockey would never thrive in the Arizona desert, but the Phoenix Coyotes team of the National Hockey League has proved them wrong. Many thousands of Arizonans are hockey fans from Canada and American cold-weather states, and they have been joined by a host of newly created fans.

The Winnipeg Jets team was moved to Phoenix in 1996 and has been playing to mostly capacity (16,200) crowds at America West Arena ever since. Average attendance at Coyote games is 15,500. The move to Arizona was accompanied by a new team name, new colors, new uniforms, and a new logo. The colors are forest green, brick red, sand, sienna, and purple. The logo is a kachina-style coyote standing with a hockey stick.

A tradition of the Coyotes is the "Whiteout," started at playoff games when the team was in Winnipeg. Fans come dressed all in white, and the result is an amazing optical effect that boosts team morale and disquiets the opposition.

The Coyotes display their community spirit through their Goals for Kids Foundation, which raises money for children's activities in many Arizona non-profit organizations. Fans may watch practice sessions at the new Cellular One Ice Den facility by paying a dollar, which goes to the Foundation.

Hogan

A hogan is a traditional Navajo building. The most common type is an eight-sided structure with a dome-like roof, where families live. Although the inside space is very open, there are specified areas where male and female family members will eat, sleep, cook, store various items, etc. The fire is built in the center, and a chimney hole in the top of the roof lets out the smoke. Hogans traditionally face east. Women and girls' activities and living areas are on the north side, and men and boys' on the south. When entering a hogan (early ones have only one "door" and no windows), one always goes to the left, to the male area.

Plans for a traditional hogan have very specific places for every piece that goes into it. Construction is done by stacking cedar logs for the walls and sealing the cracks with clay mud mixed with plant material, much like a log cabin. Poles, carefully stacked in layers to make the roof, are covered with a

Navajo hogan and weaver. From What Is Arizona Really Like? *by Reg Manning.*

very thick coating of clay to protect the hogan from the elements. The floor is compacted dirt. These houses can last for centuries. The early ones had no electricity or running water, just as many hogans on the Navajo Reservation remain today. However, those built using modern construction materials may have interior walls, electricity, phone service, running water, televisions, and even computers.

Another, smaller hogan is used for many ceremonies. It is also made of wooden poles, but is not a permanent structure and may be torn down after the ceremony.

Holbrook

The county seat of Navajo County has a rich history dating back to frontier days when cattle roamed without fences and the Atlantic and Pacific Railroad reached the area in 1881 that is now Holbrook. Today the A and P is called the Burlington Northern and Santa Fe, and Interstate 40 brings thousands of visitors to this city of 5,700 people. Historic Route 66 also ran through Holbrook. Holbrook is located on the high desert of northeastern Arizona, at an altitude of 5,069 feet. The area offers the visitor many wonders, including the Painted Desert, Petrified Forest, and a chance to see working cattle ranches, as well as Navajo people and their crafts.

Honeymoon Trail

Mormon newlyweds consider it important to "seal" their marriages in a temple of their church. Until 1927, when the Mesa temple was completed, the nearest temple was at St. George, Utah. These couples made the arduous trek in covered wagons, traveling what became known as the "Honeymoon Trail." This trail was the principal entryway into Arizona from the north in the days before the building of good roads. From the Mormon communities of Safford, St. Johns, Joseph City and other settlements, the honeymooners went through Navajo country past the beautiful Echo and Vermilion Cliffs near the Utah border, and on through Lees Ferry and Kanab, Utah, to St. George.

Horse Racing

Horse racing fans find thrills aplenty at Turf Paradise in Phoenix, Rillito Downs in Tucson, Prescott Downs in Prescott, and at smaller communities in the state. Turf Paradise has racing from early October to early May each year, and Rillito Downs is also a winter racing track. Prescott Downs has quarter horse racing on weekends throughout the summer. Arizona-bred horses compete with some of the West's finest in the major stakes races at the Phoenix and Tucson tracks. The big day for Arizona racing fans is Super Saturday at Turf Paradise, the first Saturday in February, featuring the $150,000 Turf Paradise Breeders Cup and two other highly rated stakes races.

Horse racing at Turf Paradise, Phoenix. Courtesy Turf Paradise Race Course.

George W.P. Hunt, first state governor of Arizona. Courtesy Southwest Studies, Scottsdale Community College.

Hunt, George W.P.

Young George Hunt walked into the mining camp of Globe, Arizona Territory, in October 1881, clad in overalls and leading a burro. He was virtually penniless, but the lad was burning with ambition; so much so that he made a small fortune in a mercantile business and then elbowed his way to the top of the heap in Arizona politics.

In 1910 he was elected president of the Arizona Constitutional Convention, which laid the groundwork for statehood 18 months later. Thus it was almost a certainty that he would be elected as Arizona's first state governor. A genius of practical Democratic politics, Hunt was able to build a loyal following that returned him to the governorship six more times, far more than any other Arizonan in history.

When the mustachioed 300-pounder was defeated in the Democratic primary election of 1934, there seemed to him nothing more to live for. He died not long thereafter and is buried with his wife Helen in a white pyramid on a hill in Papago Park near Tempe.

Hunting

Arizona's mountains and deserts are home to a wide variety of game animals and birds, including deer, elk, bear, mountain lion, bighorn sheep, buffalo, javelina (wild pig), dove, quail, partridge, grouse, turkey, squirrel, rabbit, coyote, fox, raccoon, bobcat, weasel and badger.

License fees in 1999 were: general hunting, $18 for Arizona residents and $85.50 for non-residents; combination hunting and fishing, $34 and $100; youth (under 21), $18 and $18. Hunting is regulated by the Arizona Game and Fish Department, 2221 W. Greenway Road, Phoenix 85023, telephone (602) 942-3000. Regional offices of the department are located in Pinetop, Flagstaff, Kingman, Yuma, Tucson and Mesa.

For information on legal hunting seasons for each of the game animals and birds, write or call the Game and Fish Department. The department also issues publications outlining rules, areas of special restrictions, and other information of interest to hunters. In the case of some protected game, drawings are held to award permits.

In Arizona, everyone needs a license to hunt big game, which includes deer, elk, antelope, wild turkey, bighorn sheep, bison, peccary, mountain lion and bear. In addition to general licenses, the state offers licenses to disabled veterans and Arizona pioneers. A person under the age of 14 may hunt wildlife other than big game without a license only when accompanied by a properly licensed person 18 or older. No more than two unlicensed children may accompany any license holder.

The Game and Fish Department offers these rules of hunting etiquette:

Do not drive on wet and muddy roads where damage to the road is likely.

Do not hunt near livestock waters where livestock is nearby.

It is illegal to camp within a quarter mile of livestock and/or wildlife watering sources.

You may not operate a motorized vehicle cross-country except for the purpose of retrieving downed big game on State Trust Land.

Do not hunt on private property without permission.

If you observe vandalism, please call 1-800-VANDALS. To report hunting rule violations, call the Operation Game Thief Hotline, 1-800-352-0700.

Insects and Spiders

Some species of invertebrates common in Arizona deserts are scorpions, millipedes and tarantulas. Many species of spiders, beetles, ants, termites, crickets, grasshoppers, flies, gnats, mosquitoes, moths, bees, wasps and butterflies live throughout the state. One insect *not* found is the firefly, or lightning bug. African honeybees, the so-called "killer bees," arrived in the southern part of Arizona several years ago. Grand western cicadas and ladybugs come out in force on hot, humid, summer days.

Some interesting species include:

Scorpions (order *Scorpionida*)

The scorpion, a desert danger. Illustration by Robert Williamson.

Although they are not spiders, scorpions are related to them. They have at least three pairs of legs, with the front pair ending in large pincers. They inject venom into their prey through a stinger on the end of their long tail, which curls up over their bodies. Desert scorpions can withstand extreme heat and very arid conditions. They only hunt at night, looking for other invertebrates that live in the ground. Shine an ultraviolet light on the desert floor some evening, and you may detect a scorpion by its strange glow. The largest is the giant hairy desert scorpion, *Hadrurus arizonensis,* at 5 1/2 inches long. Ironically, the smaller and lighter in color a desert scorpion, the more dangerous its venom to humans. Straw-colored bark scorpions, *Centruroides exilicauda,* about 1 1/2 inches long, can deliver a neurotoxin that, in rare cases, has proven fatal.

Tarantulas (family *Theraphosidae*) The tarantula is North America's largest spider, growing up to 6 inches across. Their dark, hairy bodies and long fangs make them look very fierce. However, although they release venom through their fangs to kill insects and small lizards, they are timid around people. Their bite is never fatal to humans. In adverse conditions, tarantulas can go dormant and live without food for more than two years. They can go without water for up to seven months. Males die after about eight or nine years, but female tarantulas in captivity have lived for as long as 30 years.

Red velvet-ant (*Dasymutilla magnifica*) Velvet-ants aren't really ants; they are wasps that look like ants because they have no wings. But they do have long stingers and can deliver a sting that is quite painful, but not fatal to humans. They eat another species of wasp, raiding their buried pupal chambers and laying eggs inside to provide food for their young. These insects have half-inch-long wine-red bodies covered with black hair. The abdomen of the female is rust color to yellow-orange.

Great purple hairstreak (*Atlides halesus*) In spite of its name, this butterfly is small, and it's not purple. Its wings are iridescent blue, outlined with black, and dotted with red and white. The back wings have two black "tails." The underside of the wings is brown with white, yellow, and red spots that resemble a head with antennae when they move their wings up and down. This fools birds into attacking at that end, allowing the hairstreak to escape. These insects live in the Sonoran desert and lay their eggs only on mistletoe, which the larvae eat.

Jackass Mail

The San Antonio and San Diego Mail Line, popularly known as the "Jackass Mail Line" because mules were used to pull the coaches over part of the route, began its service in July 1857. It was the first passenger and mail line to operate through Arizona and advertised "an armed escort through Indian country." Coaches left San Antonio and San Diego twice each month, and the trip took about 26 days. The line was poorly financed, passengers enjoyed few amenities, and the threat of Indian attacks discouraged all but the most adventurous. When the more ambitious Butterfield Overland Mail service was launched in 1858, the Jackass Mail Line was discontinued.

Japanese Internment

One of the unfortunate consequences of the bombing of Pearl Harbor on Dec. 7, 1941, was the internment of thousands of loyal Americans of Japanese origin. "Relocation" camps were set up at Poston, on the Colorado River, and near Sacaton on Indian reservation land southeast of Phoenix. Many of the internees lost their homes and businesses. At one time Poston, with 18,000 people, was Arizona's third largest city.

The flimsy buildings of these camps were abandoned in 1945 and all occupants were released to go about rebuilding their lives.

The military services would not accept Japanese volunteers in the early months of World War II, but later an all-Japanese Army regiment won high praise for heroic action in the European Theater of operations.

Jerome (SEE ALSO GHOST TOWNS)

They called the town "The Billion Dollar Copper Camp," and it was a good name for Jerome. During World War I, when copper was bringing top prices, the population of the town exceeded 15,000, making Jerome Arizona's third largest city at the time. Built on and around Cleopatra Hill, a treasure trove of gold, copper, and silver in Yavapai County, the town clung to the steep slopes. The big mines were the United Verde, the Little Daisy, and the United Verde Extension. The underground treasure

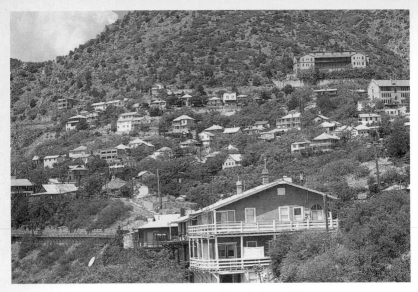

Jerome, Yavapai County, historic copper mining camp. Photo by James Tallon.

finally ran out in 1953, residents left town, and Jerome became a virtual ghost town.

In recent years, it has attracted artists, retirees, and a host of tourists and now has some 600 residents. Its Victorian-era buildings have been carefully preserved, making it a mecca for lovers of history and antiques. The old mansion once owned by James "Rawhide Jimmy" Douglas, who had purchased the Little Daisy in 1912, is now Jerome State Historic Park and open to the public.

Kartchner Caverns

One of America's largest and most colorful limestone caverns, with 2½ miles of surveyed passageways, two huge rooms and 26 smaller ones, was opened to the public late in 1999. Kartchner Caverns is located near Benson, just off State Route 90, and has been purchased by the State of Arizona as a state park. Among its special attractions are the "fried eggs"

stalagmites, the Throne Room, the "soda straws" stalactites, and slabs that look amazingly like strips of bacon.

Cavers Randy Tufts and Gary Tenen discovered the mammoth cave in 1974, on ranch land owned by James and Lois Kartchner. They kept their find a secret for 14 years, knowing that vandals and curiosity seekers would spoil its beauty if the word got out. At last they approached Governor Bruce Babbitt, who started the process by which the caverns became a state park.

During the past decade, work progressed to prepare Kartchner Caverns for visitation by the public: installation of air locks, walkways, lighting, safety features and much more. Every effort has been made to preserve the beauty and stability of the caverns, a natural wonder that took millions of years to create. Kartchner is especially significant in that it is a "living" cave, one in which the mineral formations are still growing with each tiny droplet of water.

Kingman

Kingman, a mining and ranching center since the 1880s, is the county seat of Mohave County. It is 25 miles east of Lake Mohave and within easy driving distance of Hoover Dam, Lake Mead, and Lake Havasu. Many ghost towns in the area lure seekers after western history and attest to the multitude of gold mines that yielded their riches decades ago. Tourism, copper mining, and ranching are now the chief economic pillars of Kingman. The Mohave Museum of History and Arts is a mecca for visitors. Kingman, whose population now exceeds 20,000, is also home to Mohave Community College.

Labor Force

(SEE ALSO UNION MEMBERSHIP) Especially in the two urban counties, Maricopa and Pima, there are more jobs available than qualified people to fill them. Both counties have unemployment rates below 4 percent, and the state as a whole has a rate below 5 percent.

The Arizona Department of Economic Security reports that 2,250,000 Arizonans are gainfully employed. Of those, 1,352,000 are employed in Maricopa County and 368,000 in Pima County. Per capita personal income in the state is just over $25,000 per year.

In the production industries, manufacturing leads the way with more than 220,000 employed. Construction employs 130,000, and mining 14,000. Service industries employ 640,000; retail and wholesale trade, 480,000; government, 324,000; and finance, insurance, and real estate 126,000.

Lake Havasu City

(SEE ALSO LONDON BRIDGE) Mohave County's largest community, Lake Havasu City, has over 41,000 residents. A year-around resort, it is situated on the Colorado River and is a popular water sports site. Many retirees have settled here since Lake Havasu City's founding in 1963 by chain saw manufacturer Robert McCulloch. It is best known as the home of London Bridge, which was shipped, stone by stone, from London and reassembled in 1971. Lake Havasu's major economic bases are tourism, retirement, cattle ranching, and manufacturing.

Lakes (SEE ALSO DAMS)

Newcomers to Arizona are usually surprised to learn that the state has many large lakes, more shoreline mileage than many Eastern and Midwestern states, and larger per-capita recreational boat ownership than all but a few other states. It is also surprising to discover that only little Stoneman Lake in Coconino County, and perhaps one or two others, are natural lakes. All the others have been impounded behind dams on the state's streams and rivers. Largest of Arizona's lakes are Lakes Mead and Powell, both of which extend into neighboring states.

Lake Mead. The largest man-made lake in North America, Lake Mead was created by the construction of Hoover Dam on the Colorado River. The opposite shore of much of the lake extends well into Nevada. The dam, the world's largest at the time of its completion in 1935, is as tall as a 70-story skyscraper. Lake Mead impounds the most water of any Arizona lake, and is 115 miles long. Much of it is twice as deep as Lake Erie. The Lake Mead National Recreational

Area attracts even more visitors than the Grand Canyon and is a mecca for campers, fishermen, and water sports enthusiasts.

Lake Powell. Created by 710-foot-high Glen Canyon Dam on the Colorado not far south of the Utah border, Lake Powell rivals Lake Mead in popularity. It is 185 miles long and has a shoreline of 1,960 miles. Most of the lake lies in southern Utah, but the dam, the city of Page, the western end of the lake, and the famed Wahweap campground and marina are in Arizona. The Glen Canyon National Recreation Area is administered by the U.S. Park Service. Houseboats, speedboats, and most other watercraft ply these waters, and on an evening each December their owners stage a spectacular floating light parade.

Lake Mohave. Down the Colorado, 67 miles from Lake Mead, is Lake Mohave, impounded behind Davis Dam. The northern part of the lake is colder, and ideal for trout fishing; the southern, warmer portion has striped bass. Some of the latter reach 50 pounds. The Willow Beach trout hatchery, which provides fish for several river sites, is here. Just south of the dam are the booming river resorts of Bullhead City, Arizona, and Laughlin, Nevada.

Lake Havasu. Behind Parker Dam, 89 miles south of Davis Dam, is Lake Havasu, home of several important boating regattas. Lake Havasu City is another thriving river community. Its big attraction is London Bridge,

transported from London and rebuilt here. Like other Colorado River cities, Lake Havasu City has attracted several thousand retirees, and even more vacationers.

Roosevelt Lake. The string of Salt River lakes east of Phoenix not only give the metropolitan area a stable water supply, but provide fishing, boating and camping for many thousands each year. Roosevelt Lake is behind Theodore Roosevelt Dam, the kingpin of the Salt River Project power and water complex. Downriver from Roosevelt are **Apache Lake, Canyon Lake** and **Saguaro Lake.** All are popular with water sportsmen. Other lakes and reservoirs in the Phoenix area that provide recreation for the populace include: **Lake Pleasant** (a giant storage basin for CAP water on the Agua Fria River), **Bartlett Reservoir** and **Horseshoe Reservoir** on the Verde River.

San Carlos Lake. Behind Coolidge Dam on the Gila River southeast of Roosevelt Lake is San Carlos Lake. In past years, this lake has served boaters and fishermen, but at the end of the 20th century, because of agricultural water withdrawals upstream on the Gila and several dry years, the lake has shrunk to less than 5 percent of its maximum size.

High on the Mogollon Rim east of Payson are **Woods Canyon Lake, Bear Lake, Knoll Lake, Willow Springs Lake, Chevelon Lake, Black Canyon Lake** and **Blue Ridge Reservoir.** At 7,000 feet, these water bodies freeze over in winter, but many visitors come the rest of the year.

Looking Back

1981

Arizona native Sandra Day O'Connor was the first woman appointed to the U.S. Supreme Court.

In the White Mountains to the southeast of Show Low are **Hawley Lake, Big Lake, Sunrise Lake, Becker Lake, Luna Lake, Lyman Lake Reservoir** and several other bodies of water. All are popular with sportsmen.

The Coronado National Forest uplands in southern Arizona have several lakes, including **Pena Blanca, Arivaca, Parker Canyon, Riggs** and **Rucker.** Each of them, although small, provides excellent recreational opportunities.

Many other areas of Arizona have small lakes such as Prescott's **Watson** and **Lynx Lakes,** Williams' **White Horse Lake,** and Flagstaff's **Lake Mary** and **Mormon Lake.**

And one cannot forget **Alamo Lake**, east of Parker on the Bill Williams River. It's one of the best desert fishing water bodies in the state.

Leaders, Politicians and Government Figures

Many people who have contributed to events on a national level have been Arizonans. Here is a partial listing:

Leaders.

Eleven Apache scouts and one U.S. Army soldier from Arizona won the Congressional Medal of Honor for distinguished service during the Indian Wars of the late 19th century.

World War I flying ace **Frank Luke Jr.,** (1897–1918) also won the Medal of Honor. **Sylvestre Herrera** (1917–) from Phoenix was the only Arizonan to win the Congressional Medal of Honor in World War II. **Ira Hayes** (1923–55), World War II hero, was one of the Marines who raised the U.S. flag on Mount Suribachi in Iwo Jima, in Joe Rosenthal's famous photo. He was a Pima Indian from Bapchule.

Seven Arizonans earned the Medal of Honor during the Vietnam War. They are: **Oscar P. Austin** (1948–69); **Nicky Daniel Bacon** (1945–); **Kern W. Dunagan** (1934–91); **Frederick E. Ferguson** (1939–); **Jose F. Jimenez** (1946–69); **Billy L. Lauffer** (1945–66); and **M. Sando Vargas Jr.** (1940–).

Cesar Chavez, (1927–93) Mexican American activist and labor union leader, was born in Arizona. Gemini 7 astronaut **Frank Borman** (1928–) came from Tucson, and astronaut **F. Richard Scobee** (1939–86), commander of the last Challenger shuttle mission, graduated from the University of Arizona. Business leader, real estate developer, and builder of Sun City, Arizona, **Del E. Webb** (1899–1974) has a hospital named for him, and his corporation continues to build Arizona. **Annie Dodge Wauneka** (1910–97) was the first woman and first American Indian to receive the Presidential Medal of Freedom, in 1963.

Politicians and Government Figures.

Rachel Emma Allen Berry (1859–1948) was the first Arizona woman elected to the state House of Representatives and one of the first women legislators in the United States. In 1933, **Isabella Greenway (King)** (1886–1953) became the first Arizona woman elected to Congress. Other Arizona politicians known on the national stage include **Carl Hayden** (1877–1972) U.S. Senator and member of Congress for 57 years; **Ernest W. McFarland** (1894–1984) Governor, Senator and Arizona Chief Justice; and **John J. Rhodes** (1916–) attorney and U.S. House Minority Leader.

Lorna E. Lockwood (1903–77) was the first woman Superior Court Judge in Arizona and the first woman state Supreme Court Chief Justice in Arizona and the United States. Arizona's first woman governor, **Rose Mofford** (1922–) was also Arizona's first woman Secretary of State. **Edwynne C. "Polly" Rosenbaum** (1899–) was the longest serving member of the Arizona House of Representatives, 1949–94.

Bruce Babbitt (1939–), current U.S. Secretary of the Interior, was raised in Flagstaff and is a former Arizona Attorney General and Governor. Author and former Arizona Congressman **Stewart Udall** (1920–) also served his country as Interior Secretary. His brother, **Morris Udall** (1922–98), also an author and Arizona Congressman, was an unsuccessful candidate for U.S. President.

Americans have looked to other Arizonans to run for President, but so far none has been elected. These include **John McCain** (1936–), U.S. Senator, Navy pilot, and former Vietnam POW, and **Barry M. Goldwater** (1909–98), U.S. Senator, Air Force Major General, businessman, author, photographer, and ham radio operator.

Two judges sitting today on the U.S. Supreme Court come from Arizona. They are **William Rehnquist** (1924–), Chief Justice, and **Sandra Day O'Connor** (1930–), Associate Justice and the first woman to be chosen for the Supreme Court. And **Harriet "Hattie" Babbitt** (1947–), attorney, Ambassador, and Deputy Administrator for the United States Agency for International Development, graduated from ASU.

Libraries

Arizona's three state universities have excellent research collections located in several buildings on each campus. The University of Arizona's specialized libraries have, among others, collections in medicine, law, the physical and biological sciences, engineering, agriculture, business and public administration. The Arizona State Museum on the University of Arizona campus houses both research materials and exhibits dealing with prehistoric peoples. Arizona State University and Northern Arizona University have libraries devoted to their major fields of study.

The Museum of Northern Arizona in Flagstaff is nationally known for its library and its publications on the native peoples of that area. The Department of Library and Archives in the state capitol in Phoenix is a mecca for students of Arizona history, as is the Arizona Historical Foundation in ASU's Hayden Library.

Libraries of the various Arizona Historical Society branches and affiliates throughout the state, and particularly the collections in Tucson, are a rich source of information for researchers in Arizona history.

The newly enlarged Burton Barr Phoenix Public Library is a source of pride for all Arizonans. Each city and town in the state has its own public library facility, and many communities have specialized collections appropriate for their major fields of economic or historical interest.

Literature

(SEE ALSO GREY, ZANE) Novelists and poets, inspired by Arizona's natural surroundings and interesting people, often base stories on the state. Many

Dick Wick Hall

His real name was DeForest Hall, but he liked to be called Dick and used Wick (short for Wickenburg) as a middle name because it rhymed. Arizona's most famous humorist, at least until Erma Bombeck came onto the scene, had a gas station in the desert town of Salome. He used his vivid imagination to populate the area with such characters as the Reptyle Kid, Chloride Kate, and Hall's seven-year-old frog that never learned to swim (not enough water) and carried a canteen on his back.

The Saturday Evening Post, at that time the most popular magazine in America, discovered Hall and published almost everything he had time to write. His Greasewood Golf Course, 247 miles long with a par of 52 days, became known to millions. So did his one-page mimeographed newspaper, the Salome Sun, which he handed out to customers along with travel advisories and wry humor. ✳

of these have gained national attention and prominence. Other authors have used Arizona as a getaway where they could have undisturbed writing time. Academics have done much research and written many books about Arizona's archeology, geology, Native peoples, plants and animals, and social interactions. It would be impossible to do justice to all of their fine work by attempting to list those authors here. Rather, here are some popular writers you may know:

Those who traveled in or explored Arizona in the 19th century often kept diaries, wrote articles for the eastern press, or published memoirs. For example, **James Ohio Pattie** (1804–50), a trapper, spun a fantastic yarn about his experiences in *The Personal Narrative of James O. Pattie*. **J. Ross Browne** (1821–75) wrote an account about the feared Apaches, *Adventures in Apache Country: A Tour Through Arizona and Sonora, 1864*.

Another easterner in Arizona because of the Apache Wars, **Martha Summerhayes** (1844–1926), a military wife, later reminisced about her life in *Vanished Arizona*. **John Wesley Powell** (1834–1902), a geologist and ethnologist, led several famous expeditions to

map and study the Grand Canyon. He titled one of his reports *Exploration of the Colorado River of the West and Its Tributaries*. Many others who traveled to the state to settle it have published interesting books and articles about their lives and experiences.

Zane Grey (1872–1939) lived in a cabin below the Mogollon Rim and set many of his novels about the West in the forests and rangelands there. These include *The Last of the Plainsmen, The Light of the Western Stars, Riders of the Purple Sage, To the Last Man,* and *Under the Tonto Rim.* **Sharlot Hall** (1870–1943), poet, journalist, author, and historian, traveled extensively throughout the state, collecting historical artifacts and writing about her findings for several magazines. **Harold Bell Wright** (1872–1944), minister, artist, and nationally acclaimed author, wrote most of his 18 novels while living in Tucson, from 1915–39. His best-known work is *The Winning of Barbara Worth*.

The effects of sunlight through the thin desert air fascinated art critic **John C. Van Dyke** (1856–1932), who published *The Desert: Further Studies in Natural Appearances*. Environmentalist author **John Muir** (1838–1914) discussed the Grand Canyon in his book, *Steep Trails.* And **Willa Cather** (1873–1947) set her novel *Death Comes for the Archbishop* in Arizona. Others who wrote about Arizona and the Southwest include **Mary Hunter Austin** (1868–1934), **Charles Lummis** (1859–1928) and **Frank Waters** (1902–95).

Joseph Wood Krutch (1893–1970), a New York drama critic, left the city to live in the desert near Tucson. He wrote several books about nature there, including *The Desert Year.* **Marguerite Noble**'s (1910–) novel *Filaree* chronicles the life of an Arizona woman in the first half of the 20th century.

Father Andrew M. Greeley (1928–) lectures at the University of Arizona and has written many articles on religion. He has also published 43 popular novels. Novelist **Barbara Kingsolver** (1955–) lives in Tucson and has set some of her books in Arizona, including *The Bean Trees, Animal Dreams* and *Pigs in Heaven.*

Edward Abbey's (1927–89) popular novel, *The Monkey Wrench Gang,* centers its story about environmental terrorism around Glen Canyon Dam. University of Arizona English Professor, **N. Scott Momaday** (1934–) won the Pulitzer Prize for Fiction for his novel *A House Made of Dawn.* Popular novelist and poet, **Leslie Marmon Silko** (1948–), also teaches at the U of A.

Humorist and author **Erma Bombeck** (1927–96) made her home in Paradise Valley for many years before her death. **Rita Dove** (1951–), poet and English Professor, was chosen to be the U.S. Poet Laureate while teaching at Arizona State University. And **Terry McMillan**'s (1951–) recent novel *Waiting to Exhale,* made into a movie, is about four Phoenix

London Bridge, transported from England and rebuilt at Lake Havasu City. Photo by James Tallon.

professional women. Like McMillan, **Sherman J. Alexie Jr.,** (1966–) does not live in Arizona. But his short story "This Is What it Means To Say Phoenix, Arizona," from his book *The Lone Ranger and Tonto Fistfight in Heaven,* is the basis for the movie *Smoke Signals.*

London Bridge

London Bridge, which spanned the Thames River from the 1830s to the late 1960s, now stands at Lake Havasu City on the Colorado River. The city's founder, Robert P. McCulloch, bought the bridge from the City of London for $2.6 million in 1968. The bridge was dismantled and shipped to Arizona, where it was reconstructed at a cost of $7 million. It was dedicated in 1971, amid ceremonies, which included celebrities from both Great Britain and the United States and throngs of other visitors. Scoffers derided McCulloch's purchase of the bridge as sheer folly, but it has attracted many millions of visitors to Lake Havasu City during the past quarter century and has produced tourism income far exceeding its cost.

Lost Dutchman Mine (*SEE ALSO* GOLD) Arizona

has hundreds of lost mines, many with colorful legends about their wealth and where they might be found. By far the most famous of these is the Lost Dutchman Mine, supposedly a rich gold mine in the Superstition Mountains east of Apache Junction. Several hundred magazine articles and scores of books have been written about this mine, and treasure hunters still comb the rugged mountain slopes in search of it.

Jacob Waltz, a prospector in the late 19th century, was the "Dutchman," and legend says he discovered an old Spanish gold mine in the Superstitions. He would tell no one of its location but occasionally brought nuggets to Phoenix, claiming they were from his find. Not long before he died, he is said to have left a crude map to the mine site. The map has never been found, nor has the mine. A dozen people have died looking for it, some mysteriously, during the past century. More than one skeleton has been found with bullet holes in its skull.

Lost Dutchman State Park has been established near the western base of the Superstitions. Visitors use it as a base for their searches, or just for hiking adventures.

Magazines, Selected General Interest Periodicals

The magazine most familiar to those outside of Arizona is *Arizona Highways*. Founded in 1925 as a technical journal on highway construction, the magazine soon became a publication used to promote the state. Under the editorship of Raymond Carlson, it became the unchallenged leader of state magazines in America. Many of the nation's leading photographers contributed their best scenic images to the magazine and prominent writers told the story of Arizona's natural wonders. It was the first magazine to go 100 percent to full-color photos.

Arizona Highways has now branched out into related products— books, calendars, video tapes, gifts and much more. The magazine's readership continues to be nearly 70 percent out-of-state and it is credited with attracting many thousands of new-comers to Arizona. For more information, write to: ***Arizona Highways,*** 2039 W. Lewis, Phoenix 85009.

Cover of December 1946 issue of Arizona Highways, *the first all-color general interest magazine in the world.* Cover photo by Barry Goldwater.

Other state magazines include:

Arizona Living, 5046 N. Seventh St., Phoenix 85014

Arizona's Economy, Division of Economic and Business Research, University of Arizona, Tucson 85721

Journal of Arizona History, Arizona Historical Society, 949 E. Second St., Tucson 85719

Kiva, State Museum, University of Arizona, Tucson 85721

Native Peoples, 5333 N. Seventh St., Phoenix 85040

Phoenix Magazine, 5555 N. Seventh Ave., Phoenix 85013

Tucson Lifestyle Magazine, 7000 E. Tanque Verde Road, Tucson 85715

Mammals With terrain
that varies from Sonoran desert to alpine tundra, Arizona's mammals encompass a large number of species. Lower Sonoran desert mammals include the western pipistrelle and California myotis bats, big horn sheep, mule deer, coatimundi, gray foxes, kit fixes, raccoons, coyotes, antelope, ground squirrels, kangaroo rats, jackrabbits javelinas, wild horses and burros.

Mexican Wolves

Fewer than 200 Mexican gray wolves, an extremely endangered species, survive today, mostly in zoos. However, the U.S. Fish and Wildlife Service and the Arizona Game and Fish Department have been reintroducing these animals into Arizona. Since 1998, the program has released 34 wolves into the Apache National Forest in southeastern Arizona. While there has never been a verified instance of a Mexican wolf attacking a human, they will hunt domesticated animals, so this program has been controversial. ❋

Some well-known Arizona animals include desert rabbits such as the white-tailed desert cottontail and the black-tailed jackrabbit. Cottontails eat everything from grasses to garden flowers to cacti. Jackrabbits can hop up to 10 feet and run 35 miles per hour.

Depending on the season, you can also see squirrels, mice, rats, skunks, chipmunks and white-tailed deer in the Upper Sonoran and in the pine forests at higher elevations. Prairie dogs live in the grasslands near Seligman. Around water, you will see bats, beavers, badgers and muskrats. Higher into the mountains you will find the habitats for porcupines, several species of squirrels, elk, deer, black bears, ringtails, bobcats and mountain lions. The Chiricahua fox squirrel is found only in the Chiricahua Mountains. Bobcats and mountain lions (also called cougars or pumas) live in mountain areas all over the state.

Hoofed animals prefer the mountains in summer and the desert in winter. These include the 4-to-6-foot tall mule deer, with its large ears and black-tipped tail, and elk that weigh over 900 pounds and can grow 6 to 9 feet tall. Bighorn sheep, including desert bighorns, have distinctive coiled horns and like to jump in rocky areas. The pronghorn antelope (not actually an antelope, but related more closely to the mountain goat) can run up to 70 miles per hour, making it the fastest animal in North America. This shy animal is commonly seen in Petrified Forest National Park.

Although bison and Arabian oryxes, an endangered species of antelope, are not native to Arizona and do not live in the wild, you may see herds of bison

Bighorn sheep. Photo by James Tallon.

at House Rock Buffalo Ranch and Raymond Ranch, and the world's largest oryx herd at the Phoenix Zoo. Other interesting animals found in Arizona are:

Ringtail *(Bassariscus astutus).* Arizona's state mammal, the ringtail is a cat-like animal with large eyes and ears and a 15-inch-long black and white ringed tail. They aren't really in the cat family, but are instead a type of raccoon. These nocturnal animals like rocky places from the deserts to forested lower mountain areas, and are great climbers. They eat insects, fruit and smaller mammals.

Kangaroo rat (several species of *Dipodomys*). The huge hind legs and feet of the 8-to-11-inch kangaroo rat allow it to leap up to 10 feet in one bound. When a predator grabs one by the tail, it breaks off, allowing the animal to escape. Later the tail grows back. Their coloring, like pale sand, also gives them protection. Kangaroo rats don't need to drink water, and they come out only at night, when the desert is cooler. They eat seeds, stuffing them into pouches in their cheeks and storing them underground.

Javelina *(Tayassu tajacu).* Also known as peccaries or musk hogs, these bristly, salt-and-pepper colored animals have hoofs and snouts that make them look like pigs. However, they are not related, and among several differences are the javelina's dorsal musk gland and his small, sharp tusks. Weighing about 40 to 60 pounds, these animals travel in packs of three to 40 and are found in desert or grasslands from 1,000 to 5,000 feet. They eat mostly plants such as prickly pear cactus, roots, nuts, acorns and mesquite, and palo verde beans.

Coyote *(Canis latrans).* The fabled yellow-gray coyote, a wild dog with a black-tipped tail, lives everywhere, from deserts to mountains. Social animals that travel in families, coyotes have several ways of communicating with each other, including their distinctive long howls that end with a few short yips. Desert coyotes weigh about 20 pounds and can run up to 40 miles per hour, which is helpful in hunting antelope and deer. They also eat javelinas, rabbits, rodents and a wide variety of plant material.

Mesa

Arizona's third largest city, Mesa, has grown from its 1990 U.S. Census figure of 288,000 residents to today's estimated 375,000. It is located 15 miles southeast of downtown Phoenix on slightly elevated tableland above the Salt River; thus its name, the word for "table" in Spanish.

Mesa was founded in 1878 by Mormon pioneers and was incorporated in 1883. It had a predominantly Mormon population until its period of rapid growth started at the close of World War II. The city is the home of the Arizona Temple of the Church of Jesus Christ of Latter-day Saints (Mormon), the buildings and grounds of which attract many thousands of visitors each year.

Chicago Cubs baseball fans know

Mesa's Hohokam Park as the spring training home of their team. The Cubs play in the 10-team Cactus League in February and March, and their games draw the largest crowds in the league.

Once known primarily as a farming town, Mesa now has a thriving economy also based on manufacturing, tourism, education, government, retail trade and finance. Mesa Community College, largest of the state's community colleges, is here. So is the East Valley government complex of Maricopa County. Champlin Fighter Aircraft Museum is one of five museums featuring technology, the arts, archeology and history.

Meteor Crater (SEE ALSO MOON WALKERS) Some 50,000 years ago a meteorite entered the atmosphere of our planet and plunged earthward toward the northern Arizona high desert 20 miles west of Winslow. The fiery missile exploded on impact with the force of 20 million tons of TNT, blasting a hole 4,000 feet wide and 750 feet deep.

Today Meteor Crater is one of Arizona's most visited tourist attractions. Only 5 miles south of Interstate 40, it offers walking tours to the bottom of the chasm and around its perimeter, an excellent museum of space and meteoritic science, a theater and other amenities. Memorabilia of American astronauts' moon walk training, even an actual space capsule, are on display. Wearing space suits, these space pioneers ventured into the crater to study cratering effects they soon would be encountering on the surface of the moon.

Military Although the Air Force has closed Williams Air Force Base near Chandler, one of the nation's

Frank Luke Jr.

One of the storied daredevils of World War I aviation was Frank Luke Jr. of Phoenix, whose exploits during his 39 days of combat action in France earned him the adulation of all Arizonans. Only 21 years of age, he shot down 21 German artillery observation balloons and survived several aerial dog fights. He was hailed as "the Arizona Balloon Buster" by the nation's press.

He was shot down and killed behind enemy lines, but his memory will live on in two permanent tributes to his heroism: a statue of the young aviator which stands at the entrance to the state capitol in Phoenix, and the naming of Luke Air Force Base near Glendale, one of America's major jet fighter training bases. ✳

top jet fighter training bases for half a century, Arizona still has major military installations.

Davis–Monthan Air Force Base at Tucson is one of the city's largest employers, and Luke Air Force Base near Glendale continues to be a major economic engine for the Phoenix area. The Barry M. Goldwater Air Force Range in southwestern Arizona is a remote gunnery training site for pilots of all the U.S. armed forces.

The Army's Fort Huachuca at Sierra Vista, established in 1877, played an important role in the Apache wars and in recent years has become a global communications center. Yuma is the site of the Army's desert proving ground for vehicles of many types. The U.S. Marine Air Station is another of Yuma's military bases.

Arizona's Army and Air Force National Guard headquarters are in Phoenix, and units of both National Guard organizations train in other remote locations around the state.

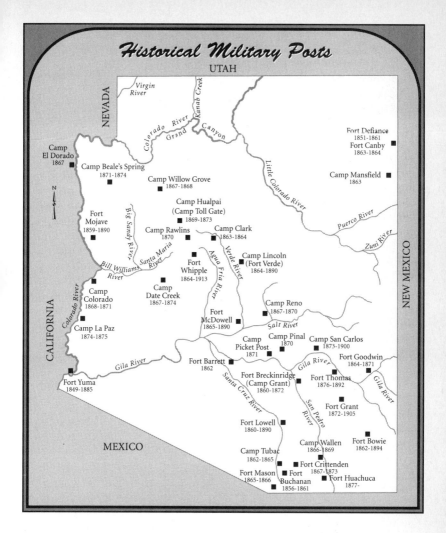

Historical Military Posts

UTAH

NEVADA

Virgin River

Colorado River

Grand Canyon

Kanab Creek

Fort Defiance
1851-1861
Fort Canby
1863-1864

Camp El Dorado
1867

Camp Beale's Spring
1871-1874

Little Colorado River

Camp Mansfield
1863

Camp Willow Grove
1867-1868

Camp Hualpai
(Camp Toll Gate)
1869-1873

Puerco River

Fort Mojave
1859-1890

Camp Rawlins
1870

Camp Clark
1863-1864

Zuni River

Big Sandy River

Santa Maria River

Fort Whipple
1864-1913

Verde River

Camp Lincoln
(Fort Verde)
1864-1890

NEW MEXICO

Bill Williams River

CALIFORNIA

Camp Colorado
1868-1871

Camp Date Creek
1867-1874

Agua Fria River

Camp Reno
1867-1870

Colorado River

Camp La Paz
1874-1875

Fort McDowell
1865-1890

Salt River

Camp Picket Post
1871

Camp Pinal
1870

Camp San Carlos
1873-1900

Fort Goodwin
1864-1871

Gila River

Fort Barrett
1862

Fort Breckinridge
(Camp Grant)
1860-1872

Gila River

Fort Thomas
1876-1892

Gila River

Fort Yuma
1849-1885

Santa Cruz River

Fort Grant
1872-1905

San Pedro River

Fort Lowell
1860-1890

Camp Wallen
1866-1869

Fort Bowie
1862-1894

MEXICO

Camp Tubac
1862-1865

Fort Crittenden
1867-1873

Fort Mason
1865-1866

Fort Buchanan
1856-1861

Fort Huachuca
1877-

Military Posts

Camp Calhoun, on the Colorado River opposite today's Yuma, was established in 1849, the first of the military posts in Arizona territorial history. Camp Yuma was opened in 1852, after steamship travel assured a means of supply. It guarded the Southern Overland Trail to California.

Fort Defiance in northeastern Arizona was established in 1851, the first of many posts manned to defend against Indian incursions. Other posts in operation before the creation of Arizona Territory in 1863 included Fort Mohave on the Colorado River, and Fort Buchanan, Camp Lowell and Fort Bowie in the southeast.

The Arizona territorial government party set up the first capital (1864) at the new Camp Whipple, north of Chino Valley. It became Fort Whipple and was moved to the present site of Prescott later that same year.

A chain of forts was built soon after the end of the Civil War: Fort Verde, Fort Apache, Camp Reno and Fort McDowell. The Apache wars of the 1870s and 1880s in southeastern Arizona brought Fort Huachuca, Fort Bowie and Fort Grant into headlines across the nation.

Mining (SEE ALSO THE FIVE C'S; GOLD; ROCKS, MINERALS, AND GEMSTONES)

The trapping of beavers in the 1820s, lured the first Americans to what is now Arizona, but mining eventually became the major occupation and economic cornerstone of the area. For many decades, Arizona's prosperity was based on its mines.

Gold was discovered along the Colorado River in the late 1850s, and several rich strikes during the 1860s—the Vulture, Rich Hill, Lynx Creek, and others—brought prospectors flooding into the new Arizona Territory. The discovery of silver in Cochise County made Tombstone a nationally known boomtown in the 1880s.

But the precious metals soon were exhausted, and copper became king in Arizona. By 1900, copper production had grown to three times the value of gold and silver combined. Today, despite the closing of many mines, Arizona still produces more copper each year than any other state. Most of the precious metals production now is a by-product of copper treatment.

Many other products of Arizona mines have contributed to the state's economy. Lead and zinc are by-products of copper production. Manganese, iron, mercury, tungsten, vanadium and uranium all have been mined in the state.

The development of extensive coal beds on the Navajo and Hopi reservations in northeastern Arizona and northwestern New Mexico in the mid-20th century was a major mining development. Most of Arizona's coal production now goes to fuel the mammoth power generators in the area.

Dr. James Douglas, a Canadian metallurgist, brought the Phelps Dodge Company of New York to Bisbee in the 1880s and built a mining empire in Arizona that still is a major force in the state's economy. Phelps Dodge developed huge open-pit copper mines at Bisbee, Morenci and Ajo, and its Douglas smelter gave birth to the town named for the canny Canadian. Later "PD," as it is known to Arizonans, took over the underground Jerome mines.

Senator William Clark of Montana, for whom Clarkdale is named, made the United Verde Mine at Jerome a winner at the turn of the century, used it to increase his wealth by $100 million, and earned for the town the nickname, "The Billion Dollar Copper Camp." Nearby Clarkdale was the home of the mines' smelter.

South of Tucson, ASARCO,

Abandoned Mines

It sounds like a gross exaggeration, but there are an estimated 100,000 abandoned mine shafts in Arizona, some 15,000 of which pose a serious danger to those who venture too near them. The Office of Arizona Mine Inspector rates the Tonopah Belmont Mine, between Wickenburg and Tonopah, as the most dangerous. One of the shafts burrows 450 feet into the earth. The Lucky Cuss Mine, southwest of Wickenburg, is rated second most dangerous.

The State of Arizona has begun an abandoned mine closure program with $80,000 in seed money from the legislature and four mining companies. Shafts are being filled in or sealed over. Two of the most recent deaths caused by abandoned mines occurred in 1990 and 1994. In the first, a boy fell to his death in the Tonopah Belmont; in the second, a man died when he drove his truck into a shaft near Payson.

Hikers are warned to stay away from open mine shafts. �֎

Mineral Production in Arizona (non-fuel production only)

Mineral	Measured in	1994 Quantity	1994 Value	1995 Quantity	1995 Value
Clays	metric tons	98,000	$452,000	100,000	$463,000
Copper	metric tons	1,120,000	2,750,000,000	1,200,000	3,600,000,000
Gemstones		n/a	3,550,000	n/a	3,760,000
Gold	kilograms	1,980	24,500,000	1,940	23,300,000
Iron oxide pigments crude	metric tons	77	62,000	77	62,000
Sand and gravel construction	thousand metric tons	34,800	166,000,000	37,000	180,000,000
Silver	metric tons	192	32,600,000	194	33,100,000
Stone, crushed	thousand metric tons	4,970	25,000,000	5,400	27,500,000
Combined value others			274,000,000		309,000,000
Total			$3,280,000,000		$4,180,000,000

Source: U.S. Department of Interior, Bureau of Mines

Anamax, Duval, and Cypress companies developed profitable copper mining operations. The Kennecott Company mine at Hayden, Magma's San Manuel mine, Inspiration and Cities Service mines at Globe-Miami, and the Cyprus mine at Bagdad have been among other major copper producers.

The combination of competition from South American mines, increasing production costs, and declining use of copper have pushed down the price and profitability of copper so drastically in recent years that many mines have closed and the industry is presently suffering in Arizona and elsewhere.

Miranda v. Arizona

Every police show on television repeats the familiar words: "You have the right to remain silent, etc." It's called "Mirandizing" an accused law breaker:

reading his or her rights before an arrest. Should an arresting officer forget to recite those rights, the accused may escape punishment.

The U.S. Supreme Court, by a 5 to 4 decision, in 1966 reversed an Arizona court's conviction of Ernesto Miranda, who had been found guilty of kidnapping and rape. Chief Justice Earl Warren wrote the decision for the majority. Although he had signed a confession of guilt, Miranda was freed on the grounds that the prosecution could not use his statements because the police had not told him of his right to remain silent, or to have a lawyer present to advise him.

The Miranda decision stunned the law enforcement community. Critics said the court, in its efforts to protect the rights of accused persons, had seriously weakened enforcement agencies. Advocates of strict law and order still decry the decision, which has over the past three decades allowed many guilty persons to escape punishment. Chief Justice Warren, however, always defended the decision because he had become increasingly concerned about methods being used by police to obtain confessions.

Montezuma Castle

The name is all wrong (Montezuma never came near the place, and it's not a castle) but Montezuma Castle is one of the most visited of Arizona's National Monuments. It is easily accessible, just off Interstate 17 about 5 miles north of Camp Verde.

This is a prehistoric cliff dwelling, four stories high, built in the 14th century. It hangs on its precipice, 80 feet above the valley floor, and Sinagua mothers must have gotten gray from worry when their children moved too near the edge. A dozen or more

Montezuma Castle National Monument..
Photo by James Tallon.

families lived in the 20 rooms of Montezuma Castle, gaining access to the living quarters by climbing long ladders.

It's well worth an hour or two of the traveler's time. So is nearby Montezuma Well, which is not a well at all but a spring-fed pond, 1,750 feet in diameter. Montezuma Well is part of the Montezuma Castle National Monument.

Monument Valley

Most Americans have seen magnificent Monument Valley, even if they have never visited Arizona. That's because it has been the backdrop for scores of moving pictures, since the classic *Stagecoach* was filmed there in 1938. It is a favorite site for tourist visits, and for good reason.

Monument Valley Tribal Park is astride the Arizona-Utah border in the Navajo Reservation, and is easily accessible in northeastern Arizona via U.S. 160 to Kayenta, and then north 45 minutes on U.S.163.

Here Nature has carved out a skyline of towering stone statues: spires, castles, skyscrapers, and fantastic shapes of many kinds. It has been called "an architect's dream

Monument Valley, northeastern Arizona.
Photo by James Tallon.

turned to stone." Guided tours are available. Those who have longed to mingle with American Indians up close and personal find Kayenta and Monument Valley an ideal answer.

Moon Walkers (SEE ALSO METEOR CRATER) The Apollo astronauts in the 1960s had been chosen for exceptional abilities as aviators, but scientists insisted that they have enough knowledge of geology to make valid observations on the surface of the moon. Among other things, they needed to be able to distinguish a volcanic crater from one made by the impact of a meteor.

The National Aeronautics and Space Agency sent its astronauts to Sunset Crater near Flagstaff to train at the site of one of the world's most recent volcanic eruptions. Explosives were set in strategic positions in the volcanic ash to simulate moon craters. A practice moon landing vehicle was brought in, and the astronauts were given a trial run in these pockmarked surroundings.

Arizona's Meteor Crater, 20 miles west of Winslow, became equally important to NASA in the training regimen of the astronauts. Earth's freshest and best-preserved impact crater was waiting to serve as a textbook for those space pioneers who would soon be inspecting craters on the moon.

Dr. Eugene Shoemaker, recognized as the top authority on cratering mechanics, set up the training program at Meteor Crater in early 1963. Among his first students were astronauts Neil Armstrong, Frank Borman, Charles Conrad, James Lovell, Thomas Stafford and James McDivitt. Armstrong and Buzz Aldrin became the first humans to walk on the face of the moon in July 1969.

Wearing their space suits, the trainees descended into Meteor Crater, handled meteorites and rocks, sat through long lectures, and, in a short time, became fairly competent in the science of meteoritics. They would find the moon's surface similar in structure.

One unexpected benefit of the moon walk training was in the testing of the astronaut's equipment. When one of the trainees ripped his space suit on a rock, he angrily declared that such a tear on the moon would have let his oxygen escape and caused his death. As a result, space suit materials of greater strength were developed.

Meteor Crater became known around the world as a result of this training. To perpetuate the memory of that era, Meteor Crater has established an Astronaut Hall of Fame and Museum, and has placed an Apollo space module for public inspection beside its picnic area.

Mountains (SEE ALSO SKIING AND SNOWBOARDING) Arizona's highest mountains are the **San Francisco**

Arizona Snow Bowl, Flagstaff. Photo by James Tallon.

Peaks near Flagstaff. **Mount Humphreys**, at 12,670 feet, is the highest of those peaks. They are snow-covered throughout much of the year, and have winter sports facilities.

The **White Mountains** of eastern Arizona also have ski runs and other winter sports amenities. **Mount Lemmon**, just north of Tucson, is a favorite of visitors in both summer and winter, and has the southern-most skiing facilities in the U.S.

Mount Graham, in southeastern Arizona, is one of the state's "sky islands" which meets the criteria of rising abruptly from the desert floor to elevations of 7,500 feet and above. Several astronomical observatories are planned for the near future on Mount Graham. This is not the place for people with heart problems or breathing difficulties, but the lookout tower at Mount Graham's Heliograph Park is the only place in Arizona where a person can drive a car above 10,000 feet.

A Phoenix landmark is **Camelback Mountain**, which resembles a camel at rest. It overlooks an affluent area of homes and resort hotels, and people of the area have banded together to prevent more buildings from being erected on its higher elevations.

East of Mesa are the **Superstition Mountains**, best known as the location of the fabled Lost Dutchman Mine. Several thousand treasure hunters have scoured the rugged wilderness of the Superstitions looking for that lost gold mine, so far without success.

In the far southeast corner of the state are the **Chiricahua Mountains** and Chiricahua National Monument, with its Wonderland of Rocks, nearly 10,000 feet in elevation. The area attracts visitors throughout the year.

Movies
It comes as a shock to most people to learn that the 1955 movie classic, *Oklahoma!*, was not filmed in the Sooner state but in the San Rafael Valley of southern Arizona. The producer and director had wanted to shoot it in Oklahoma, but there were too many oil wells, airplanes and modern development to make that location feasible.

Arizona has been a favorite locale of Hollywood producers for many decades. It was in 1939 that the movie *Arizona* was filmed on a specially constructed western set near Tucson. The territorial-era storefronts became

Gunfight at Old Tucson western movie center. Photo by James Tallon.

Tom Mix Memorial, near Florence. Photo by James Tallon.

the nucleus of today's Old Tucson, where more than 300 movies and television shows have been filmed.

Phoenix had its Cudia City movie production site and Apache Junction was the scene of many other cinematic efforts. Part of the movie *Leave Her to Heaven* was shot at Granite Dells, near Prescott, and Jerry Lewis brought his company to Tempe to film the original *Nutty Professor*. *Planet of the Apes* was created in the Lake Powell area. Every part of the state has hosted film productions from time to time.

One of the most used sites has been scenic Monument Valley, in Navajo country near the Utah border in northeastern Arizona. Zane Grey novels were made into movies here in the 1920s, and the giant rock formations have formed the backdrop for western epics from that time to the present.

Director John Ford fell in love with the area, once calling it "the most complete, beautiful, and peaceful place on earth." He returned time and again, filming such major hits as *Stagecoach*, *My Darling Clementine*, *Fort Apache*, *She Wore a Yellow Ribbon* and *The Searchers* in what became his favorite movie locale. John Wayne became a star as a result of his roles in Monument Valley productions.

Some other movies filmed in, or that are about, Arizona:

In Old Arizona (1928), *Broken Arrow* (1950), *Rio Grande* (1950), *Gunfight at the OK Corral* (1957), *Lost in America* (1985), *The Three Amigos* (1986), *Midnight Run* (1988), *Tombstone* (1993), *Boys on the Side* (1995), *Waiting to Exhale* (1995), *Jerry*

McGuire (1996), *Tin Cup* (1996), *Buffalo Soldiers* (1997), *The Postman* (1997), *Smoke Signals* (1998), *Wild Wild West* (1998), *South of Heaven* (1999) and *Three Kings* (1999).

Museums and Historical Societies

Museums. One of America's premier regional museums is the **Heard Museum** in Phoenix. Founded in 1929, it was established with a core of artifacts collected by Dwight and Maie Bartlett Heard and has since been expanded several times. Its primary emphasis is on Native American art and ethnographic objects, of which it now has 32,000, and in its library are 24,000 volumes and 50,000 photographs. An $18 million expansion of 50,000 square feet was opened to the public in March 1999. The museum now has three major galleries, an amphitheater, auditorium, education pavilion, restaurant and gift shop. More than a quarter of a million visitors come to the Heard each year.

The Heard Museum is located in downtown Phoenix at 22 E. Monte Vista Road.

Other interesting museums include:

The Amerind Foundation Museum, 2100 N. Amerind Road, Dragoon 85609

Apache County Historical Society Museum, 180 W. Cleveland, St. Johns 85936

Arizona Hall of Fame Museum, 1101 W. Washington, Phoenix 85007

Arizona Hall of Flame Museum, 6101 E. Van Buren St., Phoenix 85008

Arizona Historical Society Museum, 949 E. 2nd St., Tucson 85719

Arizona Historical Society Museum/Tempe, 1300 N. College Ave., Tempe 85281

Arizona Historical Society/Pioneer Museum, 2340 N. Fort Valley Road, Flagstaff 86001

Arizona Mining and Mineral Museum, 1502 W. Washington, Phoenix 85007

Arizona Museum for Youth, 35 N. Robson St., Mesa 85201

Arizona Science Center, 600 E. Washington St, Phoenix 85004

Arizona State Capitol Museum, 1700 W. Washington, Phoenix 85007

Arizona State Museum, Park Avenue and University Boulevard, University of Arizona campus, Tucson 85721

Arizona State University Art Museum, Mill Avenue and 10th Street, Tempe 85287

The Bead Museum, 5754 W. Glenn Drive, Glendale 85301

Bisbee Mining & Historical Museum, 5 Copper Queen Plaza, Bisbee 85603

Buckeye Valley Historical & Archaeological Museum, 116 E. Highway 85, Buckeye 85326

Casa Grande Valley Historical Society and Museum, 110 W. Florence Blvd., Casa Grande 85222

Casa Malpais Museum, 318 Main St., Springerville 85938

Cave Creek Museum, Corner of Basin and Skyline Drive, 6140 E. Skyline Drive, Cave Creek 85331

Center for Creative Photography, The University of Arizona, Tucson 85721

Champlin Fighter Aircraft Museum, 4636 Fighter Aces Drive, Mesa 85215

Clemenceau Heritage Museum, 1 N. Willard St., Cottonwood 86326

DeGrazia Gallery in the Sun, 6300 N. Swan Road, Tucson 85718

Desert Caballeros Western Museum, 21 N. Frontier St., Wickenburg 85390

Discovery Park, 1651 Discovery Park Blvd., Safford 85546

Flandrau Science Center and Planetarium, University of Arizona, Tucson 85721

Fleischer Museum, 17207 N. Perimeter Drive, Scottsdale 85255

Gila River Indian Arts & Crafts Center and Heritage Museum, P.O. Box 457, Sacaton 85247

Glendale Historical Society, Sahuaro Ranch Park, 9802 N. 59th Ave., Glendale 85302

Grace Foundation for the Preservation of Americana, P.O. Box 406, Cave Creek 85331

Grand Canyon Railway Museum, 233 N. Grand Canyon Blvd., Williams 86046

The Heard Museum North, el Pedregal Festival, Marketplace at the Boulders Resort, 34505 N. Scottsdale Road, Scottsdale 85262

International Wildlife Museum, 4800 W. Gates Pass Road, Tucson 85745

John Wesley Powell Memorial Museum, 6 N. Lake Powell Blvd., Page 86040

Little House Museum, P.O. Box 791, Springerville 85938

Mesa Southwest Museum, 53 N. Macdonald, Mesa 85201

Mohave Museum of History and Arts, 400 W. Beale St., Kingman 86401

Muheim Heritage House, 207 Youngblood Hill, Bisbee 85603

Looking Back

1988

Governor Evan Mecham was impeached, convicted, removed from office and charged with misuse of state funds.

Museum of Northern Arizona, 3101 N. Fort Valley Road, Flagstaff 86001

Museum of the Forest, 700 S. Green Valley Parkway, Payson 85541

Museum of the Southwest, 1500 N. Circle I Road, Willcox 85643

Museum of the West, 109 S. Third St., Tombstone 85638

Navajo County Museum, Navajo county Historical Society, Holbrook Branch, 100 E. Arizona, Holbrook 86025

Petersen House Museum, 1414 W. Southern Ave., Tempe 85282

Phippen Museum, 4701 Highway 89 N., Prescott 86301

Phoenix Art Museum, 1625 N. Central Ave., Phoenix 85004

Phoenix Museum of History, Heritage and Science Park, 105 N. Fifth St., Phoenix 85004

Pimeria Alta Historical Society Museum, 136 N. Grand Ave., Nogales 85621

Pioneer Arizona Living History Museum, 3901 W. Pioneer Road, Phoenix 85027

Pueblo Grande Museum & Cultural Park, 4619 E. Washington St., Phoenix 85034

Rawhide Old West Museum, 23023 N. Scottsdale Road, Scottsdale 85255

Rex Allen Arizona Cowboy Museum, 155 N. Railroad Ave., Willcox 85643

San Pedro Valley Arts and Historical Society Museum, 180 S. San Pedro, Benson 85602

Scottsdale Artists' School, 3720 N. Marshall Way, Scottsdale 85251

Scottsdale Historical Museum, 7333 E. Scottsdale Mall, Scottsdale 85251

Sharlot Hall Museum, 415 W. Gurley St., Prescott 86301

Shemer Art Center, 5005 E. Camelback Road, Phoenix 85018

Sirrine House, 160 N. Center, Mesa 85201

Smoki Museum Inc., 147 N. Arizona St., Prescott 86304

Stinson Historical Museum, 102 N. First E., Snowflake 85937

Superstition Mountain/Lost Dutchman Museum, 4650 N. Mammoth Mine Road, Goldfield 85219

Taliesin West, 12621 Frank Lloyd Wright Blvd., Scottsdale 85261

Tempe Arts Center, Mill Avenue and First Street, P.O. Box 549, Tempe 85280

Tempe Historical Museum, 809 E. Southern Ave., Tempe 95282

Tubac Center of the Arts, 9 Plaza Road/P.O. Box 1911, Tubac 85646

Tucson Children's Museum, 200 S. Sixth Ave., Tucson 85702

Tucson Museum of Art & Historic Block, 140 N. Main Ave., Tucson 85701

University of Arizona Museum of Art, University of Arizona campus, Tucson 85721

West Valley Art Museum, North 114th Avenue at Bell Road, Sun City 85373

White Mountain Archaeological Center, HC 30 Box 30, St. Johns 85936

Zane Grey Museum and Counseller Art, 408 W. Main St., Suite 8, Payson 85541

Historical Societies. State law requires the board of directors of the Arizona Historical Society, with headquarters in Tucson, to designate one or more historical organizations in each county that shall be incorporated as nonprofit organizations and are deemed to have a functioning program of historical value.

Designated societies include:

Ajo Historical Society, Ajo

Apache County Historical Society, St. Johns

Arizona Military Museum, Phoenix

Arizona Railway Museum, Chandler

Bisbee Mining and Historical Society, Bisbee

Buckeye Valley Historical and Archaeological Museum, Buckeye

Camp Verde Historical Society, Camp Verde

Casa Grande Valley Historical Society, Casa Grande

Cave Creek Museum, Cave Creek

Chandler Historical Society, Chandler

Cochise County Historical and Archaeological Society, Douglas

Colorado River Historical Society, Bullhead City

Colorado River Indian Tribal Museum, Parker

Coolidge Historical Society, Coolidge

Douglas Historical Society, Douglas

Eastern Arizona Museum and Historical Society, Pima

Gila County Historical Society, Globe

Gila River Indian Arts and Crafts Tribal Museum, Sacaton

Gilbert Historical Society, Gilbert

Glendale Arizona Historical Society, Glendale

Graham County Historical Society, Safford

Greenlee County Historical Society, Clifton

Havasupai Tribal Arts Enterprise, Supai

Hopi Cultural Center Museum, Second Mesa

Jerome Historical Society, Jerome

John Wesley Powell Memorial Museum, Page

Mesa Historical Society, Mesa

Mohave County Historical Society, Kingman

Navajo County Historical Society, Holbrook

Navajo Tribal Museum, Window Rock

Ned A. Hatathli Center, Tsaile

Northern Gila County Historical Society, Payson

Oracle Historical Society, Oracle

Phoenix Museum of History, Phoenix

Pima Air and Space Museum, Tucson

Pimeria Alta Historical Society, Nogales

Pinal County Historical Society, Florence

Pine-Strawberry Archaeological and Historical Society, Pine

Pioneer Arizona Living History Museum, Phoenix

Quartzsite Historical Society, Quartzsite

Quechan Tribal Museum, Yuma

Rex Allen Arizona Cowboy Museum, Willcox

San Pedro Valley Arts and Historical Society, Benson

Showlow Historical Society, Showlow

Skull Valley Historical Society, Skull Valley

Sulphur Springs Valley Historical Society, Willcox

Superstition Mountain Historical Society, Apache Junction

Verde Historical Society, Cottonwood

Wellton-Mohawk Fine Arts and Historical Association, Wellton

White Mountain Apache Cultural Center, Fort Apache

White Mountain Historical Society, Springerville

The Arizona Historical Society's headquarters adjoins the campus of the University of Arizona. Its address is 949 E. Second St., Tucson 85719. The AHS Maricopa County branch is in Papago Park, and its address is 1300 N. College Ave., Tempe 85281.

Among other valuable historical archives are those in the Arizona Historical Foundation on the campus of Arizona State University, Tempe; Sharlot Hall Museum, Prescott; Museum of Northern Arizona, Flagstaff; and the libraries of the University of Arizona, Arizona State University and Northern Arizona University.

National Parks and Monuments (SEE ALSO BUTTERFIELD OVERLAND MAIL; CANYON DE CHELLY; CORONADO; GRAND CANYON; MONTEZUMA CASTLE; PAINTED DESERT; SAGUARO NATIONAL PARK)

Canyon de Chelly National Monument, P.O. Box 588, Chinle 86503—Three canyons, Canyon de Chelly, Canyon del Muerto, and Monument Canyon, are scenic wonders and shelter many well-preserved cliff dwellings.

Casa Grande Ruins National Monument, 1100 Ruins Drive, Coolidge 85228—A four-story structure built of adobe earth nearly 700 years ago was the central building of a prehistoric Hohokam village.

(Continued on page 146)

Arizona Federal Lands

N

National Forests

1 Apache National Forest
2 Coconino National Forest
3 Coronado National Forest
4 Kaibab National Forest
5 Prescott National Forest
6 Sitgreaves National Forest
7 Tonto National Forest

National Parks, Monuments, Historic Sites/ Preserves/Parks, and Recreation Areas

8 Canyon de Chelly National Monument
9 Casa Grande Ruins National Monument
10 Chiricahua National Monument
11 Coronado National Memorial
12 Fort Bowie National Historic Site
13 Glen Canyon National Recreation Area
14 Grand Canyon National Recreation Park
15 Hubbell Trading Post National Historic Site
16 Lake Mead National Recreation Area
17 Montezuma Castle National Monument
18 Montezuma Well
19 Petrified Forest National Park
20 Pipe Spring National Monument
21 Saguaro National Park
22 Sunset Crater Volcano National Monument
23 Tonto National Monument
24 Tumacacori National Historical Park
25 Tuzigoot National Monument
26 Walnut Canyon National Monument
27 Wupatki National Monument

National Wildlife Refuges, Refuge Wildernesses, and National Fish Hatcheries

28 Alchesay National Fish Hatchery
29 Bill Williams River National Wildlife Refuge
30 Bueno Aires National Wildlife Refuge
31 Cabeza Prieta Refuge Wilderness
32 Cabeza Prieta National Wildlife Refuge
33 Cibola National Wildlife Refuge
34 Havasu National Wildlife Refuge
35 Imperial National Wildlife Refuge
36 Kofa National Wldlife Refuge
37 Kofa Refuge Wilderness
38 Leslie Canyon National Wildlife Refuge
39 San Bernardino National Wildlife Refuge
40 Williams Creek National Fish Hatchery
41 Willow Beach National Fish Hatchery

115° W

114° W

NEVADA

Virgin River

15

Lake Mead

16

41

Lake Mohave

Kingman

Bullhead City

Big Sandy River

40

34

93

Lake Havasu City

Lake Havasu

29

Bill Williams River

Parker

60

CALIFORNIA

Colorado River

Quartzsite

10

95

33

36

37

35

Martinez Lake

Gila River

Yuma

8

 National Forests

 National Parks, Monuments, Historic Sites/Preserves/ Parks, and Recreation Areas

 National Wildlife Refuges, Refuge Wildernesses, and National Fish Hatcheries

 Counties

31

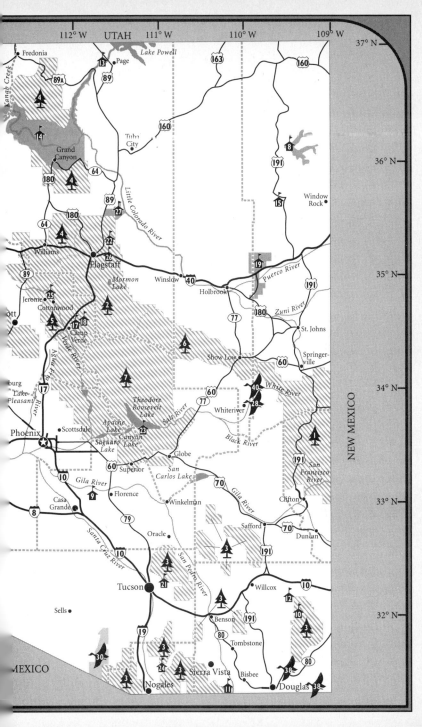

(Continued from page 143)

Chiricahua National Monument, Dos Cabezas Route, P.O. Box 6500, Willcox 85643—The Chiricahua Mountains rise spectacularly from the southeastern Arizona desert to a forested land with many strangely shaped rock formations.

Coronado National Memorial, 4101 E. Montezuma Canyon Road, Hereford 85615—The memorial overlooks a hundred miles of the route believed to have been taken by Francisco Vasquez de Coronado in his 1540 expedition of discovery.

Fort Bowie National Historic Site, P.O. Box 158, Bowie 85605—The memorial is dedicated to the preservation of the Butterfield Overland Mail Route, Apache Pass Station, Apache Spring and Fort Bowie. The fort was a focal point of military operations in southeast Arizona against Apache leaders Cochise and Geronimo.

Glen Canyon National Recreation Area, P.O. Box 1507, Page 86040—This recreation area surrounds Lake Powell in northeast Arizona. The lake has 1,960 miles of canyon-indented shoreline.

Grand Canyon National Park, P.O. Box 129, Grand Canyon 86023—One

Chiricahua National Monument. Photo by Randy Britton.

of the natural wonders of the world, the Grand Canyon draws millions of visitors from all over the globe each year. The park encompasses the course of the Colorado River and adjacent lands from Glen Canyon to Lake Mead.

Hubbell Trading Post National Historic Site, P.O. Box 150, Ganado 86505—The post has served the Navajo Nation for almost a century. Visitors come to see the extensive collection of native arts and crafts and the historic home of trader Lorenzo Hubbell and his family.

Lake Mead National Recreation Area, 601 Nevada Highway, Boulder City, NV 89005—Lake Mead, formed by Hoover Dam, and Lake Mohave, formed by Davis Dam, are both included in the Lake Mead National Recreation Area. Together they offer water sports and other outdoor recreation.

Montezuma Castle National Monument, P.O. Box 219, Camp Verde 86322—This monument has both Montezuma Castle, a five-story prehistoric cliff dwelling, and Montezuma Well, a large limestone sink from which the prehistoric Sinagua peoples irrigated their crops for centuries.

Navajo National Monument, HC 71, Box 3, Tonalea 86044—Betatakin, Keet Seel, and Inscription House are cliff dwellings of Anasazi farmers who lived in this area seven centuries ago. Some of the Southwest's best preserved native structures are available to visitors.

Organ Pipe Cactus National Monument, Route 1, Box 100, Ajo 85321—Sonoran Desert plants and animals may be seen here. The Organ Pipe Cactus is rarely found anywhere else in the United States. The monument is in southwestern Pima County.

Arizona-Sonora Desert Museum, Tucson. Photo by James Tallon.

Petrified Forest National Park, P.O. Box 2217, Petrified Forest 86028—Within the Painted Desert is a forest of colorful petrified logs, many thousands of years old. The park also encompasses Indian ruins and petroglyphs.

Pipe Spring National Monument, Moccasin 86022—A well-preserved fort and other buildings, built by Mormon pioneers in the 1870s, are featured at this national monument. A living history ranch is adjacent.

Saguaro National Park, 3693 S. Old Spanish Trail, Tucson 85730—Forests of Giant Saguaro cacti and other Sonoran desert plants, located in two sections near Tucson, lure many thousands of visitors annually.

Sunset Crater National Monument, Route 3, Box 149, Flagstaff 86004—Sunset Crater erupted during the winter of A.D. 1064–65, forming a colorful cinder cone. The cataclysmic eruption has been pictured in petroglyphs of Sinagua people who lived here at the time. The monument is just east of Flagstaff.

Tonto National Monument, HC 02 Box 4602, Roosevelt 85545—A few miles east of Theodore Roosevelt Dam, Tonto National Monument's cliff dwellings were occupied in the early 14th century.

Tumacacori National Historic Park, P.O. Box 67, Tumacacori 85640—A frontier mission church built near a site visited by Father Kino in the late 1600s, Tumacacori commemorates the "entrada" of Spanish culture into southern Arizona.

Tuzigoot National Monument, P.O. Box 68, Clarkdale 86324—The ancients who farmed the Verde Valley in the 12th and 13th centuries built a town that has been carefully preserved and is open to visitors. Tuzigoot is a remnant of that town.

Walnut Canyon National Monument, Walnut Canyon Road, Flagstaff 86004—The Sinagua people built more than 300 cliff rooms in the walls of Walnut Canyon near Flagstaff. Situated in a scenic area, the national monument is a popular stop for tourists.

Wupatki National Monument, Tuba City Star Route, N. Highway 89, Flagstaff 86004—The Wupatki community was built in the shadow of Sunset Crater near Flagstaff, and the stone pueblo ruins also include a ball field and other structures of prehistoric times.

Native Arts and Crafts
Over the centuries, Arizona's Native artisans have created many items for use in their daily activities, ceremonial times, and for personal adornment. Various tribes became known for specialty work such as pottery, baskets, blankets, carvings, and jewelry making. Traditionally, they used distinctive symbols and designs.

During the 1900s, as Native groups adjusted to relocation onto reservations and learning European American ways in Indian schools, craftspeople began to make things to sell to collectors. Because of their exposure to different cultures, artisans began to experiment with different materials and methods, such as oil painting and photography. They learned about the commercial aspects of making and selling articles that had no use other than creative expression and the enjoyment of the beholder.

Today there are so many gifted American Indian artists from Arizona (who make baskets, rugs, pottery, dolls, sculptures, jewelry, paintings, ceramics, clothing, sand paintings, and kachina dolls, and work in leather, beads, metals, and wood), that listing all of their names would be impossible. Categorizing artists is difficult, since many are involved in more than one medium or craft. Nonetheless, here are just a few of them:

Navajo blankets and weavings have long been prized, both in the state and beyond its borders. Authentic items use distinctive weaving styles, but the use of pattern and color has expanded greatly over the past century. Some well-known contemporary Navajo weavers include **Nellie Bennett, Atsuma Blackhorse, Rosann Teller Lee, Mary Lewis, Barbara Teller Ornelas, Daisy Taugelchee,** and Nellie Tsosie.

Hopi weaving used to be done only by men. One of the most famous is Otis Polelonema (1902–81). Today, women also weave, and they have also become proficient in quilt making, developing a new Hopi style.

Hopis are most famous for their kachina dolls, (also

Hopi kachina doll. Courtesy Office of the Secretary of State.

pronounced *katsinas*). Made of cottonwood root, these painted carved figures are emblematic of actual kachinas that appear in religious ceremonies. Some well-known carvers include **Delbridge Honanie "Coochsiwukioma"** (1946–) and **Brian Honyouti** (1947–).

Another important Hopi art form is pottery. The tradition of **Nampeyo,** one of the most famous Hopi potters, was continued by her daughters **Annie Nampeyo** (1918–68) and **Daisy Nampeyo** (1906–), and it is being carried on today by many of her grandchildren and other relatives. Nampeyo's work inspired a renaissance in Hopi pottery making.

Ida Redbird (1892–1971) revived the Maricopa pottery industry, and **Mary Juan** (1892–1977) is another well-known Maricopa artist. Today potters such as **Lena Meskeer** carry on the tradition and develop new art forms.

Sandpainting was originally developed as part of Navajo and Hopi religious ceremonies. Today artists also use this medium to create art forms. Best known is **Joe Ben Jr.** (Navajo).

Both the Navajo and Hopi are also famous for their jewelry designs. Some well-known artisans are **Harvey Begay** (Navajo), **Kenneth Begay** (Navajo), **Charlie Bitsuie** (Navajo), **Sherian Honhongva** (Hopi), **Andrew Humiquaptewa** (Hopi), **Michael Kabotie "Lomawywesa"** (Hopi), **James Little** (Navajo), **Verma Nequatewa "Sonwai"** (Hopi), **Ambrose Roanhorse** (Navajo), **Lawrence Saufkie "Nuvahoyti"** (Hopi), **Paul Saufkie Sr.** (Hopi), **Ray Sequatewa** (Hopi), **Charles Supplee** (Hopi-French) and **Roy Talahaftewa** (Hopi). The single most influential jewelry artist, however, was **Charles Loloma** (Hopi, 1921–91), whose

Navajo weaver Mary Lee Begay. From Arizona by Fred Hirschmann.

creative genius led the way to today's Indian jewelry designs.

Apache artisans make jewelry, but they are best known for their leather and bead work. Many tribes specialize in various types of baskets and woven plaques. **Viola Jimulla** (Yavapai Prescott, 1878–1966), was a famous basket maker and also the first woman chief among North American Indian groups.

Other artists well-known for their baskets include **Novena Cobb** (San Carlos Apache), **Rikki Francisco** (Pima), **Josephine Harrison** (Yavapai), **Nonie Havatone** (Hualapai), **Rose James** (Tohono O'odham), **Angela Lewis** (Tohono O'odham), **Edith Lopez** (Tohono O'odham), **Eugene Lopez** (Tohono O'odham), **E. Ramon** (Tohono O'odham), and **Maude Sinyella** (Hualapai).

American Indian artists from Arizona working in various media include **Cliff Bahnimptewa** (Hopi painter), **James Carter** (Mohave pottery), **Preston Duwyenie** (Hopi ceramics), **Annie Fields** (Mohave jewelry, beadwork), **Chepa Franco** (Tohono O'odham carver), **Domingo Franco** (Tohono O'odham), **Roland Golding** (Mohave/Quechan rattles), **David Johns** (Navajo painter), **David Matuz** (Yaqui photography), **Henrietta Graves Peterson** (Mohave dolls) and **Paul Wehausen** (Apache painter).

Selling items represented as "authentic Indian" arts and crafts but not actually made by Native artisans is forbidden by federal law.

Newspapers

Daily Newspapers.

Bisbee
Bisbee Daily Review, 12 Main St., Bisbee 85603

Bullhead City
Mohave Valley Daily News, P.O. Box 1209, Bullhead City 86442

Casa Grande
Casa Grande Dispatch, P.O. Box 15002, Casa Grande 85230

Chandler
Tribune, 120 W. First Ave., Mesa 85210

Douglas
Douglas Dispatch, P.O. Drawer H, Douglas 85607

Flagstaff
Arizona Daily Sun, 417 W. Santa Fe, Flagstaff 86001

Gilbert
Tribune, 120 W. First Ave., Mesa 85210

Kingman
Mohave Daily Miner, P.O. Box 3909, Kingman 86402

Lake Havasu City
Today's Herald News, 2225 W. Acoma Blvd., Lake Havasu City 86403

Mesa
Tribune, 120 W. First Ave., Mesa 85210

Phoenix
  Arizona Republic, P.O. Box 1950, Phoenix 85004
Prescott
  Prescott Courier, 147 N. Cortez, Prescott 86301
Scottsdale
  Tribune, 120 W. First Ave., Mesa 85210
Sierra Vista
  Herald, 102 Fab Ave., Sierra Vista 85635
Sun City–Sun City West
  Daily News Sun, P.O. Box 1779, Sun City 85351
Tempe
  Tribune, 120 W. 1st Ave., Mesa 85210
  State Press, P.O. Box 871502, Arizona State University, Tempe 85287
Tucson
  Arizona Daily Star, P.O. Box 26887, Tucson 85726
  Arizona Daily Wildcat, University of Arizona, Tucson 85721
  Daily Territorial, P.O. Box 35250, Tucson 85740
  Tucson Citizen, P.O. Box 26887, Tucson 85726
Yuma
  Yuma Daily Sun, P.O. Box 271, Yuma 85366

Selected Weekly Newspapers.
Ajo
  Ajo Copper News, P.O. Box 39, Ajo 85321
Arizona City
  Arizona City Independent, 1335 Sunland Gin Road, Arizona City 85223
Avondale-Litchfield Park-Goodyear
  West Valley View, 310 N. Dysart, Avondale 85323

Benson
  San Pedro Valley News Sun, P.O. Box 1000, Benson 85602
Buckeye
  Buckeye Valley News, P.O. Box 217, Buckeye 85326
Camp Verde
  Verde Independent, P.O. Box 429, Cottonwood 86326
Chino Valley
  The Review, 401 W. Palomino, Chino Valley 86323
Clifton
  The Copper Era, P.O. Box 1357, Clifton 85540
Coolidge
  Coolidge Examiner, 353 W. Central, Coolidge 85228
Cottonwood
  Verde Independent and Bugle, 116 W. Main, Cottonwood 85326
Eagar-Springerville
  The Round Valley Paper, P.O. Box 867, Eagar 85925
Eloy
  Eloy Enterprise, 710 N. Main St., Eloy 85231
Florence
  Florence Reminder Blade-Tribune, 244 N. Main St., Florence 85232
Fountain Hills
  The Times of Fountain Hills, P.O. Box 17869, Fountain Hills 85296
Glendale
  Glendale Star, 7122 N. 59th Ave., Glendale 85301
Globe-Miami
  Arizona Silver Belt, P.O. Box 31, Globe 85501
Green Valley
  Green Valley News and Sun, P.O. Box 567, Green Valley 85622

Looking Back

Feb. 14, 1912

President William H. Taft signs proclamation creating the State of Arizona.

Holbrook
Holbrook Tribune-News, 200 E. Hopi Drive, Holbrook 86025
Kearny
Copper Basin News, P.O. Box 579, Kearny 85237
Nogales
Nogales International, P.O. Box 579, Nogales 85621
Page
Lake Powell Chronicle, 3 Elm Street Mall, Page 86040
Parker
Parker Pioneer, P.O. Box N, Parker 85344
Payson
Payson Roundup, P.O. Box 2520, Payson 85541
Peoria
Peoria Times, 7122 N. 59th Ave., Glendale 85301
Phoenix
Arizona Business Gazette, 400 E. Van Buren St., Phoenix 85004
Arizona Capitol Times, 14 N. 18th Ave., Phoenix 85002
New Times, P.O. Box 2510, Phoenix 85002,
Pinetop-Lakeside
The Falcon, P.O. Box 1690, Lakeside 85929
Prescott Valley
Prescott Valley Tribune, P.O. Box 26568, Prescott Valley 86312
Safford
Eastern Arizona Courier, P.O. Box N, Safford 85546
St. Johns
Apache County Observer, 51 E. Cleveland St., St. Johns 85936
San Carlos
The Moccasin, P.O. Box 310, San Carlos 85550

San Manuel
San Manuel Miner, P.O. Box 60, San Manuel 85631
Sedona
Red Rock News, P.O. Box 619, Sedona 86339
Show Low
White Mountain Independent, P.O. Box 1570, Show Low 85901
Snowflake
Snowflake Herald, 200 E. Hopi, Holbrook 86025
Superior
Superior Sun, 467 Main St., Superior 85273
Tombstone
Tombstone Tumbleweed, 314 Toughnut, Tombstone 85638
Tucson
Tucson Weekly, 201 W. Cushing, Tucson 85701
Wickenburg
Wickenburg Sun, 180 N. Washington, Wickenburg 85358
Willcox
Arizona Range News, P.O. Box 250, Willcox 85644
Williams
Williams-Grand Canyon News, P.O. Box 667, Williams 85046
Window Rock
Navajo Times, P.O. Box 310, Window Rock 86515
Winslow
Winslow Mail, 208 W. First St., Winslow 86047

Nogales

The county seat of Santa Cruz County, Nogales sits on the U.S.-Mexico boundary line almost 4,000 feet above sea level. With its sister city, Nogales, Sonora, it comprises what is known as "Ambos (both) Nogales." The two are named for the walnut (*nogal* in Spanish) trees which were once plentiful here.

Nogales, Arizona, was settled before

From *What is Arizona Really Like?* by Reg Manning.

the arrival of the Southern Pacific Railroad in 1882 and incorporated in 1893. Pancho Villa's forces clashed with American soldiers at Nogales in 1916.

The city, with a population of more than 21,000, is a popular port of entry into Mexico. Tourism, cattle ranching, mining and international trade bolster the city's economy.

Oak Creek Canyon

Between Flagstaff and Sedona, Oak Creek comes tumbling down 2,000 feet in elevation and has carved a spectacular canyon rimmed with multi-colored rock walls. Oak Creek Canyon is one of Arizona's most celebrated beauty spots: the site of scores of movie filmings, cool pine forests, a well-stocked trout stream, campgrounds and luxury resorts.

Driving south from Flagstaff on State Route 89A, the visitor encounters a breath-taking viewpoint overlooking the canyon. From here, the twisting, descending highway is visible at a dozen different segments of S-shaped curves. Just south of the canyon, on the Sedona side, is Slide Rock State Park, where young and old shoot down a slippery slab of rock in the rushing creek, wearing out swim suits in the process.

Oak Creek Canyon suffers from a common plague: too many people camping, picnicking, photographing, fishing and hiking. But it is truly a jewel to see and remember.

OK Corral (SEE ALSO GUNFIGHTERS OF THE OLD WEST; TOMBSTONE)

Much of Tombstone's fame as a wild town originated in the Oct. 26, 1881, battle between the group led by Wyatt Earp, and the Clanton-McLaury combine. It has come down in legend as the "Gunfight at the OK Corral," although the shootout actually occurred some distance from the corral. The entire affair lasted considerably less than a minute, but it left two Earp brothers wounded and three of their antagonists dead. It proved to be only the beginning of a deadly feud that took the lives of men on both sides during the months ahead. Celebrated in story, song and movies, the Tombstone gunfight is re-enacted each year to appreciative audiences at "The Town Too Tough To Die."

Outdoor Recreation (SEE ALSO CAMPING; FISH AND FISHING; GOLF; HUNTING; LAKES; MOUNTAINS; NATIONAL PARKS AND MONUMENTS; RIVERS; STATE PARKS; TENNIS)

Arizonans live more out-of-doors than inside. An abundance of sunshine and warm weather, together with the many natural wonders to be hiked, biked, sailed and rafted, makes outdoor recreation attractive to people of all ages

Perhaps the best known of these adventures are the Colorado River rafting trips, which take hardy passengers through the Grand Canyon, over breathtaking rapids and white water, as far as Lake Mead. At Lake Mead, and farther south along the Colorado, houseboating, fishing and swimming are favorite outdoor sports.

Winter sports draw thousands of enthusiasts to the Arizona Snow Bowl near Flagstaff, and to ski resorts in the White Mountains and Mount Lemmon, near Tucson.

Hiking is so popular that the state magazine, *Arizona Highways*, publishes an account of a different hiking opportunity in each issue.

Backpacking to remote sites in mountainous and desert areas attracts many who enjoy getting back to nature. The Superstition and Chiricahua mountain wilderness lands are special favorites for backpackers. Many climbers scale precipitous mountain slopes, while others of us who are less athletic are content climbing less demanding mountain foothills near Tucson and Phoenix.

Bicyclists are on the roads everywhere, and they gather for rallies and competitions in several cities each year.

Page

The 1950s construction camp at Glen Canyon Dam lived on and became the city of Page, incorporated in 1975. It was named for John C. Page, U.S. Commissioner for Reclamation. Page now has a population of more than 9,400, and serves the many thousands of water recreation lovers who come to enjoy boating and aquatic sports at Lake Powell behind the dam. It is in Coconino County, at an elevation of 4,380 feet.

Painted Desert

Indian sand painters for centuries have obtained their colored sand from Arizona's Painted Desert, a 150-mile semi-circle on the north side of the Little Colorado River in the Navajo and Hopi reservations. It adjoins the Petrified Forest National Park, and many visitors enjoy both natural wonders together. This area was once the floor of an ocean, and its sands were dyed in brilliant colors over eons of time by minerals in the water. Reds, yellows, blues, lavenders (all the colors of the rainbow) are here. They are subdued pastels in many parts of the Painted Desert, but all are beautiful.

Perhaps the best views of the Painted Desert are from Petrified Forest National Park, and photography buffs have a field day at all the view points. So extensive and dramatic is this colorful phenomenon that it may be seen from mountains many miles away. But the park is also very intimate, with miles of hiking trails winding among the mesas and stone trees.

The Painted Desert and Petrified Forest are easily accessible from Interstate 40, some 20 miles east of Holbrook in Apache County. An excellent visitors' center is staffed by rangers who also give lectures and conduct tours.

Payson

Payson is in northwestern Gila County and is the gateway

to the forested Mogollon Rim country. Its cool summers (altitude 4,964 feet) attract tens of thousands of vacationers, many of whom have cabins in the pines nearby. Many others have chosen to retire here. Payson was settled in 1882 and was a focal point for cattle ranching in the area for many decades. Western novelist Zane Grey built a home in the forest east of Payson and wrote several books about the area. Today the city is booming, and its population now exceeds 13,000. Its rodeo, one of the oldest continuous events of its kind in the nation, is one of many summer festivals that make Payson a favorite spot for Arizonans.

Peoria

Chauncey Clark of Peoria, Illinois, bought the original townsite in 1887 and, with a group of other settlers from Peoria, named the new community after their hometown. Peoria, Arizona, remained a small farming town until recent decades, when its rapid growth sent the population soaring past the 100,000 mark.

Originally 4 miles northwest of Glendale, Peoria's growth has made one unbroken metropolitan area of those two cities and Phoenix. Now manufacturing, retirement, and other economic factors supplement agriculture in sustaining Peoria's continuing prosperity.

A notable feature of the city is its sports complex, used for spring training by both the San Diego Padres and the Seattle Mariners, as well as by Korean and Japanese baseball teams. Cowtown, an old west town, and

Looking Back

June 23, 1881

The great Tombstone fire was ignited by an exploding whiskey barrel.

nearby Lake Pleasant are other popular Peoria attractions.

Petroglyphs, Pictographs and Geoglyphs

Petroglyphs are marks made by prehistoric people, perhaps shamans, who created symbols by pecking or rubbing away the dark surface patina on rocks. Pictographs are painted symbols, typically found in shallow caves or rocky overhangs where they are protected from the elements. The word *geo* means earth. Hence, geoglyphs are earthglyphs. They are usually much larger features, such as rock alignments. Some are tamped into the ground, like wellworn dance circles, and others are raised up like mounds.

Petroglyphs are far and away the most common. No one knows for certain the meanings behind these drawings. Indistinct shapes make up the vast majority, but there are also stick figures of animals and people, circles with sunlike rays, wavy waterlike lines, crosses with outlines and endless others. It is likely that most of them were done 1,000-plus years ago. Current anthropological speculation is that they were shaman oriented; perhaps symbols recalled from vision quests; clan markers; ceremonial features as part of tribal initiations. But in any case, idle doodling they are not, and defacing them is a federal offense.

Good examples of petroglyphs can be seen at: Canyon de Chelly National Monument, Chinle; Casa Malpais

Petroglyphs: Native American art on rocks. Illustration by Robert Williamson.

Archaeological Park, Springerville; Deer Valley Rock Art Site, Phoenix; Homolovi State Park, Winslow; Lyman Lake State Park, St. Johns; Navajo National Monument, southwest of Kayenta; Painted Rock Campground, west of Gila Bend; Palatki Indian Ruins, Sedona; Petrified Forest National Park, east of Holbrook; Saguaro National Park, Tucson; South Mountain Park, Phoenix; and V-Bar-V Ranch Petroglyph site, near Camp Verde.

Phoenix

More than half of Arizona's people live in the Greater Phoenix area of the Salt River Valley in the south-central portion of the state. With its 2.9 million population (only half within the Phoenix city limits), the state capital, the county seat of Maricopa County, excellence in the arts and education, manufacturing and business prominence, five major league professional sports teams and world-class resort facilities, Phoenix is one of the dominant cities of the Southwest.

This area's first farmers, the Hohokam people (who began moving into the area about A.D. 1), constructed a network of irrigation canals that were unearthed in the 1870s to form the basis of an irrigated agricultural empire. When Theodore Roosevelt Dam was completed in 1911, the impounded waters assured Phoenix a dependable supply for the foreseeable future. The area also gets water from the Central Arizona Project canal and underground supplies. Agriculture, once the principal user of water, has declined as residential developments replaced citrus groves, cotton and alfalfa fields.

Economy. Motorola established a manufacturing plant in the Phoenix area shortly after the end of World War II, and other major semiconductor manufacturers soon followed. So did aerospace giants and makers of many other high-tech products. Clean, smokeless industry is now the economic engine of Greater Phoenix. Tourism, finance, air conditioning, Luke Air Force Base, retail trade, retirement facilities and agriculture are other major income producers.

Downtown Phoenix. Photo by James Tallon.

Arts and Entertainment. The Heard Museum, specializing in Native American and southwestern art, is a "must see" for visitors. The Phoenix Art Museum, Herberger Theater Center, Desert Botanical Garden, Symphony Hall, Blockbuster Desert Sky Pavilion, Arizona Science Center, Phoenix Museum of History, the Phoenix Zoo and the Hall of Flame Firefighting Museum are but a few of Phoenix's arts and educational facilities.

The new Bank One Ballpark hosts Arizona Diamondbacks major league baseball; America West Arena is home to the Phoenix Suns NBA basketball team; Arizona Rattlers of the arena football league; the Mercury of the WNBA; and the Phoenix Coyotes NHL hockey team. Sun Devil Stadium in neighboring Tempe hosts the Arizona Cardinals of the NFL. Eight of the 10 major league baseball teams in the spring Cactus League play in Greater Phoenix stadiums. Major golf tournaments of the PGA, LPGA and Seniors circuits are played here. Phoenix International Raceway hosts leading automobile racing events.

Universities and Colleges. Largest of the many higher educational institutions are Arizona State University's main campus in Tempe and ASU West in Phoenix, Grand Canyon University, American Graduate School of International Management in suburban Glendale, University of Phoenix, Phoenix College and other campuses of the county community college system.

Suburbs. Not long ago central Phoenix and its suburbs were miles apart. Now the 20-plus Phoenix suburbs have grown together into one great metropolitan district. Mesa, soon to reach 400,000 population, is the largest. Glendale, Scottsdale, Tempe,

Chandler and Gilbert all have well over 100,000 residents.

Pima County Cities

Much of metropolitan Tucson's population lives outside its city limits, in unincorporated Pima County locations or in suburban cities which do not adjoin Tucson.

Catalina. This community north of Oro Valley is 3,200 feet above sea level, 1,000 feet higher than Tucson. Its population is just over 5,000. Catalina is known as a starting place for horseback rides and hikes into the Catalina Mountains, climbing from open desert to alpine forest in a few hours. The community was established in 1950.

Marana. Not many years ago, Marana was 25 miles north of Tucson. Now the city limits reach Tucson's, thanks to recent annexations of land. It has more than 12,000 residents in 75 square miles of area. Primarily a farming center, it also has commercial centers and an industrial park.

Oro Valley. Incorporated in 1974, Oro Valley has a population of about 27,000. It is situated 5 miles north of Tucson, and has recently experienced substantial growth. Oro Valley is primarily a residential community, and takes pride in its family oriented lifestyle. It has five golf courses, a lighted air strip and luxury resorts. Next door to the east is Catalina State Park.

South Tucson. Less than 2 miles south of Tucson's central business district is South Tucson. More than 80 percent of its residents are of Hispanic origin, and the town has a delightfully Latin aura. Its Mexican restaurants are famous, and visitors enjoy the several annual fiestas celebrating Mexican-American culture. South Tucson's population has remained stable at about 5,500.

Pioneers and Settlers (SEE ALSO BUFFALO SOLDIERS; CORONADO; GILA TRAIL; BARRY GOLDWATER; HONEYMOON TRAIL; SAN XAVIER DEL BAC MISSION; TUBAC)

Once those from other parts of the world discovered the land that we now call Arizona, life in this area was never the same for its original inhabitants. The reasons outsiders had for moving here varied greatly, but most sought basic things such as land, a better life, or a cure for respiratory ailments such as asthma or tuberculosis. Many people, from many cultures and backgrounds, have contributed to the growth and development of the state we see today.

Some of the most important include:

African Americans. Since 1539, when the black slave Esteban became the first non-Indian to visit Arizona, men and women of color have played significant roles in the building of the state. It is not commonly known, but many of the cowboys in early territorial days were former slaves who came west to start new lives in freedom. During the Apache Wars of the 1870s and 1880s, "Buffalo Soldiers" stationed at Fort Huachuca made up some 20 percent of the military force in the territory.

Bill and Ann Neal began a freighting business in Tucson and later added cattle ranching to their enterprises. But with the 1895 opening of their resort, the Mountain View Hotel, they became pioneers in Arizona's fledgling tourist business.

Because a majority of Arizonans in the early decades of the 20th century were transplants from southern states, Arizona had segregated schools, residential areas, and recreational facilities. But such African American leaders as the Rev. George Brooks and Dr. Lincoln Ragsdale, aided by many prominent Anglo activists, succeeded in integrating the schools and breaking down racial barriers in housing during the 1950s and 1960s.

Asian Americans.

Chinese miners and railroad builders took on many of the most dangerous jobs that were necessary to these industries in early times. An unknown number of Chinese men suffered serious injury or death. Survivors often opened laundries or restaurants in Phoenix or Tucson, and many Chinese turned to agriculture to make a living. Today many of their descendants still own family farms in Maricopa and Pima counties.

Settlers from Japan did not begin to arrive in Arizona until about 1890. They, too, worked at dangerous or menial labor, but their children later cultivated crops on family farms. Most Japanese Americans from Arizona had to go to internment camps during World War II.

Jews.

Jewish pioneers played major roles in the economic development of Arizona Territory. They came with the first prospectors for gold and silver, but soon found that there was more money to be made from supplying the miners than from seeking out the minerals.

Philip Drachman came to America, along with fellow Polish Jews Michel and Joseph Goldwater, in 1852. Drachman settled in Tucson in 1863 and established a mercantile business there. He married Rosa Katzenstein and they became the parents of Harry Arizona Drachman, believed to be the first white child born in Arizona Territory.

AZ if?!

One old-timer swears that Arizona started going downhill when people started going to the bathroom indoors and cooking outdoors.

Later Drachmans have been prominent in Tucson civic affairs for many decades.

Brothers Michel and Joseph Goldwater arrived in California in 1852, and beginning in 1860 the Goldwaters were leading merchants in La Paz, Ehrenberg, Prescott, Phoenix and other Arizona cities. Michel's sons Morris and Baron established the Goldwater's department stores, and Baron's son Barry became a prominent U.S. Senator and presidential candidate. Barry, however, was brought up in the Episcopal faith.

Many of Phoenix's other early commercial pioneers and civic leaders were Jews, including the Rosenzweigs, Goldbergs, Korricks and Diamonds. In Tucson, the Zeckendorfs, Levis, Steinfelds and Mansfelds were among that city's mercantile and developmental leaders. Jewish pioneers were prominent in the history of communities throughout the state. One of the best-known was Sol Barth, who was a prominent figure in the town of St. Johns in Apache County.

Mexican Americans. Although today's Arizona made up the northern part of the land claimed by Spain, and later Mexico from 1821–54, very few settlers ventured north of the tiny outpost of Tucson until at least 1850. This is because Indians from various tribes waged war relentlessly on anyone attempting to mine or farm their lands. Only settlements or mining camps protected by army garrisons could survive.

Eventually, however, Mexican citizens brought their families to live in Tucson and Phoenix, and they pioneered in small towns all over the state. They formed the core of the infant mining industry, knew how to grow crops in the Sonoran Desert, and brought their skills in managing huge herds of cattle in arid grasslands.

Because the U.S. government was in the process of resettling all of the various Indian tribes onto reservations during the latter half of the 19th century, Latino culture predominated in Arizona Territory at that time. However, once the railroads were completed, white Europeans from the East began to come to Arizona in large numbers. By 1900, Mexican Americans were in the minority.

When Arizona became a state in 1912, its constitution did not, as it had for African Americans, mention segregation of Mexican Americans. However, many schools, churches and businesses did have this policy. Groups such as the League of United Latin American Citizens (LULAC) worked during the Civil Rights era to desegregate schools and provide for equal employment opportunities.

Mormons. When Brigham Young had established his community of the Church of Jesus Christ of Latter-Day

Latter-day Saints Temple, Mesa. Photo by James Tallon.

Saints, commonly called the Mormons, in the Great Salt Lake Valley of Utah, he began to send numerous colonies of settlers into neighboring territories. Arizona was a particularly fruitful field for these pioneers, who established many communities that have grown and prospered to this day.

Mesa, the largest of these cities, is the site of the Arizona Temple of the Mormon faith and until recent years was predominantly Mormon in population. Safford, the county seat of Graham County; St. Johns, the county seat of Apache County; and Heber in Navajo County are among Arizona cities with large percentages of Mormon residents.

Mormon pioneers were devoted to agriculture, and their descendants retain a love of the land.

In the late 19th century, the Mormon practice of polygamy antagonized many Arizona citizens, but multiple marriage has been outlawed in the church for more than a century. Today almost every Arizona community has one or more Mormon wards (churches).

Other European Americans. Most Europeans who came to Arizona in the 19th century didn't stay long. They hunted and trapped, mined gold and silver, or served with the U.S. Army. Then they returned to their homes. Many came through on their way to Mexico or California. The end of the Apache Wars in 1886 and the completion of railroad lines into major towns made European Americans more interested in bringing their families to the Territory. Many made their homes in northern Arizona, where the weather was more temperate and the rainfall more plentiful than in the south. There they could have large cattle spreads and large farms.

Since the end of the 19th century, European Americans have been the dominant cultural group in Arizona. Phoenix, the capital city, attracted merchants, professional people, and farmers. People also came to Tucson to farm and run businesses, and the University of Arizona enticed those from the academic world. Mining towns have gone through many boom and bust cycles, depending on the current prices for various ores. Because Arizona is such a new state, many "old pioneer families," whatever their cultural heritage, go back only a few generations.

Pioneers Home and Disabled Miners Hospital

The Arizona Pioneers Home and Disabled Miners Hospital, an agency of the State of Arizona, is in Prescott. It was founded in 1911.

Applicants to the Pioneers Home must be at least 65 years of age, a resident of Arizona for 30 years, and a U.S. citizen for 5 years. Disabled miners must be at least 60 years of age. There are presently 135 residents in the two categories. The home is fully occupied, and there is a waiting list for admission. The address is 300 S. McCormick St., Prescott 86303; (520) 445-2181.

Place Names— Where Did That Name Come From?

The origin of the name "Arizona" has been debated for more than a century. One version is that it comes from the Papago, *ali shonak*, meaning "little spring." Another is that it came from the region the early Spanish settlers called "Arizonac," along today's border with Mexico. The town of Arizonac was a shipping point for mines in the district.

What the name did NOT come from is a fairly widespread notion that it was a contraction for "arid zone." That Arizona is, but its aridity did not inspire its name.

Seven Arizona counties are named for Native American tribes (Pima, Navajo, Apache, Yuma, Mohave, Maricopa, Yavapai). Cochise bears the name of a famous Apache chief. Two (Santa Cruz and La Paz) are Spanish. Pinal is so named because of pine trees on its uplands. Two others (Graham and Greenlee) bear names of pioneers. Gila County was named for the river that crosses Arizona from New Mexico to the Colorado River. The name "Gila" was given to the river in Spanish colonial days. And Coconino, the largest, is a misspelled version of a Hopi word designating the Havasupai and Yavapai Indians.

Some of Arizona's place names have strange origins:

Show Low, the gateway to the White Mountain communities, got its name when two ranchers played a game of Seven-Up, in which a low hand may win. "Show low and you take the ranch," declared one. His opponent did just that, and the community was later built on his ranch. The city's main street is named "Deuce of Clubs."

Why is a tiny hamlet in the southern Arizona desert far from civilization. Many passing motorists asked the town storekeeper "Why are you living way out here?" And she often answered "Why not?"

Flagstaff, largest of northern Arizona cities, was so named because a group of New England pioneers stopped at the site on July 4, 1876, and wanted to celebrate the nation's hundredth birthday. So they trimmed the branches off a pine tree and tacked a homemade Stars and Stripes to its top.

Polygamy Creek, in Apache County, was the home of Mormon pioneer Jacob Noah Butler, who settled there with his two wives and 22 children.

Tombstone's name came from an admonition given prospector Ed Schieffelin that if he ventured out into hostile Apache territory in southeast Arizona "all you will find out there is your own tombstone." But Schieffelin was a daring man. He braved the danger and was rewarded with a rich silver find, in a mine he called the Tombstone. The town that grew up there became one of the wickedest and most fascinating in Wild West history.

Doubtful Canyon in Cochise County was named by planners of the Butterfield Stage route just before the Civil War. They said they were doubtful that the stage could get through without everybody being massacred by the Apaches.

How about the state's two biggest cities?

Phoenix was named by a well-educated Englishman named "Lord" Darrell Duppa. He noted that the Salt River Valley had for more than 1,400 years been the home of the Hohokam Indians, who dug a network of canals along the Salt River but disappeared in the mid-15th century. The Phoenix bird of mythology rose from its own ashes, Duppa said, so Phoenix would be an appropriate name for this newborn community.

Tucson is a rough rendering of a Papago word, *chuk* (black) *shon* (base). It refers to Sentinel Peak on the edge of Tucson, which has a dark stone base. Tucson citizens over the decades have wasted many an hour correcting uninformed visitors who insist on calling it "Tuck-son." But with the city's emergence as a major American metropolitan center, and with the correct pronunciation used on TV across the land, the problem is much diminished.

Those who try to attach Spanish names to Arizona locales sometimes wind up looking a bit stupid. Examples: *Picacho* Peak north of Tucson means "Peak" Peak in Spanish; and Table *Mesa* southeast of Prescott means Table "Table."

Oh, well . . .

Plants (*SEE ALSO* CACTI; TREES AND SHRUBS) From algae to pine trees, plant life in Arizona has adapted to the

---

Looking Back

June 28, 1994

The hottest day on record in Arizona was 128°F at Lake Havasu City.

161

various climates, soils, and elevations. In each different area, you can see various grasses and wildflowers.

Arizona's deserts make up about 40 percent of the land area. Here annual rainfall is usually 10 inches or less, so plants have evolved in often-ingenious ways to withstand high temperatures, drought conditions and sudden heavy rains. For example, annual wildflowers store seeds in the soil. Here they stay dormant, sometimes for decades, until they sense the right conditions. Then they sprout and grow quickly to the flowering stage.

In the Sonoran Desert, if there has been enough winter rain and the temperature is just right, annual species produce brilliantly colored flowers in March, April and May. Many years there are very few flowers, but about every 10 years, ideal conditions cause billions of seeds to grow. The desert floor is on fire with dense carpets of yellow goldfields, orange Mexican poppies, rose-purple owl clover, purple lupines, pink-lilac desert five spots, red-purple sand verbena, royal blue larkspur and delphiniums. Perennials add their notes to the chorus, too, from light

Agave plant. Illustration by Robert Williamson.

pink funnel lilies, to yellow-orange desert mariposas, to the magenta flowers of strawberry hedgehog cacti.

The desert produces such perennial plants as giant saguaros, ocotillos, barrel cacti, agaves, prickly pears, chollas, yuccas, creosote bushes, jojoba shrubs, saltbush (desert

holly), bursage, mesquite trees, ironwood trees and paloverde trees. Many plants that do well in Arizona deserts have been brought from other parts of the world. These include most palm trees (only the desert palm, found in desert mountain canyons, is native to Arizona), eucalyptus trees, olive trees, birds of paradise, pyracanthas, natal plums and oleanders.

In riparian areas, (around lakes and streams), reeds, grasses, and cattails proliferate, as well as cottonwood and willow trees. In the higher deserts, where the plants are used to an occasional dusting of snow, grasses, sagebrush, manzanita bushes, and oak, juniper, and piñon pine trees join cacti and desert shrubs.

There is more snow and rainfall at higher elevations, so junipers, Gambel oaks, Douglas firs and many other trees are found here in abundance. Huge stands of ponderosa pine trees characterize these areas. You can also see ferns, cattails and sego, and mariposa lilies.

Above 8,000 feet, fir trees—such as Douglas, white, and subalpine—dominate, and you also see stands of quaking aspens and blue and Engelmann spruce trees in the forests. Ferns, lilies and Rocky Mountain iris love the cool shade of the woodland floors.

Spruce, fir, and bristlecone pine trees are the dominant plants above 9,500 feet. This area has a shorter growing season and colder winds than most, so trees tend to be shorter and more twisted than you will see elsewhere.

Above the timberline (11,500–12,000 feet) there are no trees. Only hardy plants that like very cold weather can grow here, such as lichens, grasses, sedges and alpine wildflowers.

Politics In 1912, when Arizona became the 48th state, Democrats controlled both the state government and Congressional delegation. Democratic registration was more than double that of Republicans. Forty years later, in 1952, Democrats still held both U.S. Senate seats and both House seats. They held a wide edge in voter registration.

But things were beginning to change. Newly arrived residents, a majority of them from Republican states in the Midwest, were beginning to narrow the gap. That was the year Barry Goldwater dared to run against Ernest W. McFarland, the majority leader of the Senate, and young John Rhodes took on House veteran John R. Murdock. Both Republican upstarts shocked the political pundits at the polls in November with victories over the heavily favored Democrats . Republican Howard Pyle, who had upset a favored opponent in the governor's race two years earlier, was re-elected in 1952.

Senator Carl Hayden, who served in Congress for 56 years, was the only Democrat of national stature who continued to be re-elected during the years of the Republican resurgence.

Arizona State Capitol, Phoenix. Photo by James Tallon.

Chairman of the all-powerful Senate Appropriations Committee and President Pro-tem of the Senate, Hayden was so great an asset to Arizona that he never had a serious challenge.

Arizona has been a two-party state for four decades. Democrats have won the governorship and other major state offices on many occasions, and the party has been successful in county and local elections, particularly outside heavily Republican Maricopa County. But Maricopa County is where more than half of all Arizonans live.

In the 1998 general election, Arizona sent five Republicans and one Democrat to the U.S. House of Representatives; kept two Republicans (John McCain and Jon Kyl) in the Senate; and elected Republican Jane Dee Hull as governor. Both the Senate and House in the Arizona Legislature have Republican majorities.

No Arizonan has yet been elected President, but several have made strong bids. Goldwater was the

Population (within city limits)

Leading Cities*	1990	1999	% Change 1990–99
Phoenix (Maricopa)	983,403	1,240,775	26.1
Tucson (Pima)	405,390	475,450	17.2
Mesa (Maricopa)	288,091	374,560	30.0
Glendale (Maricopa)	148,134	208,095	40.4
Scottsdale (Maricopa)	130,069	204,660	57.3
Chandler (Maricopa)	90,533	169,000	86.6
Tempe (Maricopa)	141,865	161,995	14.1
Peoria (Maricopa)	50,168	101,235	101.9
Gilbert (Maricopa)	29,188	100,850	245.5
Yuma (Yuma)	54,923	69,055	25.7
Flagstaff (Coconino)	45,857	60,880	32.7
Sun City (Maricopa)	38,126	50,000	31.1
Lake Havasu City (Mohave)	24,363	41,045	68.4
Sierra Vista (Cochise)	32,983	40,680	23.3
Prescott (Yavapai)	26,592	35,785	34.5
Avondale (Maricopa)	16,169	32,270	99.5

*Ranked by 1999 population, counties in parenthesis.
Sources: Arizona Department of Economic Security and U.S. Census Bureau

Population Age Distribution—1998

Age	Arizona (%)	United States (%)
0–14	22.72	21.65
15–19	6.90	7.11
20–24	6.86	6.54
25–54	41.87	43.84
55–64	8.26	8.12
65+	13.83	12.74

Sources: Arizona Department of Economic Security and U.S. Census Bureau

Republican candidate in 1964. Mo Udall and Bruce Babbitt later mounted campaigns for the Democratic nomination. In 2000, Senator McCain was a viable candidate in the Republican ranks.

Population Trends

(SEE ALSO ETHNIC DISTRIBUTION)
Arizona's rate of population growth ranks first or second in the nation (Nevada and Arizona often exchange positions). The 1990 U.S. Census revealed that the state population had grown by 34.92 percent during the previous decade, and growth has been nearly as dramatic in the 1990s. Maricopa County, home of Phoenix and its satellite cities, had nearly 2.9 million of Arizona's total of 4.8 million in 1999 estimates. Pima County, with Tucson, had 836,000 people.

Projections made by the Arizona Department of Economic Security predict a state population of 5.54 million by the year 2005. In that year, says the forecast, Maricopa County will have 3.3 million and Pima 944,000. Pinal County, with a projected 2005 population of 185,000, is a distant third. Yavapai, in fourth place, will have 176,000 and Mohave 171,000. The least populated county in the state is Greenlee, with only 8,900.

At the time of statehood, in 1912, mining was king in Arizona and the copper producing counties were legislation establishing Arizona Territory on Feb. 24, 1863.

Poston became the first delegate to Congress from the Arizona Territory, serving in 1864–65. In later years his fortunes sagged, and he died in Phoenix nearly penniless.

He is buried under a pyramid atop a small hill north of Florence.

among the most populous. Cochise County had more residents than Maricopa at that time. Tucson, with a population of 13,200, was Arizona's biggest city, leading Phoenix by 2,000.

There are startling differences in the ages of residents in the counties. Yavapai, often ranked as one of the best retirement counties in the nation, had a median age of 42.4 in the 1990 Census. At the other end of the spectrum was Apache, with 23.4. Other young populations are in Coconino, 26.2, and Navajo, 26.5. The two urban counties are midway between: Maricopa with 32.0 and Pima with 32.8.

In territory days, men outnumbered women by a 10 to l margin. Today, women are in the majority, although only slightly.

Poston, Charles

He is revered as the "Father of Arizona," a title he was glad to bestow on himself. His full name was Charles Debrille Poston and he came to Arizona from Kentucky in 1854 with the foresight of a visionary and the canny energy of a land promoter. With Samuel Heintzelman, then commander of Fort Yuma, he started mining operations in Tubac and began lobbying Congress to create Arizona Territory from the western half of New Mexico Territory. His efforts, and those of Heintzelman and others, were crowned with success when President Lincoln signed the

Pow Wow

A pow wow is a gathering of American Indians. Singing, music, dancing and eating are very important activities carried on at pow wows, but visiting old friends, making new ones, preserving cultural heritages and celebrating life make these festivals eagerly awaited highlights of peoples' lives. Some activities commonly seen in addition to traditional dances are: rodeos, carnivals and various competitions such as hoop dancing and horse racing.

Prescott

(SEE ALSO THE CAPITAL ON WHEELS) Prescott, the first capital of Arizona Territory, is the county seat of Yavapai County. Known as the "Mile High City" and often as "Everybody's Home Town," Prescott has an ideal year-round climate and a friendly, small town atmosphere. It was founded in 1864, when Fort Whipple was moved here to protect the new territorial government and the gold miners in the nearby Bradshaw Mountains from Indian depredations. History abounds in Prescott. The Sharlot Hall Museum is located in the first territorial governor's mansion: ornate Victorian homes have been preserved in the central city; and courthouse square and neighboring Whiskey Row are other remnants of a past era. Ranching, tourism, small

*Historic Courthouse Square, Prescott.
Photo by James Tallon.*

manufacturing operations and mining all contribute to the economy of this city of more than 35,000 people. Neighboring Prescott Valley and Chino Valley add their thousands to the area's population.

Prisons

The storied Arizona Territorial Prison, perched on a cliff overlooking the Colorado River at Yuma, was opened in 1876. Between that time and 1909, when it was replaced by a new prison at Florence, the Yuma facility was celebrated in frontier lore as one of the hell-holes of the West. In actuality, except for the oppressive heat, it was one of the more humane and best-run prisons of the era. Today it is one of Arizona's most visited state parks.

Before the Yuma prison was opened, lawbreakers were confined in a wide variety of jails across the territory, including caves and adobe shacks. In some remote mining camps, lawmen simply chained prisoners to a tree while awaiting trial.

The prison at Florence was Arizona's main state correctional facility until recent years. In 1968, when the Arizona Department of Corrections was created, the state had only three facilities: the Florence prison, the state industrial school at Fort Grant, and the Arizona Youth Center in Tucson. The total state prison population was less than 1,700. Now that population has swelled to more than 25,000. The newest state prison, 13 miles south of Buckeye, is named for former Department of Corrections director Sam Lewis. Opened in 1999, it is the state's largest, with 4,150 beds in buildings erected on 337 acres.

The Department of Corrections is responsible for these prisons: Perryville, west of Phoenix; Florence; Winslow; Lewis, in Buckeye; Yuma; Phoenix; Douglas; Tucson; Safford; Eyman, at Florence; Marana; Florence West; and Phoenix West. The Marana, Florence West and Phoenix West prisons are contracted facilities.

Joe Arpaio

Joe Arpaio, sheriff of Maricopa County, has earned a national reputation as perhaps the toughest sheriff in the West. His county jail in Phoenix is one of the most austere, and he wants prisoners to be sure they never come back for a return visit.

Among his innovations: "Tent City," a collection of tents in which prisoners sweat out the 110°-plus heat in summer and occasional cold in winter; issuance of pink underwear to his convicts; denial of coffee and the reading of girlie magazines; chain gangs on outside work projects; and many others that have made him wildly popular with many voters and condemned by others. Arpaio enjoys his frequent television exposure, but has received several death threats. ✳

Pronunciation

Guide

To those unfamiliar with Southwestern words, particularly those of Spanish or Indian derivation, it may be difficult to pronounce them correctly. Here are a few of the most common, and the most frequently mispronounced, of these words:

Agave (Ah-GAH-vay)
Ajo (AH-ho)
Anasazi (Ah-nah-SAH-zee)
Camino del Diablo (Cah-MEE-no del
    Dee-AHB-lo)
Canyon de Chelly (Canyon duh SHAY)
Casa Grande (Cah-sah-GRAHN-day;
    more commonly Casa Grandy or
    CASS-uh Grand)
Chihuahua (Chee-WAH-wah)
Chiricahua (Cheery-CAH-wah)
Cholla (CHOY-yah)
Cochise (Co-CHEES)
Coconino (Co-co-NEEN-o)
Gila (HEE-lah)
Hohokam (Ho-ho-KAHM)
Hopi (HO-pee)
Huachuca (Wah-CHOO-cah)
Hualapai (WALL-ah-pie)
Kachina (Kah-CHEE-nah)
Kaibab (KIE-bab)
Kino (KEE-no)
Marcos de Niza (MAHR-cos duh
    NEE-sah)
Mecham (MEE-kam)
Mesa (MEH-sah; more commonly
    MAY-sah)
Mesquite (Mes-KEET)
Moeur (Moore)
Mogollon (Mug-EE-own; some say
    MO-go-yon)
Mohave (Mo-HAH-vee)
Navajo (NA-va-ho)
Ocotillo (Oh-co-TEE-yo)
Oraibi (Oh-RYE-bee)
Paiute (PIE-yoot)
Paloverde (PAH-lo VAIR-day)
Pinaleño (Pee-nah-LAIN-yo)
Rio Salado (REE-o Sah-LAH-do)

Saguaro (Sah-WHAR-oh)
San Xavier (Sahn-HAHV-ee-air)
Sierra (See-AIR-ah)
Sinagua (Sin-NAHG-wah)
Tempe (Tem-PEE)
Tequila (Tuh-KEEL-ah)
Tubac (TOO-bock)
Tucson (TOO-sahn)
  (Tumacacori (Toom-ah-CAH-co-ree)
  (Wupatki (Woo-PAHT-kee)
Yaqui (YAH-kee)
Yavapai (YAHV-ah-pie)

Public Transportation (SEE

ALSO AIR TRAVEL; RAILROADS) Because Arizonans rely primarily on their automobiles, public transportation in the state's major cities is limited. Tucson and the Phoenix complex of cities do their best to encourage the use of buses, but urban sprawl has made bus travel inconvenient or impossible for a majority of people. Both Tucson and Phoenix have set up "park and ride" facilities to encourage bus travel, but they are not widely used.

Railroads, a principal public transportation a century ago, now carry only a few passengers. There are no underground rail facilities and no elevated rails.

To move the steadily increasing automobile traffic load in the Phoenix area, an extensive web of freeways has been built in recent years. Tucson has, for the most part, resisted the freeway option. Interstate freeways—I-10, I-17, I-19 and I-40—are heavily traveled.

Radio Stations

Apache Junction, KVVA-FM 107.1
Benson, KAVV-FM 97.7
Bisbee, KWCD-FM 92.3

Bullhead City, KBAS-AM 1490
  KFLG-AM 1000
  KFLG-FM 102.7
Casa Grande, KLVA-FM 105.5
Chandler, KMLE-FM 107.9
Chinle, KFXR-FM 107.3
Clifton, KCUZ-AM 1490
  KWRQ-FM 102.1
Coolidge, KCKY-AM 1150
Cottonwood, KYBC-AM 1600
  KVRD-FM 105.7
  KZGL-FM 95.9
Douglas, KAPR-AM 930
  KDAP-AM 1450
  KDAP-FM 96.5
  KEAL-FM 95.3
Flagstaff, KAFF-AM 930
  KVNA-AM 690
  KAFF-FM 92.9
  KFLX-FM 105.1
  KMGN-FM 93.9
  KVNA-FM 97.5
Gilbert, KBZR-FM 103.9
Glendale, KGME-AM 1360
  KKFR-FM 92.3
  KOAZ-FM 103.5
Globe-Miami, KIKO-AM 1340
  KJAA-AM 1240
  KHOT-FM 100.3
  KIKO-FM 106.1
  KQSS-FM 98.3
  KRXS-FM 97.3
Green Valley, KGVY-AM 1080
  KFMA-FM 92.1
  KGMS-FM 97.1
Holbrook, KDJI-AM 1270
  KZUA-FM 92.1
Kearny, KZLK-FM 105.3
Kingman, KAAA-AM 1230
  KGMN-FM 99.9
  KRCY-FM 105.9
  KZZZ-FM 94.7
Lake Havasu City, KFWJ-AM 980
  KBBC-FM 101.1
  KJCC-FM 92.7
  KNLB-FM 91.1

  KZUL-FM 105.1
Mesa, KFNN-AM 1510
  KXAM-AM 1310
  KDKB-FM 93.3
  KJZZ-FM 91.5
  KZZP-FM 104.7
Nogales, KNOG-FM 91.1
  KZNO-FM 98.3
Page, KPGE-AM 1340
  KXAZ-FM 93.5
Parker, KLPZ-AM 1380
  KWFH-FM 90.1
Payson, KMOG-AM 1420
  KRIM-FM 104.3
Phoenix, KASA-AM 1540
  KCWW-AM 1580
  KFYI-AM 910
  KHEP-AM 1280
  KIDR-AM 740
  KISO-AM 1230
  KOY-AM 550
  KPHX-AM 1480
  KPXQ-AM 960
  KSUN-AM 1400
  KTAR-AM 620
  KVVA-AM 860
  KXEG-AM 1010
  KBAQ-FM 89.5
  KESZ-FM 99.9
  KFLR-FM 90.3
  KHCT-FM 96.9
  KKLT-FM 98.7
  KMJK-FM 106.9
  KNIX-FM 102.5
  KOOL-FM 94.5
  KPHF-FM 88.3
  KYOT-FM 95.5
  KZON-FM 105.5
Prescott, KNOT-AM 1450
  KYCA-AM 1490
  KAHM-FM 102.1
  KGCB-FM 90.9
  KNOT-FM 99.1
Safford, KATO-AM 1230
  KFMM-FM 99.1

Looking Back

June 9, 1919

The first municipal airport in the United States opened in Tucson.

KXKQ-FM 94.1
Scottsdale, KSLX-AM 1440
   KSLX-FM 100.7
Sedona, KAZM-AM 78
   KQST-FM 102.9
   KSED-FM 107.5
Show Low, KVSL-AM 1450
   KVWM-AM 970
   KFRM-FM 96.5
   KVWM-FM 93.5
Sierra Vista, KLTW-AM 1420
   KNXN-AM 1470
   KKYZ-FM 101.7
   KZMK-FM 10.9
Springerville, KRVZ-AM 1400
   KQAZ- FM 101.7
Sun City, KEDJ-FM 106.3
Tempe, KUKQ-AM 1060
   KUPD-FM 97.9
Tolleson, KRDS-AM 1190
   KXEG-AM 1010
Tuba City, KTBA-AM 1050
   KGHR-FM 91.5
Tucson, KCEE-AM 940
   KCUB-AM 1290
   KFFN-AM 1490
   KFLT-AM 94.9
   KNST-AM 790
   KSAZ-AM 580
   KTKT-AM 990
   KTUC-AM 1400
   KTZR-AM 1450

KVOI-AM 690
KXEW-AM 1600
KHYT-FM 107.5
KIIM-FM 99.5
KKHG-FM 104.1
KLPX-FM 96.1
KMXZ-FM 94.9
KRQQ-FM 93.7
KWFM-FM 92.9
KXCI-FM 91.3
Whiteriver, KNNB-FM 88.1
Wickenburg, KBSZ-AM 1250
   KRDS-FM 105.3
   KSWG-FM 94.1
Willcox, KHIL-AM 1250
   KWCX-FM 98.3
Williams, KYET-AM 1180
Window Rock, KTNN-AM 660
   KWIM-FM 102.7
Winslow, KINO-AM 1230
Yuma, KJOK-AM 1400

Railroads

Before the coming of the first railroads to Arizona in the late 1870s and early 1880s, transportation around the territory varied from the nearly impossible to the slow and uncomfortable. Early arrivals came by foot, on horseback, in stagecoaches in steamboats—even on camels.

But after the first rails were laid from California into Yuma in 1877,

Railroad trestle over Canyon Diablo near Winslow, ca. 1885. Courtesy Southwest Studies, Scottsdale Community College.

travel became immeasurably faster and more pleasant. The Southern Pacific rails reached Tucson in early 1880. Shortly thereafter the Atlantic and Pacific Railroad started laying track across northern Arizona.

No other economic factor was more important to the settling and civilizing of Arizona than the railroads. Many connecting railroads briefly thrived and then faded during the latter years of territorial status, but the two originals (by then the A & P had become the Santa Fe) lived on. The importance of rail service steadily ebbed as automobile, truck and airline service came into being. Although essential to certain industries, today railroads are a relatively minor factor in Arizona's transportation picture.

As the new millennium began, neither of the two railroads provide passenger service. The Southern Pacific is now the Union Pacific, and the Santa Fe is now the Burlington Northern and Santa Fe. Only Amtrak offers interstate passenger service from Tucson or Flagstaff. Nonetheless, railroads continue to be a major mover of freight to and through the state.

Not to be overlooked, short "fun" passenger lines operate between Williams and the Grand Canyon, along the Verde River near Clarkdale, and from Benson in Cochise County. They offer not only a close-up view of some excellent country, but entertainment, food and drink.

Ranching (SEE ALSO COWBOYS; THE FIVE C'S)

Cattle. Many of the great cattle ranches of the past have been sold or subdivided, but ranching still thrives in many parts of Arizona. Arizona has 790,000 head of cattle, producing cash receipts of $458 million. The state's

Cowboy roping calf, Tombstone. Photo by James Tallon.

120,000 dairy cows produce 2.4 billion pounds of milk each year.

Cattle ranchers are becoming fewer in number, and those who continue in this chancy business battle drought, government regulation, a decreasing labor pool, encroaching civilization, corporate meat producers, low cattle prices, and environmentalists who seek to drive them off their leased lands in public forests and ranges. But it is likely that a stubborn few will survive well into the 21st century and beyond.

Sheep. The earliest Spanish probably brought the first sheep into Arizona in the 17th century. Father Kino brought more in the early years of the 18th. For more than two centuries, sheep raising was an important part of Arizona's economy.

Juan Candelaria drove Merino sheep from New Mexico into northern Arizona in the late 1860s and made his headquarters at Concho in Apache County. Flagstaff later became a center for the sheep industry, and the Babbitt brothers were among the first cattlemen to break the old taboo and raise sheep in addition to their cattle. The Daggs brothers of Coconino County had 50,000 sheep at one time, and cowman Dan Fain of Yavapai County claimed to own more than 70,000 sheep. Few Anglos were willing to endure the hardships and isolation of the sheepherder, so Basque herders were brought in from Europe and became key figures in the industry.

In 1876, aided by the coming of the railroad, some 200,000 pounds of wool were shipped from Tucson. For many years, the trek of sheep from the Apache County highlands to the warm Salt River Valley in the fall, and back north in the spring, was a spectacular annual event. But today, the sheep industry has almost disappeared from Arizona, a victim of synthetic fabrics replacing wool and the decline in the demand for mutton.

Reptiles and Amphibians

Many people outside of Arizona believe that huge poisonous reptiles lurk around every part of the state. Most of these creatures, however, are small, non-venomous, and prefer to stay hidden whenever possible. Common desert animals include several species of rattlesnake, kingsnakes, gopher snakes, Arizona alligator lizards, horned lizards, western banded geckos, western whiptails and collared lizards.

Some exceptions are the chuckwalla, which, although harmless, grows 10 to 16 inches long, and the 10-to-17-inch desert iguana. The Gila monster, which lives in the southern deserts, is the only venomous lizard

Gila monster.
Illustration by
Robert Williamson.

Spadefoot Toads

Spadefoot toads (genus Scaphiopus) lead amazing lives. They dig under the desert soil as deep as 3 feet and can remain in a dormant state for up to two years. Each hind leg has a black, sharp-edged digging tool. A summer thunderstorm awakens them, and they quickly tunnel upward at night. Thousands emerge and find a summer pool. There they rehydrate, eat and look for mates (just like happy hour at a singles bar). The young hatch in 12–36 hours and grow from tadpoles to adults in just 7–15 days. They have to hurry—summer pools don't stay for long. With the pool drying rapidly, the young spadefoots bury themselves in solitary burrows, and the cycle begins anew. ✳

in the United States. It grows 18 to 24 inches long and has a heavy body with beadlike skin patterns in red, black and yellow.

Water areas are home to Sonoran box turtles, Gilbert kinks, spadefoot toads, Arizona tiger salamanders, canyon treefrogs, bullfrogs and rattlesnakes.

Although most Arizona snakes are harmless, a rattlesnake bite can be painful and occasionally fatal to humans. Eleven species of rattlers live in Arizona. All have flat, triangular heads and can be found in many places, from low deserts to mountains 11,000 feet high.

Interesting animals in these groups include:

Arizona tree frog (*Hyla eximia*) This small frog, 3/4 to 2 inches long, is the state amphibian. They are usually green but are sometimes gold or bronze, with a white belly. What makes tree frogs different from other frogs is the pads on their toes that they use for climbing. They live in the mountains above 5,000 feet elevation and can climb a tree as high as 75 feet. Most of the year is spent hibernating, but summer rains bring them out to breed and eat insects.

Arizona ridgenosed rattlesnake *(Crotalus willardi willardi)* Arizona's state reptile was the last species of rattlesnake to be discovered in the United States, in 1905. It rarely grows longer than 24 inches. The name comes from the ridge on each side of its nose. Its brown color and white facial stripes help the rattler to hide in the leaves on the floor of southeastern Arizona forests. Lizards are the primary food, along with centipedes and small rodents. Its venom has never been known to be fatal to humans. This species is protected, and it is illegal to catch or kill them.

Desert tortoise *(Gopherus agassizii)* This desert animal grows up to 9–15 inches long, weighs 20 pounds, and can live in captivity as long as 70 years. By digging burrows underground, they can live where ground temperatures are more than 140°F. Their homes also protect them from freezing during the winter months, when they are dormant. They don't need much water, because they get most of what they need from the plants they eat. Their dark-gray, helmet-like shells protect them from predators and extreme desert conditions. Urban development is shrinking their habitat, and these gentle animals are protected by law against being collected or killed.

Western coral snake *(Micruroides euryxanthus)* Coral snakes, relatives of the Indian cobra, have very powerful venom. However, their heads and fangs are so small they rarely do damage to humans. They only grow to about 13–22 inches long. The markings on their bodies are distinctive black and red bands, each separated by narrow white or yellow rings. They hunt at night for snakes and lizards and spend the warm days buried underground. They are found in the Sonoran Desert and the highlands below 5,800 feet.

Retirement Communities (*See also* Green Valley; Prescott; Scottsdale; Tucson)

Arizona cities and towns routinely appear on lists of America's "best retirement communities." The 1999 edition of *Retirement Places Rated*, the fifth edition written by retirement guru David Savageau, places four Arizona cities among his top 10.

Wickenburg, a town of 5,000 people in northwestern Maricopa County, is listed as No. 4 in the nation. The first three are Fort Collins/Loveland, Colorado; Charleston Sea Islands, South Carolina; and Henderson/Boulder City, Nevada. Other Arizona cities on the top 10 are No. 7, Scottsdale; No. 8, Tucson; and No. 9, Prescott/Prescott Valley.

Savageau rated 187 communities on six factors: cost of living, climate,

Green Valley retirement community, south of Tucson. Photo by James Tallon.

Town Lake at Rio Salado, Tempe. Photo by Wesley Holden.

crime, availability of services, job prospects, and leisure living. Arizona placed the most communities in the top 10. Florida had two. To the surprise of many, California and Texas failed to make the elite 10. Savageau's May 1999 appearance on the televised *Today* show to announce this year's winners brought a flood of calls that tied up little Wickenburg's telephone lines for hours.

Retirement communities have become a vital part of Arizona's economy in recent decades. Sun City, Sun City West and Sun City Grand west of Phoenix have a combined population of more than 60,000. Pima County's Green Valley has 25,000. Many other Arizona cities have sizable retiree populations.

Rio Salado
Nearly a billion gallons of water, some from the Colorado River via Central Arizona Project canals and the rest from Salt River Project lakes, poured into the dry Salt River bed in Tempe during the summer of 1999 to form Town Lake. The 2-mile lake is impounded behind huge inflatable rubber dams and is the central feature of the Rio Salado project, one of the most ambitious recreational creations in the Southwest.

Thirty years in the planning, Rio Salado will have a lush green belt, wildlife habitat, resort hotels, golf courses, specialty shops, excursion boats and other amenities. Because the Salt River sometimes floods, the dams were designed to be deflated to allow the overflow to move down the channel without causing damage to adjoining structures. Pumps recirculate the water that seeps into holding basins below the lake.

Rivers (SEE ALSO DAMS)
The **Colorado River**, which enters north central Arizona from Utah and forms most of the state's western boundary, is by far the most important of the

173

Rivers, Creeks, and Lakes

state's streams. Some 90 percent of Arizona's land is drained by rivers which eventually empty into the Colorado. Once a mighty stream, the Colorado has been tamed by numerous dams during the past seven decades and now virtually disappears before it reaches the Gulf of California in northern Mexico.

In the north, the **Little Colorado River** flows from its headwaters in the White Mountains to the Colorado River just inside the east boundary of

Grand Canyon National Park. The **Bill Williams River** in western Arizona empties into the Colorado at the southern end of Lake Havasu.

Second only to the Colorado in importance in territorial times was the **Gila River**. Entering Arizona from southwestern New Mexico, it crosses the entire southern part of the state and empties into the Colorado near Yuma. The Gila valley served as a major highway for those entering the area, from the heyday of the beaver trappers in the 1820s, to the Mormon Battalion in 1846, to the California Column in the early days of the Civil War, and to the stagecoaches and wagons of later decades.

The Gila was dammed in the 1920s and has flowed only intermittently through much of its course ever since.

The **Salt River**, principal tributary of the Gila, has been a key to the present growth and prosperity of central Arizona. Its waters have been impounded behind a series of dams by the Salt River Project, and provide water and power for metropolitan Phoenix. Most important of the Salt River's tributaries is the **Verde**, which enters the Salt from the north. It too has been controlled by dams.

Two rivers, the **Santa Cruz** and the **San Pedro**, flow northward into the Gila in southeastern Arizona. The Santa Cruz, which flows past Tubac and Tucson, was a principal highway for Spanish explorers, missionaries and settlers nearly three centuries ago. The San Pedro valley, it is believed, provided the path for Coronado's army of exploration in 1540 and has been a vital force in the development of Cochise County communities.

Many smaller streams, such as the **Hassayampa**, **Agua Fria**, **Puerco**, **White** and **Black**, have played roles of varying importance in Arizona history and still lure sportsmen, vacationers and a variety of wildlife species.

Rocks, Minerals, and Gemstones

(*SEE ALSO* GOLD) Because of various geologic processes that have occurred in Arizona over time, many interesting, beautiful, and valuable rocks, minerals, and gemstones are found throughout the state. Volcanic activity has produced rocks such as granite, basalt and obsidian in a form Arizonans call Apache tears. And the effects of wind and water have exposed colorful and interesting layers of sedimentary rock such as sandstone, shale and limestone.

Arizona also is rich in deposits of minerals. There are over 500 types. One of Arizona's nicknames is the "Copper State" because more copper is mined here than in any other state. In 1997, Arizona's copper production was 65 percent of the U.S. total. Copper and its by-products make up over 80 percent of the state's non-fuel commercial mineral production. Molybdenum, silver, perlite, gold, gypsum, lime, salt, sand and gravel, and gemstones make up most of the rest. Various kinds of quartz are quite common. Lead, zinc, manganese, iron, mercury, tungsten, vanadium and uranium are also present in small quantities.

Coal production is Arizona's second most important mineral enterprise. At the present, all of this comes from high-quality coal strip-mined in central Navajo County. The Navajo and Hopi Nations lease some of their lands for the Kayenta and Black Mesa mines.

Arizona also leads the nation in the value of gemstones. Commercial production is valued at about $4 million per year. Private rockhounds collect this much and more each year. Turquoise, peridot and petrified wood are among the most valuable semi-precious gemstones, but others include amethyst, chrysocolla, malachite, fire agate, azurite, smithsonite, jasper, opal, garnet, wulfenite and onyx.

Turquoise, the primary stone used in traditional Southwestern Native American jewelry, is a phosphate of aluminum and copper. The copper gives it a distinctive sky blue to blue-green color. Arizona is one of only a few places in the world where one can find turquoise, usually in conjunction with copper mines.

About 90 percent of the world's production of peridot comes from the San Carlos Apache Reservation east of Globe. The gem is a transparent lime to olive-green color.

Navajo and Apache Counties supply most of the gem-quality petrified wood. Federal law prohibits the taking of petrified wood from public lands, so most comes from the owners of private lands. It is frequently shaped into stones for jewelry, bola ties, belt buckles, bases for desk sets and even coffeetable tops.

Looking Back

1852

The steamboat *Uncle Sam* left Yuma, launching Colorado River travel.

Arizona may be the only state that produces gem quality amethyst. Commercial quantities of the purple gem come from the Four Peaks Amethyst Mine. Rockhounds also find a few here and there in a number of other sites around the state. Deep red pyrope garnets, often called Arizona rubies, are collected from two sites on the Navajo Reservation. Common garnets, some of good quality, are found in many places. Pima County is the site of some nice aquamarines. These clear, light blue gems are found by rockhounds, but not commercially mined.

Apache tears are small pieces of obsidian (a volcanic glass), that are usually tumble-polished into an oval shape. They can be translucent to opaque, black to gray in color, and are found in greatest quantity in the Superior area. They look nice as pendants or set in silver jewelry and contrast dramatically with white onyx from the Kingman area.

Rock collecting is a very popular activity in Arizona. Hunters also find geodes and fossils. Some good sites for successful collecting are the Apache Nitrogen Plant near Benson, Diamond Point near Payson, and Hull Mine near Yuma.

Gold panning can be fun for the whole family, too. You won't strike it rich, but you'll see some beautiful country and get some exercise. Although there are several popular spots, two places allow unlimited panning: Lynx

Lake Panning Area near Prescott and Lake Pleasant Regional Park northwest of Phoenix.

Gem and mineral shows are popular winter activities in the desert. The tiny town of Quartzsite, in western Arizona, attracts more than a million visitors during January and February to its various rock, gem and mineral shows. One of them, the Annual Pow Wow, Gem and Mineral Show, typically draws 250,000 people.

Thousands of dealers, buyers and hobbyists come from all over the world to attend Arizona's premier rock exhibition, the Tucson Gem and Mineral Show, held the second week of February. The 2000 show, in its 46th year, featured over 200 dealers in minerals, rocks, gems, jewelry and fossils, each showing the best of their collections.

Rodeos
The name comes from the Spanish *rodear,* "to encircle, or round up." Old-time cowboys often referred to their cattle roundups as "rodears." The correct pronunciation of the word "rodeo" is "ro-DAY-oh," but these events are more commonly called "RO-dee-ohs."

Rodeos started more than a century ago as friendly competitions among cowboys to determine who was most proficient in the cowboy arts: roping, riding, tying, bulldogging and the rest. Then they became spectator events, and finally major productions drawing thousands of paying customers to huge arenas.

In Arizona, rodeos are held annually in communities large and small, in all parts of the state. Two of the oldest in the world, dating back to the 1880s, are held in Prescott and Payson, attract top professionals. Phoenix and Tucson host the best-attended rodeos. So

important are they to community life that schools are dismissed in some Arizona towns during the events. Rodeos traditionally open with a parade of horsemen and women, the rodeo queen and her court, stagecoaches, bands, clowns and dignitaries. Music, dancing and feasting are all a part of Rodeo Week activities.

The most popular rodeo competitions include bronc riding, calf roping (even tiny tots show their prowess in this event), bulldogging steers to the ground and bull riding. Bulls are often ferocious and have gored many a cowhand after he was unseated. To protect them, rodeo clowns rush in and try to distract the animals from their mayhem.

Safford
The county seat of Graham County is named for the third governor of Arizona Territory, Anson P.K. Safford, who is credited with establishing Arizona's first public school system. This city of an estimated 9,600 population is the trading center for the fertile Gila Valley agricultural area. Located in southeastern Arizona, it has several neighboring communities: Thatcher, Central, Pima and Solomon, among others. Safford offers visitors a variety of vacation attractions, including nearby Mount Graham (10,713 feet), the Coronado National Forest, Roper Lake State Park and the historic copper mining towns of Clifton and Morenci.

Saguaro National Park
Saguaro cacti grow only

in the Sonoran Desert, and the stately sentinel of the desert has been adopted as Arizona's most recognizable symbol. The most extensive saguaro cactus forest in the world is protected in the Saguaro National Park, in two sections to the east and west of Tucson.

The park was designated as Saguaro National Monument in 1933, to protect the deteriorating forest. It was elevated to its present status as Saguaro National Park in 1994. Facilities, services and program activities have been steadily improved for several decades. U.S. Park Service rangers are on hand to conduct tours and lecture on many phases of desert life.

Saguaro National Monument, Tucson. Illustration by Robert Williamson.

The park contains 50 varieties of cactus in addition to saguaros. More than 2,700 other plant species also thrive there, as well as a wide variety of desert animals. Some of the saguaros in the park are 150 years old and grow to a height of 40 feet. In the Signal Hill picnic area of the western portion of the park are a number of petroglyphs created by prehistoric Hohokam people. Indians are permitted to harvest the fruit of the saguaros, which they use to make jellies, syrups and wines.

The Visitor Center is at 3693 S. Old Spanish Trail in Tucson. The eastern park is at the foot of the Rincon Mountains and the western park is in the shadow of the Tucson Mountains.

Visitors are welcome every day of the year except Christmas, from sunrise to sunset.

Salt River Project

Former President Theodore Roosevelt, who spoke at the 1911 dedication of Roosevelt Dam (later renamed "Theodore Roosevelt Dam") declared that its construction was second only to the building of the Panama Canal among his administration's achievements.

The great dam, with Roosevelt Lake behind it, was the keystone of the Salt River Project, which has provided water and power for central Arizona's phenomenal population explosion. Four other dams on the Salt River northeast of Phoenix have since assured a regulated supply of water for domestic, agricultural and industrial use.

President Roosevelt spearheaded the movement to create reclamation projects in the arid western states and

Apache Lake on Salt River. Photo by James Tallon.

territories. The 1902 National Reclamation Act for the first time made the federal government a partner in damming rivers and creating lakes. The Salt River Water Users Association, composed of water users in the Salt River Valley, was formed nine months later. Construction of Roosevelt Dam began in 1905. A tortuous road known as the Apache Trail was carved through the mountain and used to haul supplies and huge blocks of granite to the site. The dam was completed in 1911, a year before Arizona became the 48th state. By 1955, the federal government had been completely repaid for its investment in the reclamation project by those who benefited from it.

Recently the original masonry dam was encased in concrete and heightened by 70 feet to provide additional water storage capacity.

San Xavier Mission, near Tucson. From *What is Arizona Really Like?* by Reg Manning.

San Xavier del Bac Mission

One of the most beautiful of all Spanish missions in the American Southwest is San Xavier del Bac, 9 miles south of Tucson. Father Eusebio Kino laid the foundations for a church near the present site in 1700. The structure we see today took 14 years to build, 1783–97. Widely known as "The White Dove of the Desert," it is a blending of Moorish, Byzantine, and late Mexico Renaissance architecture. The church and its many paintings, statuary and other art objects are photographed by thousands of visitors each year. The statue of St. Francis Xavier is an object of pilgrimage to many. Two lion-like images on either side of the communion rail represent the Lions of Castile and are a tribute to the reigning family in Spain during the late 18th century.

Scottsdale

Known around the world for its luxury resorts, its art colony, its professional golfers, and its superlative shopping facilities, Scottsdale has a special place among Arizona cities. One of Phoenix's eastside suburbs, Scottsdale is just north of Tempe and south of Carefree. Scottsdale has grown from a small town to a city of 204,000 since 1951, when it was incorporated. In 1993 it was voted America's "Most Livable City" by the U.S. Conference of Mayors.

Sedona

Sedona, in Arizona's red rock country along Oak Creek, is

Oak Creek crossing near Sedona. Photo by James Tallon.

Sunrise Ski Lodge, White Mountains. Photo by James Tallon.

situated in an area of spectacular beauty. It is 30 miles south of Flagstaff, straddles the boundary between Yavapai and Coconino counties, and is surrounded by the Coconino National Forest. Sedona has long been a mecca for artists, writers and photographers, and is a favorite retirement community. Tourism is its major business. Fine hotels, restaurants and shopping centers attract many thousands of visitors. Its elevation of 4,240 feet affords a temperate year-round climate. It has an estimated population of more than 10,000 residents.

Sierra Vista
Cochise County's largest city, Sierra Vista, now has a population of more than 40,000 and is growing fast. It is situated at the foot of the Huachuca Mountains, at an altitude of 4,626 feet, just outside the U.S. Army's huge base, Fort Huachuca, the major economic force in the area.

In addition to housing thousands of military and civilian personnel from the fort, Sierra Vista is home to a large retiree population. The town also profits from tourism, ranching and trade. Both the University of Arizona and Cochise College have campuses in Sierra Vista.

Skiing and Snowboarding
Although regarded as a desert state by most Americans, Arizona has surprisingly excellent skiing to lure winter visitors. Skiing and other winter sports are enjoyed throughout the White Mountains in eastern Arizona, as well as on San Francisco Peaks near Flagstaff, Bill Williams Mountain, Mogollon Rim country and other areas of high elevation. The southernmost ski resort in America is on Mount Lemmon, less than an hour's drive north of Tucson.

The White Mountain Apache tribe has developed a popular ski facility, Sunrise Park, a half-mile up the road from Sunrise Lake Lodge. But the state's best-known ski resort is the Arizona Snow Bowl, near Flagstaff. These facilities attract thousands of winter sports enthusiasts each year.

Ski Resorts.

Arizona Snowbowl & Flagstaff Nordic Center, P.O. Box 40, Flagstaff 86002

Mount Lemmon Ski Valley, P.O. Box 612, Mount Lemmon 85619

Sunrise Park Resort, P.O. Box 217, McNary 85930

Williams Ski Area, P.O. Box 953, Williams 86046

Speed Limits
In 1987 Governor Evan Mecham posed for photographers while changing a speed limit sign on Interstate 10 from 55 to 65 miles per hour. It was a highly popular move for Arizona drivers who had been wasting time for years in getting to their destinations on freeways that were engineered for the higher speeds. Since that time, speed limits on most portions of Arizona freeways have been raised to 75 miles per hour. In congested areas the speed limit is 65 and within metropolitan limits it is still 55.

On non-freeway roads within Arizona cities, large and small, speed limits are set by local governments. Main arteries in the cities generally have 45 miles per hour limits, and other streets are set at 25 to 40. In Arizona's school zones, the limit is 15 and strictly enforced.

There has been a recent trend toward the use of photo radar to enforce speed limits in the cities, with resulting crowds at traffic courts.

State Government
(*SEE ALSO* CONGRESSIONAL REPRESENTATIVES; ELECTED OFFICIALS; POLITICS) Arizona has a government of three branches: executive, legislative, and judicial.

Executive Branch

Governor. The governor is the chief executive officer and, unlike the case in most other states, there is no lieutenant governor. Instead, the secretary of state serves in the absence of the governor and succeeds him/her upon the death, resignation, removal or disability of the governor.

Arizona's governor transacts all executive business and may require written information from state officers on any subject relating to the duties of their offices. The governor is commander in chief of the state military forces except when they are called into federal service. Every bill passed by the legislature must be presented to the governor for approval or disapproval (veto). The governor may grant pardons and commutations of sentence to those convicted of offenses, with the exception of treason.

Secretary of State. The secretary of state is no mere vice-governor. The secretary is the chief elections officer and certifies the names of candidates for state offices; oversees the placing of initiative and referendum measures on the ballot; tests the voting equipment in each county before elections; conducts canvasses for both the primary and general elections; and certifies recognition of new parties.

The secretary of state issues many official state publications, commissions notaries public, registers lobbyists, certifies numerous commercial rules of operation, registers charitable organizations and conducts a myriad of other supervisory activities.

Secretaries of state who have succeeded to the office of governor are Sidney P. Osborn, Dan E. Garvey, Wesley Bolin, Rose Mofford and the present governor, Jane Dee Hull.

Attorney General. The attorney general is the chief administrator of the Department of Law. He/she and the assistant attorneys general are legal advisors for the Executive Department and state agencies. The Department of Law has four divisions: Administrative, Civil, Criminal, and Human Services. The attorney general must have practiced law for five years, and must devote full time to the office. He/she must not engage in the private practice of law during the term of office.

State Treasurer. The state treasurer serves as the state's chief financial officer and is responsible for the prudent receipt, safekeeping, investing and disbursement of state funds. At the request of the legislature, the state treasurer gives a written report on the condition of the state treasury. In addition, a monthly report is submitted to the governor.

Superintendent of Public Instruction. The superintendent of public instruction directs the Department of Education, which provides services to more than 230 school districts in the state. The superintendent is by law a member of the Arizona Board of Regents (universities), State Board of Directors for Community Colleges, State Board of Education, State Board of Vocational and Technological Education, and the State Board for Charter Schools.

State Mine Inspector. Established in territorial days because of frequent deaths and injuries in mines, the office of mine inspector is responsible for maintaining safe conditions in Arizona mines. Each mine is inspected every year and citations are issued to ensure compliance with Arizona mining laws.

Corporation Commission. The three members of the Arizona Corporation Commission regulate public utilities, maintaining a fair balance between rates charged to the public and income earned by the utility providers. The commission registers corporations doing business in the state and monitors their required filings of information. The commission is responsible for ensuring the integrity of the securities marketplace in Arizona.

Legislative Branch

The Arizona Legislature, composed of the Senate and House of Representatives, convenes annually in January at the state capitol in Phoenix. It has one senator and two representatives from each of the 30 legislative districts of the state. The legislature was controlled by Democrats until the 1950s, when the influx of Republican newcomers to the state started shifting the balance. Today Republicans are in control of both the Senate and House.

Judicial Branch

The Arizona Supreme Court, with five justices, has supervision of all other courts in the state. The Supreme Court may review decisions of the intermediate appellate court. It regulates activities of the State Bar, reviews charges of misconduct against attorneys, and serves as the final decision-making body in disciplinary cases.

Thieving Thirteenth

Of all the territorial legislatures of the Old West, none surpassed Arizona's Thirteenth Legislature, remembered as the "Thieving Thirteenth," for chicanery, drinking ability, physical combat—and a legacy of good deeds that lives on to this day. It met in the spring of 1885 at the capital, Prescott, and its members were wooed by well-heeled lobbyists who kept the liquor and under-the-table payoffs flowing.

So extravagant were the lawmakers that they spent their operating budget 10 times over and appropriated money so wildly that two grand juries were later assembled to charge them with malfeasance. But they managed to create today's Arizona State University and the University of Arizona, establish the first hospital for the insane in the territory, provide for railroads and bridges, and lay the groundwork for institutions that still serve Arizonans well. ✦

The Arizona Court of Appeals, established in 1965, has jurisdiction in all matters appealed from superior courts.

The Superior Court of Arizona is the general jurisdiction court and has a division in each of the 15 counties. It hears all cases except small claims, minor offenses or violations of city ordinances.

Lower courts: These are limited jurisdiction courts and are of two types—municipal and justice of the peace.

State Officials

Governors of Arizona

Governor Served	Party	Dates Served
George W.P. Hunt	Dem.	1912–17
Thomas E. Campbell	Rep.	1917–
George W.P. Hunt	Dem	1917–19
Thomas E. Campbell	Rep.	1919–23
George W.P. Hunt	Dem.	1923–29
John C. Phillips	Rep.	1929–31
George W.P. Hunt	Dem.	1931–33
Benjamin B. Moeur	Dem.	1933–37
Rawghile C. Stanford	Dem.	1937–39
Robert T. Jones	Dem.	1939–41
Sidney P. Osborn	Dem.	1941–48
Dan E. Garvey	Dem.	1948–51
Howard Pyle	Rep.	1951–55
Ernest W. McFarland	Dem.	1955–59

Governors of Arizona
continued

Governor Served	Party	Dates Served
Paul Fannin	Rep.	1959–65
Samuel P. Goddard	Dem.	1965–67
John R. "Jack" Williams	Rep.	1967–75
Raul Castro	Dem.	1975–77
Wesley Bolin	Dem.	1977–78
Bruce Babbitt	Dem.	1978–87
Evan Mecham	Rep.	1987–88
Rose Mofford	Dem.	1988–91
J. Fife Symington	Rep.	1991–97
Jane Dee Hull	Rep.	1997–

Secretaries of State

Secretary of State	Dates Served
Sidney P. Osborn	1912–18
Mit Simms	1919–20
Ernest R. Hall	1921–22
James H. Kerby	1923–28
J.C. Callaghan	1929–died 1929
I.P. Frazier	1929–30
Scott White	1931–32
James H. Kerby	1933–38
Harry Moore	1939–died 1942
Dan E. Garvey	1942–48
Curtis Williams	1948–49
Wesley Bolin	1949–77
Rose Molford	1977–88
Jim Shumway	1988–91
Richard Mahoney	1991–95
Jane Dee Hull	1995–97
Betsey Bayless	1997–

Attorneys General

Attorney General	Dates Served
George Purdy Ballard	1912–14
Wiley E. Jones	1915–20
W.J. Galbraith	1921–22
John W. Murphy	1923–28
K. Berry Peterson	1929–32
Arthur T. LaPrade	1933–34
John L. Sullivan	1935–36
Joe Conway	1937–44
John L. Sullivan	1945–47
Evo DeConcini	1947–
Fred O. Wilson	1949–52
Ross F. Jones	1953–54
Robert Morrison	1955–58
Wade Church	1959–60
Robert Pickrell	1961–64
Darrell F. Smith	1965–68
Gary K. Nelson	1968–74
N. Warner Lee	1974–
Bruce Babbitt	1975–78
John A. LaSota Jr.	1978–
Bob Corbin	1979–91
Grant Woods	1991–99
Janet Napolitano	1999–

State Parks (SEE ALSO CIVIL WAR IN ARIZONA; KARTCHNER CAVERNS; LOST DUTCHMAN MINE; MILITARY POSTS; OAK CREEK CANYON; TOMBSTONE; TUBAC; YUMA)

Arizona established its state parks system in 1957. It is governed by the Arizona State Parks Board, composed of the state land commissioner and six volunteer members appointed by the governor. The first state parks were historic sites: Tubac Presidio State Historic Park and the Tombstone Courthouse. State parks have some 250 full and part-time employees and hundreds of volunteers.

Today's Arizona state parks:

Alamo State Park. Offers anglers one of the best desert fishing lakes in the state. It is in Mohave County, accessed via 38 miles of paved road off U.S. Route 60.

Boyce Thompson Arboretum State Park. One of the Southwest's premier botanical gardens is in this park, 3 miles west of Superior along U.S. Route 60.

Buckskin Mountain State Park, and River Island Unit. This park is 11 miles north of Parker, off State Route 95 in La Paz County. It offers camping, water sports and scenery.

Cattail Cove State Park. On the shore of Lake Havasu in La Paz County, this park is for boaters. Its campsites are available only by boat. It is located upstream from the boat launch area at Buckskin Mountain State Park.

Catalina State Park. Catalina, at the base of Mount Lemmon near Tucson, offers something for everyone: canyon hikes, camping, bird watching and riding trails. It is reached off State Route 77.

Dead Horse Ranch State Park. Located in the Verde Valley at Cottonwood, Dead Horse Ranch offers fishing, camping, hiking and equestrian activity.

Fools Hollow Lake Recreation Area. Just outside Show Low, the gateway to the White Mountains in Navajo County, Fools Hollow Lake offers cool summer camping among the tall pines with a variety of outdoor activities.

Fort Verde State Historic Park. One of the best preserved cavalry posts of the Southwest, Fort Verde offers self-guided tours and an excellent museum. It is in the center of downtown Camp Verde, 3 miles east of Interstate 17 in Yavapai County.

Homolovi Ruins State Park. Walk in the footsteps of ancient cultures here. One can learn about those who came before the white man at this

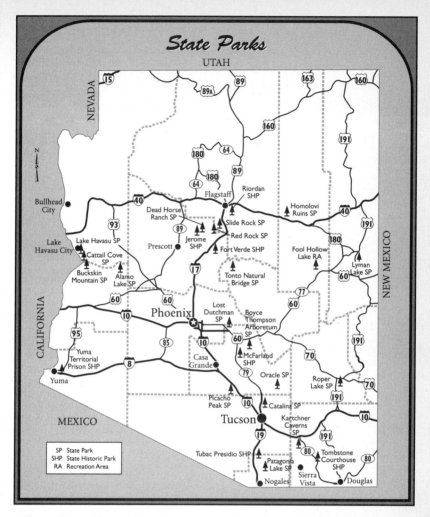

State Parks

park, 5 miles northeast of Winslow off State Route 87.

Jerome State Historic Park. The Douglas Mansion is the site of a fine museum on a hill overlooking the once-bustling mining camp of Jerome, along State Route 89A in Yavapai County.

Kartchner Caverns State Park. One of America's natural wonders, these caverns have recently been opened to the public. The park is near Benson, off State Route 90. Access is limited to this living cavern, so advance reservations are recommended.

Lake Havasu State Park. This Colorado River park features water sports near the famous London Bridge. It is in Lake Havasu City, just north of the bridge.

Lost Dutchman State Park. At the base of the Superstition Mountains 5 miles northeast of Apache Junction, this park is an excellent campground for those wishing to hike into those mountains

Patagonia Lake State Park, southern Arizona. Photo by James Tallon.

in search of the legendary Lost Dutchman Mine.

Lyman Lake State Park. Located near Arizona's northeastern border in Apache County, 2-mile-long Lyman Lake is home to a small herd of buffalo. It offers camping, fishing and water sports. It is a mile off Highway 180, 11 miles south of St. Johns.

McFarland State Historic Park. Ernest W. McFarland was a U.S. senator, Arizona governor and state supreme court justice. His hometown of Florence honors him in this museum.

Patagonia Lake State Park. Southern Arizona boaters and fishermen love Patagonia Lake. It is 2¹/₂ miles long and is located north of State Route 82 between Patagonia and Nogales.

Picacho Peak State Park. Just off Interstate 10 at the base of Picacho Peak is the site of the westernmost Civil War battle, fought in 1862. Hiking trails, picnicking, camping, wildflowers in season and history await the visitor.

Red Rock State Park. Located southwest of Sedona, in some of nature's most spectacular beauty, this park is a nature center for environmental education. Rangers conduct hikes and programs.

Riordan Mansion State Historic Park. Located on the campus of Northern Arizona University in Flagstaff is the home of the pioneer Riordan families, furnished as it was at the turn of the century.

Roper Lake State Park. Located near Mount Graham, 4 miles south of Safford in Graham County, this park offers camping, nearby fishing, water fun and a rock-lined natural hot spring.

Slide Rock State Park. One of scenic Oak Creek Canyon's most popular features is Slide Rock, with its natural water slide that delights young and old. The park is 7 miles north of Sedona off State Route 89A.

Sonoita Creek State Natural Area. A flourishing riparian area near Nogales, the area has steep canyons and teems with wildlife. Particularly in autumn, Sonoita Creek is one of Arizona's most picturesque waterways.

Tombstone Courthouse State Historic Park. Located in the storied town of Tombstone, off U.S. Route 80, this park gives visitors a look at the history of a wild and wonderful territorial mining town.

Tonto Natural Bridge State Park. Mineralized water and the ages have combined to create this spectacular natural travertine bridge. It is 13 miles northwest of Payson, off State Route 87.

Tubac Presidio State Historic Park. Spanish pioneers first occupied Tubac nearly two and a half centuries ago. The town's long history is told in its museum. Tubac is 45 miles south of Tucson along Interstate 19.

Verde River Greenway. Wildlife thrives among stands of cottonwood trees along the Verde River in this hideaway. Bird watching is great here. The park is adjacent to Dead Horse Ranch State Park at Cottonwood.

Yuma Crossing Historic Park. This 20-acre park on the banks of the Colorado River in Yuma was an important river crossing for Quechan Natives, Spanish explorers, 49ers, steamboat captains and military men. It has a visitors center, museum and amphitheater.

Yuma Territorial Prison State Historic Park. Hear the whisper of ghosts in the prison cells and visit the museum. The park overlooks the Colorado River in Yuma, not far off Interstate 8.

Statehood Battle

Arizona languished as a territory for almost half a century, from its separation from New Mexico Territory in February 1863 to its admission as the 48th state of the Union in February 1912. During almost all of that seemingly endless time, delegations of pioneer Arizonans made frequent pilgrimages to Washington, D.C., to secure statehood, only to be turned back each time empty handed.

Why was Arizona kept so long in second-class status when other western territories managed to place their state stars on the American flag in a much shorter time?

There were many reasons. Lack of population was one. Arizona Territory had only 4,573 inhabitants ("excluding Indians," as the census takers noted) in 1864. The so-called "Apache menace" was another. Its remote location and limited transportation facilities kept the territory unknown to most Americans who lived in what was referred to by Arizonans as "the states."

But there was another more important reason that militated against Arizona statehood in the halls of Congress: except for the Cleveland administrations, the Republican Party ruled in Washington from the Civil War to the eve of World War I, and Arizona Territory was heavily Democratic. Republican leaders kept Arizona in thralldom to prevent the sure election of two more Democratic senators.

In a gesture of fairness, Republican Senator Albert Beveridge of Indiana,

AZ if?!

Coconino County in northern Arizona is big enough to hold all of Massachusetts, Rhode Island and Connecticut, and still have a few square miles left over.

chairman of the Committee on Territories, brought two colleagues with him in 1902 for a whirlwind visit to Oklahoma, New Mexico and Arizona territories, all candidates for statehood. They paused a few hours in a few Arizona communities, ignored the booming mines and irrigated farmlands, and returned to Washington with a most unflattering report.

Later Beveridge proposed that Arizona and New Mexico be admitted as a single state, with its capital at Santa Fe. Infuriated Arizonans turned down the idea by a 5 to 1 margin in a 1906 election. They even turned on one of their idols, Teddy Roosevelt, who supported the Beveridge plan, and the Phoenix city council voted to change the name of Roosevelt Street to Cleveland Street.

Finally, in 1909, the tide began to turn when President Taft visited Arizona Territory and returned to Washington convinced that it was at last ready for statehood.

He signed an enabling act for that purpose in 1910, and jubilant Arizonans held an election the following year to ratify a newly crafted state constitution.

There was still a big hurdle to clear. That constitution provided for popular election and recall of judges, something Taft could not stomach. He refused to approve the new constitution until the offending section was removed. So Arizona went back to the polls, approved the changes Taft demanded, and held an election for state officials in late 1911.

All that was now lacking was the president's signature on the Arizona statehood proclamation. He was scheduled to sign it, and thus set off wild celebrations throughout the new state, on Feb. 12, 1912. But that was

Lincoln's birthday, a federal holiday. Taft declined to sign on Feb. 13, deeming that date an unlucky one. But at last, on the morning of Feb. 14, he affixed his signature to the document.

True to their reputation for stubborn independence, Arizona voters returned to the polls not long after statehood was granted and amended their constitution to provide for the election and recall of judges. By then, of course, it was too late for President Taft to do anything about their insolence.

Steamboats on the Colorado (SEE ALSO DAMS; RIVERS)

An unusual kind of steamboat was assembled at the mouth of the Colorado River during the fall of 1852, one that drew only 22 inches of water. Christened *Uncle Sam*, it was the first of many river craft to navigate the river as far north as today's Lake Mead for 55 years. Steamboats carried many thousands of emigrants, soldiers, and fortune seekers upriver and served as the principal means of entry into western and central Arizona.

Uncle Sam was 65 feet long, with side-wheeler paddles powered by a 20-horsepower wood-burning engine, and could carry only 35 tons of freight and passengers. The craft was piloted by Captain James Turnbull. Its shallow draft was necessary to permit the boat to pass over the countless shoals that appeared and disappeared almost overnight along the river route.

Indians supplemented their income for decades by cutting mesquite trees on the riverbanks and selling the wood to fuel the boats, leaving the shores denuded for 300 miles.

The Colorado, in that era before the

The Aztec plies the Colorado River near Yuma, ca. 1892. Courtesy Southwest Studies, Scottsdale Community College.

building of the upstream dams, was a powerful river that battered the frail boats unmercifully. Many were stranded atop sandbars for long periods, and others struck rocks and sank. Against the current, a boat needed weeks to reach ports as much as 300 miles to the north, but only a few days to return.

A second boat, *General Jesup,* 104 feet long with a 50-horsepower engine, replaced *Uncle Sam* as the king of the steamboats in 1854. Many other boats entered the lucrative freighting and passenger arena, and the exploits of their colorful captains became the stuff of Arizona territorial legend.

The arrival of the Southern Pacific Railroad in 1877 brought serious competition and river traffic gradually declined. When Laguna Dam was built not far north of Yuma in 1907, it brought Colorado River steamboating to an end.

Taliesin West
Frank Lloyd Wright, considered the premier American architect of the 20th century, had his offices and architectural school at Taliesin, in Spring Green, Wisconsin, for many years before building Taliesin West north of Scottsdale in 1939, as his winter headquarters. Located on 600 acres in the shadow of the nearby McDowell Mountains, it was built from native materials. "Our new desert camp belonged to the Arizona desert as though it had stood there during creation," Wright once declared.

Thousands of visitors come to participate in tours of the buildings and surroundings. Taliesin West, now a National Historic Landmark, is the international center for the Frank Lloyd Wright Foundation and the design firm, Taliesin Architects.

Taxes
Arizona collects several kinds of taxes, including personal income tax, estate tax, property tax, and tax on vehicle licenses. The personal income tax is levied by the state on individuals earning income in

Arizona. While there is no inheritance tax, estates over $600,000 are currently subject to taxation. In 1996, depending on the type of property, the state assessed taxes ranging from $3.68 to $16.37 per $100 of the estimated value of buildings and land. Household goods and personal property are not subject to state taxes. Annual vehicle license taxes are based on a percentage of retail price, and the assessed value goes down each year thereafter.

The state also levies a tax of 5 percent on all retail sales, except those for food and prescription medications. Several of the counties add a 0.5 percent to 0.7 percent tax, and many cities add from 1 percent to 2 percent on top of that. These are subject to change. For example, in early 2000, Phoenix charged a 1.3 percent city sales tax, but in March the voters approved 0.4 percent more for expanding the public transportation system. The state adds 18 cents per gallon to the price of gasoline or diesel fuel, which helps pay for highway construction and maintenance.

Television Stations

Flagstaff, KNAZ (2) NBC
Kingman, KMOH (6)
Greater Phoenix, KAET (8) PBS
    KASW (61) WB-FCN
    KNXV (15) ABC
    KPAZ (21) TBN
    KPHO (5) CBS
    KPNX (12) NBC
    KSAZ (10) Fox
    KTVK (3) ABC
    KUTP (45) UPN
Prescott, KUSK (7)
Tucson, KGUN (9) ABC
    KHRR (40) Telemundo
    KMSB (11) Fox
    KOLD (13) CBS
    KUAT (6) PBS

    KVOA (4) NBC
Yuma, KSWT (13) CBS
    KYMA (11) NBC

Tempe (SEE ALSO RIO SALADO)

Once known only as a small college town, Tempe has blossomed into a many-faceted city with a booming industrial park, research centers, fine hotels and the state's largest shopping mall. Still its primary claim to fame is as the home of Arizona State University, with a main campus enrollment of 44,000. The city adjoins Phoenix on the southeast. Tempe plays host to the Fiesta Bowl football classic each year, and Sun Devil Stadium is the home of the Arizona Cardinals of the National Football League. The Rio Salado recreational development, opened in late 1999, includes a large lake, parks, hotels and other amenities. Primarily a residential community over the years, it has been honored with All-American City status. Its population is more than 160,000.

Tennis

Arizona's sunny weather makes the state a natural site for tennis. In addition to hundreds of private facilities, the metropolitan Phoenix area has more than 550 public courts, 12 tennis schools (including the famous John Gardiner Tennis Ranch, with 21 courts), and 42 tennis resorts. Tucson has courts at six of its resorts; Sedona has two, and several other communities have at least one.

Major national tournaments for junior and senior professionals are played in Arizona throughout the year, and celebrity charity exhibitions are popular. The Association of Tennis Professionals (ATP) tour comes each March to the Princess Resort in

Tombstone's Bird Cage Theater, popular 1880s entertainment center. Courtesy Southwest Studies, Scottsdale Community College.

Scottsdale for the Franklin Templeton Tennis Classic. That event attracts more than 60,000 spectators and 70 million worldwide television viewers.

Tucson's Randolph Tennis Center hosts the Doubletree Copper Bowl Tennis Open in early January, the CIGNA Celebrity Tennis in April, and the Penn Arizona Doubles Championship in mid-September.

Tombstone (SEE ALSO
GUNFIGHTERS OF THE OLD WEST;
OK CORRAL) No town in Arizona territorial history is better known than Tombstone, the rowdy silver mining camp that was called the most sinful town between New Orleans and San Francisco in the 1880s. Visitors still flock to the Bird Cage Theater, Boot Hill Cemetery, and the OK Corral, where the Earps and Clantons shot it out in a brief gun battle that spawned a hundred books and movies.

Tombstone, once the county seat of Cochise County, should have died when its mines closed down, but it has survived as a tourist mecca and health resort, with a population of 1,660.

Tourism (SEE ALSO THE FIVE
C'S; OUTDOOR RECREATION) Estimates show that in 1997, 27 million tourists visited Arizona. Of these, more than 2.5 million of them came from places outside the United States. Lake Mead National Recreation Area and Grand Canyon National Park are the most visited attractions. The next three most popular destinations are: Saguaro National Park, Glen Canyon National Recreation Area and Canyon de Chelly National Monument.

The top activities for visitors are: sightseeing and visiting national and state parks (16 percent); visiting historic sites (14 percent); hiking or biking (11 percent); camping

(8 percent); visiting a museum or attending a play (8 percent); and watching a sporting event (7 percent).

Day Trips

Arizonans and visitors alike love to pile the family into the car and spend a day visiting some of the attractions of the state. Arizona offers scores of such trips, but these are especially enticing, from cities in the south, central and north.

From Tucson: Trip 1. After an early breakfast, drive south 9 miles on Interstate 19 to the famed San Xavier Mission, one of the architectural masterpieces of North America. Take the Valencia Road West exit a short distance to Mission Road. The white twin-towered church is visible for miles, rising majestically from the desert in the San Xavier Indian Reservation. It is known fondly to millions as the "White Dove of the Desert." Father Kino built the original church 2 miles away in the early 1700s. The present structure was built in the late 18th century, and contains many art masterpieces and a glimpse into Spanish colonial history.

Leave the church on Mission Road and proceed, via Ajo Way and Kinney Road, to Old Tucson, a theme park and western movie location. Old Tucson stands at the junction of Kinney Road and Gates Pass Road, not far west of downtown Tucson. It was originally built as the set for the 1939 movie classic, *Arizona*, starring William Holden and Jean Arthur. More than a hundred films and many television shows have been filmed here. The park has western storefronts, a stagecoach, a narrow gauge railroad and much more. Western melodramas, strolling mariachi musicians and gunfights in front of a saloon enliven your stay.

If you still have energy enough, make a stop at the western segment of Saguaro National Park a few miles to the northwest. The world's most extensive Saguaro cactus forest is preserved in this portion of the park, and in the other half on Tucson's east side.

The saguaro is Arizona's symbol,

and you'll see it in scores of forms: in jewelry, paintings, clothing and about anyplace else you can think of. There is a 9-mile drive that is well worth taking, and a mile-long nature trail.

Trip 2. Now that you know your way to Tucson's west side, return via Gates Pass Road to the Arizona-Sonora Desert Museum, located between Old Tucson and Saguaro National Park. This showplace has earned its ranking among the nation's leading museums, partly because it is much more than a museum. It is a zoo, a botanical garden, geology laboratory and living desert classroom as well. The Congdon Earth Sciences Center tells how the Sonoran Desert was formed, and even boasts an imitation limestone cavern. You'll find all the common desert animals and flora in this amazing museum, as well as mountain lions, black bears and Mexican parrots.

You could spend several days at the Arizona-Sonora Desert Museum, but this is a one-day trip. So drive on to Sabino Canyon in the Santa Catalina foothills on Tucson's northeast side. Here you'll enjoy waterfalls, desert flora, creeks, picnic areas and hiking trails. If your time and energy permit, visit the Flandrau Planetarium on the U of A campus for an evening showing of the night sky. It's truly amazing! Top it all off with dinner in one of Tucson's famed Mexican restaurants and you'll have a day to remember.

From Phoenix: Trip 3. Phoenix and the Valley of the Sun have much to offer, and it may require several days to touch even the high spots. Start with downtown Phoenix, a cultural and sports treasure trove. If you're a sports fan you will enjoy visiting the downtown complex featuring the new

Arizona Biltmore Hotel, Phoenix, one of the state's premier resorts. From Arizona by Fred Hirschmann.

domed baseball stadium, Bank One Ballpark (BOB to its friends), home to the Arizona Diamondbacks of the National League. A stone's throw away is America West Arena, where the Phoenix Suns of the National Basketball Association play. The Phoenix Coyotes of the National Hockey League also call AWA their home, as do the Arizona Rattlers of arena football and the Phoenix Mercury of the WNBA. Historic Heritage Square, with its Victorian homes, is nearby, as is Symphony Hall, home of the Phoenix Symphony Orchestra. The Herberger Theater, the Phoenix Museum of History and the Science Museum are all in the vicinity. Art lovers will want to visit the Phoenix Art Museum, and everyone will enjoy the Heard Museum and Phoenix Public Library.

Take Central Avenue all the way south to its ending, and you will enter Phoenix South Mountain Park. At

Rawhide

A few minutes' drive north of Scottsdale is one of the Southwest's most popular pseudo-western villages, Rawhide. Visitors from all over the world come to see wooden sidewalks, frontier saloons and all the other trappings of 19th-century Arizona.

Good guys shoot bad guys in confrontations on the Rawhide streets. Dance hall girls perform to the music of tinny pianos. Gamblers ply their trade at green baize tables.

The food is good, too, especially the barbecues prepared by cowboy chefs, and the entertainment at these affairs is always memorable. ✳

nearly 17,000 acres, this is the largest municipal park in the world. Drive to the lookout at the top and enjoy the 100-mile view, from the White Tank Mountains in the northwest, to the Four Peaks Wilderness Area in the northeast.

Along the Phoenix/Scottsdale border, on Galvin Parkway, is the renowned Desert Botanical Garden and the Phoenix Zoo. The Garden has more than 10,000 different plants from all the deserts of the world, and the Zoo is the largest privately financed zoo in the United States. Both are world-class attractions.

Nobody could hope to spend any appreciable time in all these attractions during a one-day trip, but you can make your choices from this menu.

Trip 4. Want to get out of the city? Drive 25 miles north on I-17 to the well-marked exit for the Pioneer Arizona Living History Museum. Here you'll find a bustling pioneer village, with store buildings, a Victorian mansion, school, opera house and stagecoach station. Next, go south a couple of miles on I-17 to the Carefree Highway exit and drive 8 miles east to the towns of Cave Creek and Carefree. Cave Creek was a mining camp in the 1880s and now it's a quiet residential enclave. Nearby Carefree is a newer, planned community, with

high-priced homes, the world's largest sundial, fine restaurants and a wonderful shopping area.

Go south from Carefree on Scottsdale Road toward the glamour city of Scottsdale, perhaps stopping mid-way at the western theme town of Rawhide, where you can see many of the attractions offered by Old Tucson (see Trip 1.) Scottsdale has more world-class resort hotels, great golf courses, art galleries, shops and millionaires than any other city of its size in the West.

Scottsdale adjoins Phoenix on the northeast, and Tempe is just south of Scottsdale. Tempe is the home of Arizona State University, one of the nation's largest universities, and the new Rio Salado complex of hotel, business, and recreational facilities centered around the 2-mile long Town Lake. From here, Phoenix is only 20 minutes to the west.

From Flagstaff: Trip 5. Northern Arizona offers scenic beauty on every hand. This trip really should take at least two days, but you can squeeze some of it into 24 hours. First, drive northwest from downtown Flagstaff on U.S. Route 180, passing Mount Humphreys (Arizona's highest), the Arizona Snow Bowl, and the Museum of Northern Arizona en route. Come back later and enjoy them all. It's only

78 miles on Route 180 through pine forests and rolling hills to the South Rim of the Grand Canyon. One of the world's seven natural wonders, the Grand Canyon is an experience you'll never forget.

When you leave the South Rim, drive east on State Route 64, past breathtaking views of the Canyon to the still-active trading post at Cameron. Turning south on U.S. Route 89, you'll see Navajo Indians selling their wares along the way. A little more than 20 miles down Route 89 is the turnoff to Wupatki National Monument, a well-preserved community of structures built in the 12th and 13th centuries by the Sinagua Indians. Continue on the loop road to nearby Sunset Crater National Monument. The crater cone and surrounding lava fields look as though it erupted yesterday, and geologically speaking, it did, in the winter of 1064–65. The rangers at the Wupatki visitor center will explain it all. Your return trip to Flagstaff from here takes only half an hour.

Trees and Shrubs

Arizona has many native varieties of trees and shrubs. Creosote bushes are seen everywhere in the deserts, up to 4,000 feet. Stands of these perennial shrubs cover thousands of square miles. Other desert shrubs include ocotillo, bird-of-paradise, New Mexico locust, jojoba, desert fir, desert honeysuckle, bursage and desert broom. Desert trees include acacia, paloverde, mimosa, ironwood, mesquite and desert catalpa.

In the higher deserts and mountain foothills, shrub-like oak trees, junipers and piñon pines grow. Shrubs in the high desert areas include hackberry, barberry, Arizona rosewood, sumacs,

Ocotillo is native to the desert. Illustration by Robert Williamson.

poison ivy, soapberry, deerbrush, buckthorn, quinine bush, ocotillo, yellow trumpet bush, bouvardia and sand sagebrush.

Temperatures are cooler and rainfall greater in the highest elevations. Ponderosa and other long-needled pines, Douglas fir and aspen flourish here. There are also Arizona walnut, alder, Arizona white oak, Palmer oak, black oak, mulberry, mountain mahogany, arbutus, ash and elder. Shrubs include bouvardia, hawthorn, Arizona rose, poison ivy, smooth sumac, red-osier dogwood, cliff-rose, manzanita and Rocky Mountain blueberry.

Around lakes, rivers, streams and springs are often found cottonwoods, sycamores, maples and willows. Above 9,500 feet and up to the timberline, forests contain spruce, fir and bristlecone pine trees.

Mistletoe is a parasitic plant that grows on both shrubs and trees. It may weaken, or even kill, its host. The leafless desert mistletoe grows on desert trees and shrubs (such as mesquite, acacia, paloverde and ironwood) that live below 4,000 feet. The bright-green mistletoe with white berries that we use for Christmas prefers cottonwoods, willows, sycamores and oaks. Juniper mistletoe is parasitic on several species of juniper, at elevations of 4,000–7,000 feet. Dwarf mistletoe likes it even higher and grows on spruce trees.

Some interesting Arizona shrubs and trees are:

Arizona Cypress (*Cupressus arizonica*). Outside of California, this is the only native true cypress in North America. It is an evergreen that grows naturally in mountain canyons along the Mexican border, from 3,500 to 8,000 feet. It is also popular for ornamental planting. Its blue-green leaves resemble those of a juniper, but its cones are bigger. The trees can grow to 90 feet in height. The trunk branches very close to the ground, and the bark is thin, dark brown-gray, and rough.

Bristlecone Pine (*Pinus aristata*). A scattering of these hardy trees grow on rocky ridges swept by cold winds, from 9,500 feet to the top of the timberline at about 12,000 feet. In Arizona, they only grow on San Francisco Peaks. They become gnarled and twisted by extreme weather conditions. Each scale of the 4-inch-long cones is tipped with a curved bristle. They grow very slowly, but these trees can live for over 1,000 years. The oldest one in Arizona is more than 1,400 years old.

Manzanita (Genus *Arctostaphylos*). This evergreen shrub has several varieties, all with distinctive smooth,

Looking Back

April 15, 1862

The westernmost battle of the Civil War was at Picacho Pass, north of Tucson.

red bark and bright green, rounded leaves. Its white or pink flowers bloom from March to June. The reddish-brown berries look like little apples. (*Manzanita* means "little apple" in Spanish.) The plants grow 3–6 feet high, at elevations from 4,000 to 8,000 feet. The greenleaf manzanita (*Arctostaphylos patula*) grows only on the Navajo Reservation and the North Rim of the Grand Canyon.

Paloverde (Genus *Cercidium*). There are two species of paloverde in Arizona, blue and foothill paloverde (also called yellow paloverde). Both are state trees, and both have smooth, green bark. (*Paloverde* is Spanish for "green stick.") The blue variety (*Cercidium floridum*) has tiny dull, bluish-green leaves, while the foothill (*Cercidium microphyllum*) is a signature plant of the Sonoran Desert and has delicate yellowish-green leaves that are larger than the blue. Their yellow flowers usually bloom from April to May. They are found in desert areas from 500 to 4,000 feet in elevation.

Ponderosa Pine (*Pinus ponderosa*). This is Arizona's most abundant species of pine. It is also the most important tree for the lumber and construction industries. These mature trees have distinctive rusty-orange bark that splits into broad plates and smells like vanilla. They may grow to 125 feet in height and 3 feet across. These trees grow in Arizona high country, at elevations from 5,000 to 8,500 feet. The forest running about 200 miles along the Mogollon Plateau is the largest stand of ponderosa in the West.

Tubac (*SEE ALSO* POSTON, CHARLES*)

The Spanish presidio of Tubac was established in 1752 and was the first European community in Arizona. Tubac, 22 miles north of today's Mexican border city of Nogales, was commanded by Captain Juan Batista de Anza, who in 1775 led an expedition from the presidio to open a route to California. The following year he established a presidio in northern California that became the modern city of San Francisco.

The Tubac presidio was moved to Tucson in 1775, and the old fort fell into disrepair. But in 1856 Charles Poston, revered as the "Father of Arizona," arrived and rebuilt it. Poston, who ruled the community as its *alcalde*, or mayor, later wrote: "I was legally authorized to celebrate rites of matrimony, baptize children, grant divorces, execute criminals, and declare war." Arizona's first newspaper was published there in 1859.

Today Tubac is a mecca for history buffs and art lovers. There are more than 30 art galleries in the little town.

Tucson (*SEE ALSO* ASTRONOMY; THE CAPITAL ON WHEELS*)

Tucson, one of America's fastest-growing cities, now has a metropolitan population of more than 750,000. It is an exciting mix of contrasts: a modern city of world-class arts, science, education, and entertainment, blended with many centuries of history.

The city is known as the astronomy center of America, with Kitt Peak National Observatory, Steward Observatory, Flandrau Science Center and Planetarium and several astronomical research centers.

The Hohokam Indians appeared in this area at the time of Christ. Father Eusebio Kino made his first visit here

Downtown Tucson, Pancho Villa statue in foreground. From Arizona by Fred Hirschmann.

in 1694, and in 1775 Hugo O'Connor founded the walled presidio which became today's Tucson. The city was part of Mexico until the Gadsden Purchase of 1854, and was briefly claimed by the Confederacy in 1862. Tucson was the capital of Arizona Territory from 1867 to 1877, and it is still the county seat of Pima County.

Tucson lies along the Santa Cruz River in the shadow of the Santa Catalina and Rincon Mountains, at an altitude of 2,410 feet. Mount Lemmon, in the Santa Catalinas, rises to a height of 9,100 feet and offers skiing and other snow sports in winter. The city's proximity to Mexico gives Tucson a definite Hispanic flavor, as evidenced in its festivals, restaurants, street names and the fact that one Tucsonan in seven is of Latino, mostly Mexican, heritage.

Major attractions.
Arizona-Sonora Desert Museum is rated by the *New York Times* and

Parade magazine as one of best zoos and museums in the world.

Mission San Xavier del Bac, on the Tohono O'odham Indian Reservation is among the most beautiful Spanish missions in the Americas.

Saguaro National Park, with units both east and west of Tucson, has the world's largest collection of Saguaro cactus.

Old Tucson, the western town built in 1939 for the filming of the movie *Arizona*, is a tourist mecca and the site of more than 200 motion picture filmings.

Pima Air and Space Museum is the largest privately funded air museum in the world, with 180 airplanes representing America's civil and military flight history. **Colossal Cave**, east of the city, attracts many thousands.

University of Arizona. Founded in 1885, the university has achieved national prominence in many scientific fields, including astronomy, medicine and archaeology,

It has 14 colleges, 87 doctoral programs and 8 schools, including the only state-supported medical school.

Colleges. Pima Community College has five campuses serving metropolitan Tucson. Private colleges include the University of Phoenix, Parks College, Prescott College, Tucson University and several technical training institutions.

Economy. Tucson's major employers, in order, are the University of Arizona, Davis-Monthan Air Force Base, Raytheon Missile Systems, Carondelet Health Network, Tucson Medical Center HealthCare, BHP Copper, ASARCO Copper, Phelps Dodge, American Airlines, IBM Storage Systems Division, Teletech, Tucson Electric Power, Burr-Brown Semiconductors and First Data Teleservices Division.

Transportation. Tucson is on I-10 and I-19. It is served by 45 freight trucking lines. Eleven airlines serve the city at Tucson International Airport. The Union Pacific Railroad crosses the southern portion of the state through Tucson.

Arts and Entertainment. Visitors enjoy five major Tucson resorts. The city has an opera company, symphony orchestra, ballet and theater companies. The Arizona State Museum, Tucson Museum of Art, Arizona Historical Society Museum and the International Wildlife Museum are major attractions.

There are 40 golf courses, a professional baseball stadium, rodeos, greyhound and automobile racing and PGA and LPGA annual golf tournaments.

Union Membership

Percentage of non-agricultural wage-and-salary workers who are members of unions:

Year	U.S.	Arizona
1995	14.9	8.0
1996	14.5	5.9
1997	14.1	7.0
1998	13.9	6.5

Union Membership

	1990	1998
Civilian Labor Force	1,726,000	2,272,388
Employed	1,634,000	2,178,306
Unemployed	92,000	94,082
Unemployment Rate	5.3%	4.1%

Source: Arizona Department of Economic Security

Universities and Colleges

Arizona has a number of institutions of higher learning, both public and private.

Universities

State Universities.

Arizona State University, Main Campus, Tempe 85287

ASU East, 6001 S. Power Road, Mesa 85206

ASU West, 4701 W. Thunderbird Road, Phoenix 85069

Arizona's largest state university has its Main Campus in Tempe, 9 miles east of downtown Phoenix. Other campuses are ASU West, in west Phoenix; ASU East, at the former Williams Air Force Base east of Chandler; and the ASU Extended Campus in downtown Phoenix. Television and correspondence courses serve thousands around the state.

The Main Campus has some 44,000 students; ASU West 5,000 junior, senior and graduate students; and the new ASU East more than 1,000.

Situated in the heart of Arizona's population center, this is the state's urban university and is rated as a Research I institution. ASU offers 86 undergraduate, 97 masters, and 52 doctoral or terminal degree programs.

Arizona State University was founded in 1885 as a normal (teacher-training) school and offered its first classes in 1886. In later years it was upgraded to a teachers college and then a liberal arts college. By a vote of the state electorate in 1958, its name was changed to Arizona State University.

ASU Main has these colleges: Architecture and Environmental Design, Business, Education, Engineering and Applied Sciences, Liberal Arts and Sciences, Fine Arts, Nursing, Public Programs, Law, Honors College, and Graduate College. ASU West has Arts and Sciences, Education, Human Services, and Management. ASU East has Agribusiness and Technology.

The university's most renowned cultural landmark is Grady Gammage Memorial Auditorium, the final architectural masterpiece of Frank

Lloyd Wright. The auditorium hosts major symphony orchestras, dramatic companies and entertainment headliners throughout the year and has helped make ASU's College of Fine Arts one of the most respected in the nation.

ASU's men's and women's athletic teams, known as the Sun Devils, compete in the Pacific Ten Athletic Conference and have won national championships in many sports. The men's baseball teams have been NCAA champions five times, its football teams twice have gone to the Rose Bowl, and its women's teams are perennial national titleists in golf, archery, and several other sports.

The university's athletic complex ranks with America's finest. Sun Devil Stadium, seating 73,000, is shared with the New Year's Day Fiesta Bowl and the National Football League games of the Arizona Cardinals.

Northern Arizona University, Main Campus, Flagstaff 86011

NAU-Yuma, P.O. Box 6236, Yuma 85366

The newest and smallest of Arizona's state universities is Northern Arizona University, located in the heart of Flagstaff. In addition to the main campus, the university offers degree programs at NAU-Yuma, in southwestern Arizona. Several other Arizona communities host NAU educational offerings.

In contrast to the huge enrollments on the campuses of the other two state universities, Northern Arizona University has 14,000 students in Flagstaff, 660 in Yuma, and nearly 4,000 in other cities. NAU also is unique in its 7,000-foot main campus elevation, where winter comes early and snow sports may be enjoyed as many as six months each year.

Although its traditional emphasis has been on teaching and public service, NAU has developed impressive research programs in recent years. Its Colorado Plateau Research Station, Bilby Research Center, and Social Research Laboratory are examples of that effort.

NAU awards bachelors, masters, and doctoral degrees. The university's colleges are: Arts and Sciences, Business Administration, Ecosystem Science and Management, Engineering and Technology, Excellence in Education, Health Professions, Social and Behavioral Sciences, and Graduate. Other academic entities are the School of Hotel and Restaurant Management, School of Performing Arts, and Women's Studies Program.

Established in 1899 as a teacher-training institution, it broadened its offerings and scope to become first a college and then a university. Clara M. Lovett, long-time history professor and current president of NAU, became the first woman president of an Arizona university in 1994.

Northern Arizona athletic teams are known as the Lumberjacks, in recognition of Flagstaff's historic role as a center for the lumbering industry. The university's most prominent athletic facility is the Walkup Skydome, site of both football and

AZ if?!

Famed story teller Cap Hance loved to tell gullible Grand Canyon visitors about the time he skied across the canyon on top of frozen fog.

basketball home games. This domed arena provides comfortable seating for patrons in the coldest weather. NAU teams compete in the Big Sky Conference.

The proximity of the Arizona Snow Bowl winter sports facility is a major attraction for skiing enthusiasts among the student body, faculty and staff.

University of Arizona, Main Campus, Tucson 85721

Sierra Vista Off-Campus Center, Sierra Vista 85635

During the past five decades of rapid growth, the University of Arizona, founded in 1885, has become one of the nation's leading state universities.

Looking Back

1775

The Spanish presidio moved from Tubac to Tucson.

Its colleges are Agriculture, Architecture, Business and Public Administration, Education, Engineering and Mines, Fine Arts, Graduate College, Honors Center, Humanities, Law, Medicine, Nursing, Pharmacy, Science, Social and Behavioral Sciences, and the University College. The University offers more than a hundred undergraduate majors.

There are 155 buildings, with Southwestern architecture and red tiled roofs, on its 351-acre campus in mid-town Tucson. Broad lawns, gardens, palm trees and desert plants enhance the appearance of the campus.

The university's undergraduate enrollment now is about 26,000. Graduate students number more than 8,000. More than 2,200 of its students are from foreign countries. This is a residential institution, and most students live on or near the campus.

Faculty members number more than 1,500, and 94 percent have doctoral degrees.

The student-faculty ratio is 18 to 1.

Because it was designated as Arizona's land grant institution when it was founded, the University of Arizona has always had a strong program of agricultural assistance to the state's counties. Research on U of A experimental farms has been of great value to farmers and stockmen, both in the state and beyond its borders.

University of Arizona men's and women's athletic teams rank with the nation's best. The men's basketball team won the national collegiate championship in 1997, and has advanced to the coveted Final Four three times. U of A men's baseball and golf teams have won national titles. The women's softball team has won the national championship five times. In 1997–98, 14 of the 18 university teams, known as the Wildcats, earned berths in NCAA post-season competition.

The computer age has transformed student research and study methods at the University of Arizona. All residence halls now offer Internet connections. Homework assignments are available electronically, and all freshmen are assigned e-mail accounts.

Private Universities and Colleges.
American Graduate School of International Management, 15249 N. 59th Ave., Glendale 85306

Chapman University, 10640 N. 28th Drive, Phoenix 85029; P.O. Box 15132, Davis Monthan Air Force Base, Tucson 85707

Devry Institute of Technology, 2149 W. Dunlap, Phoenix 85021

Dine Community College, (Formerly Navajo CC), P.O. Box 126, Tsaile 86556

Embry-Riddle Aeronautical University, 3200 N. Willow Creek Road, Prescott 86301

Grand Canyon University, 3300 W. Camelback Road, Phoenix 85061

Keller Graduate School of Management, 2149 W. Dunlap Ave., Phoenix 85021

Midwestern University, 19555 N. 59th Ave., Glendale 85308

Ottawa University-Phoenix, 2340 W. Mission Lane, Phoenix 85021

Prescott College, 220 Grove Ave., Prescott 86301

Tucson University, 110 S. Church St., Tucson 85701

University of Advancing Computer Technology, 4100 E. Broadway Road, Phoenix 85040

University of Phoenix, 4605 E. Elwood, Phoenix 85072

1811 S. Alma School Road, Mesa 85210

15601 N. 28th Ave., Phoenix 85023

7001 N. Scottsdale Road, Scottsdale 85210

5099 E. Grant Road, Tucson 85711

1350 N. Kolb Road, Tucson 85715

Fort Huachuca Education Center, Fort Huachuca 85613

Western International University, 9215 N. Black Canyon Highway, Phoenix 85021

Frank Lloyd Wright School of Architecture, Taliesin West, Scottsdale 85261

Community Colleges

Arizona Western College, P.O. Box 929, Yuma 85364

La Paz Center, 1120 16th St., Parker 85344

Central Arizona College, 8470 N. Overfield Road, Coolidge 85228

Aravaipa Campus, Star Route, Box 97, Winkelman 85292

Superstition Mountain Campus, 273 Old West Highway, Apache Junction 85219

Chandler-Gilbert Community College, 2626 E. Pecos Road, Chandler 85225

Cochise College, 4190 W. Highway 80, Douglas 85607

Sierra Vista Campus, 901 N. Colombo, Sierra Vista 85635

Coconino County Community College, 3000 N. Fourth St., Flagstaff 86003

Eastern Arizona College, 3714 W. Church St., Thatcher 85552

Gila Pueblo Campus, P.O. Box 2820, Globe 85502

Estrella Mountain Community College Center, 3000 N. Dysart Road, Avondale 85323

Gateway Community College, 108 N. 40th St., Phoenix 85034

Glendale Community College, 6000 W. Olive Ave., Glendale 85302

Maricopa County Community College District, 2411 W. 14th St., Tempe 85281

Mesa Community College, 1833 W. Southern Ave., Mesa 85202

Mohave Community College, 1971 Jagerson Ave., Kingman 86401

Lake Havasu Campus, 1977 W. Acoma Blvd., Lake Havasu City 86403

Mohave Valley Campus, 3400 Hwy 95, Bullhead City 86442

North Mohave Center, 480 S. Central, Colorado City 86021

Northland Pioneer College, District Office, P.O. Box 610, Holbrook 86025

Painted Desert Campus, 993 E. Hermosa Drive, Holbrook 86025

White Mountain Campus-Show Low, P.O. Box 610, Holbrook 86025

Sun City West, a retirement community west of Phoenix. Photo by James Tallon.

Silver Creek Campus-Snowflake, P.O. Box 610, Holbrook 86025

Little Colorado Campus, Winslow, P.O. Box 610, Holbrook 86025

Paradise Valley Community College, 18401 N. 32nd St., Phoenix 85032

Phoenix College, 1202 W. Thomas Road, Phoenix 85013

Pima Community College, 4905 E. Broadway Blvd., Tucson 85709

Community Campus, 401 Bonita Ave., Tucson 85709

Desert Vista Campus, 5901 S. Calle Santa Cruz, Tucson 85709

Downtown Campus, 1255 N. Stone Ave., Tucson 85709

East Campus, 8181 E. Irvington Road, Tucson 85709

West Campus, 2202 W. Anklam Road, Tucson 85709

Rio Salado Community College, 2323 W. 14th St., Tempe 85281

Scottsdale Community College, 9000 E. Chaparral Road, Scottsdale 85250

South Mountain Community College, 7050 S. 24th St., Phoenix 85040

Yavapai Community College, 1100 E. Sheldon, Prescott 86301

Verde Valley Campus, 601 Black Hills Drive, Clarkdale 86324

Western Maricopa Cities

For the past two decades, Phoenix's Westside cities have been experiencing amazing growth. Beyond the larger cities of Glendale and Peoria to the west lie: Litchfield Park, Avondale, Tolleson, Buckeye, El Mirage, Goodyear, Surprise, Wickenburg and the Sun City retirement communities.

Most of these were established as centers of farming operations in the early years of this century. Luke Air Force Base, opened in 1941, has long been a major economic force for this area, and the first of the large Sun City communities began in 1960.

Agriculture still is important, as are manufacturing and resort hotels.

White Mountain Communities
Arizona's White Mountain country in Navajo County has dense forests, four-season climate, many lakes and streams, and winter temperatures that plunge below zero. To many visitors who picture Arizona as primarily desert, this area comes as a surprise.

Its several booming communities offer outdoor recreation all year around, including skiing and other winter sports.

Alpine. Situated well above 8,000 feet in altitude, Alpine has Arizona's lowest temperatures on many days. Snow sports, fishing, hunting and golf are all popular here. Its Winter Fest celebration draws many visitors each year.

Show Low. The western gateway to the White Mountain area is Show Low, with a population of more than 8,000. It is the commercial hub of the area, and a favorite retirement and vacation mecca.

Snowflake–Taylor. Settled by Mormon pioneers more than a century ago, these agricultural communities are noted as excellent places for family living. They lie north of Show Low, midway between that city and Holbrook.

Pinetop–Lakeside. These two cities, a few minutes drive southeast of Show Low, have some of Arizona's best golf courses, fishing lakes and camping. They have excellent tourist accommodations and good restaurants.

Springerville–Eagar. At the eastern end of the White Mountain playground, near the New Mexico border, are the cities of Springerville and Eagar. Hunters and fishermen flock here in season. The towns are in Round Valley, where Mormon settlers first made their homes in the late 1870s.

Window Rock
Window Rock, in eastern Arizona's Apache County, is the capital of the Navajo Nation. It was established in 1936 as the Central Agency headquarters to consolidate the several agencies around the reservation. Situated at an altitude of nearly 7,000 feet, Window Rock has cool summers and cold winters. The town is named for a wind-scoured opening in a sandstone cliff that overlooks the administration buildings of Navajo Tribal Headquarters. Navajo craft shows and ceremonies attract many visitors.

Winslow
Winslow, in Navajo County, is on busy I-40 and the Burlington Northern and Santa Fe Railroad main line across northern Arizona. It once had railroad shops and district offices, and relied primarily on the railroad for its livelihood. Today it has a more broad-based economy, with tourism, trucking, ranching and trade of particular importance. The city, first settled in 1881 and incorporated in 1900, has a population of more than 11,000 and is on the high desert of the Colorado Plateau, at nearly 5,000 feet above sea level.

World War II
(SEE ALSO BATTLESHIP ARIZONA; JAPANESE INTERNMENT; MILITARY) Four years of World War II provided more impetus for Arizona growth than had the previous half century. First, starting in 1941, came the flood of military installations that brought uniformed

men by the thousands into posts across the state. Defense plants blossomed at about the same time, bringing thousands of civilians. When the hostilities ended, airmen who had trained at Arizona bases and civilian technicians who had worked there returned in a torrent of new residents.

Luke Field, opened in early 1941 west of Glendale, trained more than 13,000 Army Air Corps pilots during the war. Williams Field, east of Chandler, was another major flight training base, as were Mesa's Falcon field and Thunderbird I and II in Glendale and Scottsdale, respectively. The Naval Air Facility at Litchfield Park tested and delivered Navy airplanes.

In Tucson the municipal airport, Davis-Monthan Field, was taken over by the Army. It was, and still is, an important installation. Nearby Ryan Field and Marana Air Base teemed with trainees, and Marana instructed more than 10,000 men before it was deactivated. Smaller flight training bases sprang up in other communities.

The Army's ground forces, under the command of General George Patton, trained for desert warfare at Camps Bouse, Hyder, and Horn in western Arizona. Historic Fort Huachuca near the Mexican border got new life and continues as a major communications installation today. West of Flagstaff the Army established an ordnance depot at Bellemont called the Navajo Army Depot.

The price of copper and other metals soared, reviving the lagging mining industry. Agriculture and other economic endeavors benefited as well.

Manufacturing had been a minor component of Arizona's economy until the end of World War II, when Dr. Daniel Noble brought the first Motorola, Inc. plant to Phoenix. A dozen other semiconductor manufacturing giants soon followed Motorola to central Arizona. In Tucson, Howard Hughes gave a huge boost to the local economy with his aircraft components plants. Manufacturing now is a primary economic engine of the state.

World War II changed the face of Arizona and launched an era of previously unimaginable growth that has continued to this day.

Yuma
The seat of Yuma County is situated along the Colorado River at the mouth of the Gila River and just north of the border with Mexico. Rich in history, Yuma was a crossing site for 49ers heading for California gold, a base for steamboats, and the site of the territorial prison. Now a city of almost 70,000 residents, Yuma is the center of a rich agricultural empire. Tourism, light manufacturing, trade, and the nearby Yuma Proving Ground and Marine Air Station bolster the economy. Arizona Western College and Northern Arizona University offer degree programs.

Zanjero
In Arizona's irrigated farming areas, an important figure is the *zanjero* (pronounced san-HAIR-oh)—the person who opens and closes the canals and ditches to give the farmer the amount of water to which he is entitled. The word comes from the Spanish *zanja*—ditch.

Water providers such as the Salt River Project release water from the storage lakes to major canals that run for many miles across the land and are as wide and fast-running as rivers. The zanjero opens the gates to smaller canals, sometimes called laterals, from which the farmer takes his allotted quota into his own ditches.

The water user who neglects to keep his ditches cleared of weeds, or who is not on hand (often in the middle of the night) to be sure his water is received and distributed as he wants it, may lose his precious allotment. Large farms hire their own zanjeros to get the job done.

Today's irrigation canals are concrete lined to preserve the water. A half century ago, before there were swimming pools in many residential yards, young people did their swimming in the canals. Some even rode water skis, hitching a rope behind a truck that sped along the canal-side roads. But modern concerns for health and safety have caused the canal companies to forbid such recreational use of their waterways.

Zip Codes

City	County	Zip Code (*=multiple)
Ajo	Pima	85321
Alpine	Apache	85920
Apache Junction	Pinal	85220*
Arizona City	Pinal	85223
Ash Fork	Yavapai	86320
Avondale	Maricopa	85323
Bagdad	Yavapai	86321
Bapchule	Pinal	85221
Bellemont	Coconino	86015
Benson	Cochise	85602
Bisbee	Cochise	85603
Black Canyon City	Yavapai	85324
Bouse	La Paz	85325
Buckeye	Maricopa	85326
Bullhead City	Mohave	86430
Bylas	Graham	85530
Cameron	Coconino	86020
Camp Verde	Yavapai	86322
Carefree	Maricopa	85377
Casa Grande	Pinal	85222*
Cashion	Maricopa	85329
Catalina	Pima	85738

City	County	Zip Code (*=multiple)
Cave Creek	Maricopa	85331
Central	Graham	85531
Chambers	Apache	86502
Chandler	Maricopa	85224*
Chandler Heights	Maricopa	85227
Chinle	Apache	86503
Chino Valley	Yavapai	86323
Chloride	Mohave	86431
Clarkdale	Yavapai	86324
Clifton	Greenlee	85533
Colorado City	Mohave	86021
Concho	Apache	85924
Congress	Yavapai	85332
Coolidge	Pinal	85228
Cortaro	Pima	85652
Cottonwood	Yavapai	86326
Crown King	Yavapai	86343
Dateland	Yuma	85333
Dewey	Yavapai	86327
Douglas	Cochise	85607*
Dragoon	Cochise	85609
Duncan	Greenlee	85534
Eagar	Apache	85925
Ehrenberg	La Paz	85334
El Mirage	Maricopa	85335
Elfrida	Cochise	85610
Elgin	Santa Cruz	85611
Eloy	Pinal	85231
Flagstaff	Coconino	86004*
Florence	Pinal	85232
Fort Apache	Navajo	85926
Fort Defiance	Apache	86504
Fort Huachuca	Cochise	85613
Fort McDowell	Maricopa	85264
Fort Mohave	Mohave	86427
Fort Thomas	Graham	85536
Fountain Hills	Maricopa	85268*
Fredonia	Coconino	86022
Gadsden	Yuma	85336
Ganado	Apache	86505
Gila Bend	Maricopa	85337
Gilbert	Maricopa	85234*
Glendale	Maricopa	85301*
Globe	Gila	85501
Golden Valley	Mohave	86413
Goodyear	Maricopa	85338
Grand Canyon	Coconino	86023
Green Valley	Pima	85614
Greer	Apache	85927
Happy Jack	Coconino	86024

City	County	Zip Code (*=multiple)	City	County	Zip Code (*=multiple)
Hayden	Gila	85235	Pima	Graham	85543
Heber	Navajo	85928	Pine	Gila	85544
Hereford	Cochise	85615	Pinetop	Navajo	85935
Higley	Maricopa	85236	Portal	Cochise	85632
Holbrook	Navajo	86025	Poston	La Paz	85371
Hotevilla	Navajo	86030	Prescott	Yavapai	86301*
Huachuca City	Cochise	85616	Prescott Valley	Yavapai	86314
Humboldt	Yavapai	86329	Quartzsite	La Paz	85346
Indian Wells	Navajo	86031	Queen Creek	Maricopa	85242
Iron Springs	Yavapai	86330	Rillito	Pima	85654
Jerome	Yavapai	86331	Rio Rico	Santa Cruz	85648
Joseph City	Navajo	86032	Rio Verde	Maricopa	85263
Kayenta	Navajo	86033	Roll	Yuma	85347
Keams Canyon	Navajo	86034	Roosevelt	Gila	85545
Kearny	Pinal	85237	Sacaton	Pinal	85247
Kingman	Mohave	86401	Safford	Graham	85546
Lake Havasu City	Mohave	86403*	Sahuarita	Pima	85629
Lake Montezuma	Yavapai	86342	St. David	Cochise	85630
Lakeside	Navajo	85929	St. Johns	Apache	85936
Laveen	Maricopa	85339	Salome	La Paz	85348
Litchfield Park	Maricopa	85340	San Carlos	Gila	85550
Lukachukai	Apache	86507	Scottsdale	Maricopa	85251*
Mammoth	Pinal	85618	Second Mesa	Navajo	86043
Many Farms	Apache	86538	Sedona	Coconino	86336
Marana	Pima	85653	Seligman	Yavapai	86337
Maricopa	Pinal	85239	Sells	Pima	85634
Mayer	Yavapai	86333	Show Low	Navajo	85901
McNary	Apache	85930	Sierra Vista	Cochise	85635
Mesa	Maricopa	85201*	Snowflake	Navajo	85937
Miami	Gila	85539	Solomon	Graham	85551
Morenci	Greenlee	85540	Somerton	Yuma	85350
Mormon Lake	Coconino	86038	Sonoita	Santa Cruz	85637
Mount Lemmon	Pima	85619	Springerville	Apache	85938
Munds Park	Coconino	86017	Stanfield	Pinal	85272
Naco	Cochise	85620	Strawberry	Gila	85544
New River	Maricopa	85027	Sun City	Maricopa	85351*
Nogales	Santa Cruz	85621	Sun City West	Maricopa	85375
Oatman	Mohave	86433	Supai	Coconino	86435
Oracle	Pinal	85623	Superior	Pinal	85273
Overgaard	Navajo	85933	Surprise	Maricopa	85374
Page	Coconino	86040	Tempe	Maricopa	85281*
Paradise Valley	Maricopa	85253	Thatcher	Graham	85552
Parker	La Paz	85344	Tolleson	Maricopa	85353
Patagonia	Santa Cruz	85624	Tombstone	Cochise	85638
Paulden	Yavapai	86334	Tonalea	Coconino	86044
Payson	Gila	85541	Tonopah	Maricopa	85354
Peoria	Maricopa	85381*	Topock	Mohave	86436
Peridot	Gila	85542	Tsaile	Apache	86556
Phoenix	Maricopa	85001*	Tuba City	Coconino	86045
Picacho	Pinal	85241	Tubac	Santa Cruz	85646

Zip Codes *continued*

City	County	Zip Code (*=multiple)
Tucson	Pima	85726*
Wenden	La Paz	85357
Whiteriver	Navajo	85941
Wickenburg	Maricopa	85390
Wikieup	Mohave	85360
Willcox	Cochise	85643
Williams	Coconino	86046
Window Rock	Apache	86515
Winslow	Navajo	86047
Woodruff	Navajo	85942
Yarnell	Yavapai	85362
Young	Gila	85554
Youngtown	Maricopa	85363
Yucca	Mohave	85363
Yuma	Yuma	85364*

Zoos and Gardens

Many Arizona communities take great pride in their local zoos or gardens. Some, like Arizona Sonora Desert Museum and Navajo Nation Zoological and Botanical Park, combine aspects of both a garden and a zoo. Most have education and conservation programs, and many have become vital in the preservation of certain threatened or endangered species.

Children's Park, Phoenix Zoo. Photo by James Tallon.

Zoos.

Arizona Sonora Desert Museum, 2021 N. Kinney Road, Tucson 85743

Heritage Park Zoo, 1403 Heritage Park Road, Prescott 86301

Navajo Nation Zoological & Botanical Park, P.O. Box 9000, Window Rock 86515

Out of Africa, No. 2 S. Fort McDowell Road, Fountain Hills 85269

The Phoenix Zoo, 455 N. Galvin Parkway, in Papago Park, Phoenix 85008

Reid Park Zoo, 22nd Street and Country Club, 1100 S. Randolph Way, Tucson 85716

Wildlife World Zoo, 16501 W. Northern, Litchfield Park 85340

Gardens.

The Arboretum at Flagstaff, 3.8 miles S. Woody Mountain Road, Flagstaff 86002

Boyce Thompson Arboretum State Park, 37615 Highway 60, Superior 85273

Desert Botanical Garden, 1201 N. Galvin Parkway, Phoenix 85008

Tohono Chul Park, 7366 N. Paseo del Norte, Tucson 85704

Tucson Botanical Gardens, 2150 N. Alvernon Way, Tucson 85712

News Highlights, 1999–2000

The following is a collection of news events from mid-1999 to mid-2000. *The Great Arizona Almanac* credits the *Arizona Republic,* Arizona's largest newspaper and the only one sold throughout most of the state, as the primary source for this overview of a year in the life of a state.

Arizona Legislator Shoots from the Lip.
Over the years, Arizona has experienced many public figures who make controversial statements or take unpopular stands. The latest is State Rep. Barbara Blewster, a Republican from Dewey, in the north-central part of the state. Blewster, a member of the John Birch Society, has made national headlines after her derogatory remarks about Jews, blacks, American Indians and homosexuals. After the April 1999 shootings at Columbine High School in Littleton, Colorado, Blewster said that allowing teachers to carry guns in their classrooms would deter people from opening fire in schools. Also, she has proposed that Arizona secede from the Union if the federal government passes any more laws restricting gun use and ownership.

Senator John McCain Runs for President.
Arizona's senior senator, John McCain, announced in April 1999, that he was a candidate for the Republican nomination for President of the United States. While he conducted a successful campaign for almost a year, participating in several debates and winning the New Hampshire primary and delegates in several other states, McCain put his candidacy *on hold* in March 2000. He stopped short of endorsing the front-runner, Governor George W. Bush of Texas, saying that he first wanted to talk with Bush about including campaign finance reform in the Republican platform for November's election.

'Sleepwalking' Man Found Guilty of Murdering His Wife.
Scott Falater, a Phoenix engineer accused of stabbing his wife Yarmila 44 times and holding her head under water in their backyard swimming pool in January 1997, was convicted of her murder in 1999 and sentenced to life in prison without the possibility of parole. Falater had a history of sleepwalking and claimed that he was asleep as he assaulted his wife.

Although puzzled by the lack of a clearly established motive, jurors said they had no choice but to find him guilty because Falater had hidden his bloody clothing after the attack. They thought his actions were too complicated for someone who was sleepwalking to have carried out.

The two, high-school sweethearts, had been married for 20 years and had two teen-age children. The children and Falater's mother-in-law testified on his behalf at his pre-sentencing hearing, which is why, people believe, he was not sentenced to death.

Explosives Stolen from Mine.
In December 1999, 1,000 pounds of explosives were stolen from the M.C. Sandstone Quarry near Drake, about 20 miles south of Ash Fork and 20 miles southwest of Flagstaff, in northern Arizona. The theft included 750 pounds of fuel-soaked ammonium nitrate and 250 pounds of dynamite, materials used in the mining industry. Also stolen from the quarry, owned by

3 Wins Mining Company, were detonator cord and blasting caps.

Investigators from the Coconino County Sheriff's Department and the Federal Bureau of Alcohol, Tobacco and Firearms checked leads all over the state, but were unable to find the perpetrators or the explosives. Arizona's laws regulating mining explosives are relatively loose, according to the State Mining Inspector's Office, and the legislature has resisted pressure to pass laws that oversee the use of explosives more closely. Phil Howard, Arizona's Assistant Mine Inspector, said the office will lobby the legislature for stricter laws, since he believes the theft of these materials shows the need for them.

USAA To Open Corporate Operations Center in Phoenix.
On Dec. 29, 1999, Governor Jane Dee Hull welcomed the announcement by USAA (United Services Automobile Association) that they have purchased 500 acres of land in northern Phoenix. The company plans to build offices that would employ 500 to 600 people by 2001. The USAA's plans fit in well with the governor's Growing Smater program for new development in Arizona, Governor Hull said. The new corporate campus will provide recreational facilities, a day-care center and a clinic for its employees. Based in San Antonio, USAA is the nation's sixth-largest insurer, providing insurance and financial services to more than 3 million clients, 91 percent of whom are members of the United States military services and their families.

First Peoples' 'Thunder in the Desert' Fair Ushers in New Millennium.
Native groups from around the world gathered in Tucson from the end of December 1999 through the first week in January 2000 for "Thunder in the Desert: the First Peoples' World Fair and Pow Wow." Some 150 American Indian tribes were represented, as well as groups from Canada, Mexico and Australia. They gathered to sing, dance, celebrate the new millennium, and show pride in their cultures, most of which have existed for much longer than 2,000 years. Thunder in the Desert was among the celebrations featured on ABC TVís New Year's Eve/millennium coverage.

Clinton Creates Two New National Monuments in Arizona.
President Bill Clinton visited Arizona on Jan. 11, 2000, to proclaim the creation of two new national monuments: the Agua Fria National Monument and the Grand Canyon-Parashant National Monument.

In the 71,100-acre Agua Fria National Monument alone, there are at least 450 pre-historic sites, containing petroglyphs and other evidence of man's habitation. The Agua Fria National Monument lies in central Arizona, about 40 miles north of downtown Phoenix. While the federal Bureau of Land Management already oversees the land, monument status will afford the archeological sites better protection from vandalism and encroaching development.

The new Grand Canyon-Parashant National Monument is located on the Colorado Plateau in northwestern Arizona, along the North Rim of the Grand Canyon. Its 1,014,000 acres also include part of the Lake Mead National Recreation Area. The monument contains incomparable geological, biological, archaeological and historical resources that could be threatened by mining interests and other economic development. The National Park Service and the Bureau of Land Management will continue to co-manage the area, with heavier emphasis on preserving its scientific treasures. Both new national monuments will be closed to off-road vehicle use, and new mining and geothermal leases will not be granted in these areas.

Navajo-Hopi Land Dispute Closer to Settlement. For more than 100 years, some members of the Navajo and Hopi Nations have made claims to land in northeastern Arizona that both people groups have occupied for hundreds of years. Although the federal government granted the disputed land to the Hopis in the 1880s, no one had been able to work out a fair arrangement for its use.

In 1958, the Hopi Tribe sued the Navajo Tribe over land rights. After many years of court hearings and negotiations, Congress passed the Navajo-Hopi Land Dispute Settlement Act in 1996. In its provisions, Navajos who lived on land given to the Hopis were given a deadline of Feb. 1, 2000, to move or to sign an Accommodation Agreement with the Hopi Nation. The Accommodation Agreement creates a 75-year lease for Navajo homeowners, with an option to renew.

People who chose to move off the land were entitled to relocation compensation from the federal government. Those who neither moved nor signed the agreement were subject to eviction, but courts are continuing to conduct hearings on individual cases. The conflict and resulting lawsuit has attracted international attention, and many people from other countries have expressed their opinions for or against the partition of the land. Some have even traveled to the area to protest in person.

Eighth F-16 Crashes Over Arizona. On Feb. 16, 2000, an F-16 Fighter jet crashed during a training mission over Arizona, marking the eighth such accident in 16 months. All of the planes, all F-16s, have gone down in remote areas, most near Gila Bend in southwestern Arizona or near Luke Air Force Base west of Phoenix. Although many investigations have been conducted, no one has definitively determined why so many F-16 crashes have occurred. In four instances, engine problems were identified. Another ran off the end of the runway at Luke and crashed. Each of the airplanes cost the taxpayers $20 million. In all cases, the pilots escaped serious injury.

Arizona Democrats Participate in First Ever Internet Voting. On March 11, 2000, Arizona Democrats voted in a primary election to select their candidate for President of the United States. At stake were 31 delegates to the Democratic National Convention. Although electors could mail in their ballots or vote at a polling place, as usual, the 2000 primary was the first time they could choose to vote online. This method of voting was implemented and presided over by Election.com, the company hired to provide online voting services. Overall, more than 77,000 people voted, more than doubling the previous record for a presidential primary in Arizona. Of those, almost 36,000 chose to use the Internet. Vice President Al Gore received 77 percent of the votes, to former Senator Bill Bradley's

20 percent. However, just before the election, Bradley announced his withdrawal from the race.

Record-Setting Drought Conditions Over Arizona. As a rule, Arizona does not get much rain or snow, but records for dry conditions were set in 1999–2000. From late September 1999 to early January 2000, more than 100 days, the entire state received no measurable precipitation. On Jan. 2, Phoenix and central Arizona received a trace of rain (.01 inches), and a few inches of snow fell in the high country. The next precipitation did not fall until the first week in March 2000, when some places received over 2 inches of rain in two days. The same storm dumped up to 2 feet of snow in the higher elevations, which brought great glee to the ski areas that had been closed for lack of snow. March 2000 was the latest in the year that the ski areas had ever opened.

Through the winter, many northern Arizona communities had had to cancel winter festivals, or at least the activities that required snow. The lack of precipitation also meant that few desert wildflowers bloomed in the spring, and higher-than-normal fire danger was expected throughout the summer and fall of 2000.

Controversial AIMS Testing Begins. Like many states, Arizona has devised a standardized test to determine whether or not its students have learned enough to graduate from high school. The Arizona exam is called AIMS (Arizona Instrument to Measure Standards), and every student must pass all of its sections before being granted a high school diploma. In 1999, some 45,000 high school sophomores throughout the state took a sample form of the test. Barely 30 percent of them passed the writing section, while 61 percent passed the reading portion. Only 11 percent could do the required math.

Beginning in 2000, the Arizona State Legislature mandated that all Arizona secondary school sophomores take the test. Once the students have passed a section they won't have to take it again. Students may re-test in a subject that they didn't pass, but they must have acceptable scores in all subjects to graduate in 2002.

Many parents, school districts, and media groups asked that the Arizona Department of Education release copies of the test for public scrutiny, but Lisa Graham Keegan, State Superintendent of Public Instruction, said that to do so would compromise the integrity of the exam. Minority groups and those living in rural areas have complained that the questions unfairly favor white, urban students, and many are planning lawsuits to force re-evaluation of the test.

Suggested Reading and Web Sites

August, Jack L. Jr. *Visions in the Desert.* Fort Worth, Texas: Christian University Press, 1999.

Bayless, Betsey. *Arizona Blue Book 1997–98.* Phoenix: Office of Secretary of State, 1997.

Bret Harte, John. *Tucson: Portrait of a Desert Pueblo.* Woodland Hills: Windsor Publications, 1980.

Cheek, Lawrence W. *A.D. 1250.* Phoenix: Arizona Highways Books, 1994.

Cook, James E. *Arizona Trivia Book.* Baldwin Park: Gem Guides, 1991.

Dedera, Don. *The Cactus Sandwich.* Flagstaff: Northland Press, 1986.

Dedera, Don, and Randy Irvine. *You Know You're an Arizonan When.* Payson: Prickly Pear Press, 1993.

Granger, Byrd. *Arizona's Names.* Tucson: Treasure Chest, 1983.

Hirschmann, Fred. *Arizona.* Portland, Ore.: Graphic Arts Center Publishing, 1990.

Hopkins, Ernest, and Alfred Thomas. *The ASU Story.* Phoenix: Southwest Publishing Co., 1960.

Iverson, Peter. *Carlos Montezuma.* Albuquerque: University of New Mexico Press, 1982.

James, Henry. *Territorial Tales.* Marcelline: Walsworth Publishing, 1980.

Kavanagh, James. *The Nature of Arizona.* San Francisco: Waterford Press, 1996.

Leverton, Bill. *On The Arizona Road.* Phoenix: Golden West, 1968.

Manning Reg. *What Is Arizona Really Like?* Phoenix: Reganson, 1968.

Martin, Douglas. *An Arizona Chronology.* Tucson: University of Arizona Press, 1963.

Nutt, Frances. *Dick Wick Hall.* Flagstaff: Northland Press, 1968.

O'Reilly, Sean, ed. *Grand Canyon.* San Francisco: Travelers Tales, 1999.

Phillips, Ed. *2000 Arizona Almanac.* Phoenix: KTAR Radio, 2000.

Ruffner, Budge. *Ruff Country.* Payson: Prickly Pear Press, 1994.

Shadegg, Stephen. *Arizona Politics.* Tempe: Arizona State University, 1986.

Shelton, Richard. *Going Back to Bisbee.* Tucson: University of Arizona Press, 1992.

Sheridan, Thomas E. *Arizona: A History.* Tucson: University of Arizona Press, 1995.

Smith, Dean. *The Goldwaters of Arizona.* Flagstaff: Northland Press, 1986.

Sonnichsen, C. L., *Tucson*, Norman, University of Oklahoma Press, 1982.

Spencer, Guynne. *Places to Go with Children in the Southwest.* San Francisco: Chronicle Books, 1990.

Stocker, Joseph. *Travel Arizona.* Phoenix: Arizona Highways Books, 1987.

Tallon, James. *Arizona's 144 Best Campgrounds.* Phoenix: Arizona Highways, 1996.

Trimble, Marshall. *Arizona: A Panoramic History.* New York: Doubleday, 1977.

_____. *Arizona 2000.* Flagstaff: Northland Press, 1999.

Varney, Philip. *Arizona Ghost Towns and Mining Camps.* Phoenix: Arizona Highways, 1994.

Wagoner, Jay. *Arizona Territory.* Tucson: University of Arizona Press, 1970.

_____. *Early Arizona.* Tucson: University of Arizona Press, 1975.

Walker, Henry, and Don Buffkin. *Historical Atlas of Arizona.* Norman:

University of Oklahoma Press,
1979.
Wormser, Richard. *Tubac*. Tubac:
Tubac Historical Society, 1975.
Wright, Barton. *Hopi Kachinas*.
Flagstaff: Northland Publishing
Company, 1977.
Wyllys, Rufus K. *Arizona*. Phoenix:
Hobson and Herr, 1950.

Web Sites to Check Out for Additional Information

If you like to surf the Internet, you'll get good results from using the keywords "Arizona" and whatever activity or location interests you. Most cities and towns have both official and unofficial web sites, as do many resorts and chambers of commerce. All counties, universities and colleges have home pages.

Some Internet addresses to use when seeking general information are:

www.arizonaguide.com/
www.arizonahighways.com
www.accessarizona.com/
www.azoutdoors.com/
www.desertusa.com/
gorp.com/gorp/location/az/
www.azcentral.com/
www.azstarnet.com/
www.yumasun.com/
www.prescottaz.com/
www.azreporter.com/
www.the-observer.com/
www.grandcanyontourguide.com/
www.paysonroundup.com/
www.kingmandailyminer.com/
www.pinalonline.com/
http://my.ispchannel.com/~leszekp/
rockart/arizona.html
http://gosouthwest.about.com/
travel/
www.arizonatourism.com/

Appendix: Arizona Constitution, Article 2—Declaration of Rights

SECTION 1 FUNDAMENTAL PRINCIPLES; RECURRENCE TO. A frequent recurrence to fundamental principles is essential to the security of individual rights and the perpetuity of free government.

SECTION 2 POLITICAL POWER; PURPOSE OF GOVERNMENT. All political power is inherent in the people, and governments derive their just powers from the consent of the governed, and are established to protect and maintain individual rights.

SECTION 2.1 VICTIMS BILL OF RIGHTS. (A) To preserve and protect victims rights to justice and due process, a victim of crime has a right:

To be treated with fairness, respect, and dignity, and to be free from intimidation, harassment, or abuse, throughout the criminal justice process.

To be informed, upon request, when the accused or convicted person is released from custody or has escaped.

To be present at and, upon request, to be informed of all criminal proceedings where the defendant has the right to be present.

To be heard at any proceeding involving a post-arrest release decision, a negotiated plea, and sentencing.

To refuse an interview, deposition, or other discovery request by the defendant, the defendant's attorney, or other person acting on behalf of the defendant.

To confer with the prosecution, after the crime against the victim has been charged, before trial or before any disposition of the case and to be informed of the disposition.

To read pre-sentence reports relating to the crime against the victim when they are available to the defendant.

To receive prompt restitution from the person or persons convicted of the criminal conduct that caused the victim's loss or injury.

To be heard at any proceeding when any post-conviction release from confinement is being considered.

To a speedy trial or disposition and prompt and final conclusion of the case after the conviction and sentence.

To have all rules governing criminal procedure and the admissibility of evidence in all criminal proceedings protect victims' rights and to have these rules be subject to amendment or repeal by the legislature to ensure the protection of these rights.

To be informed of victims' constitutional rights.

(B) A victim's exercise of any right granted by this section shall not be grounds for dismissing any criminal proceeding or setting aside any conviction or sentence.

(C) "Victim" means a person against whom the criminal offense has been committed or, if the person is killed or incapacitated, the person's spouse, parent, child or other lawful representative, except if the person is in custody for an offense or is the accused.

(D) The legislature, or the people by initiative or referendum, have the authority to enact substantive and procedural laws to define, implement, preserve and protect the rights guaranteed to victims by this section, including the authority to extend any of these rights to juvenile proceedings.

(E) The enumeration in the constitution of certain rights for victims shall not be construed to deny or disparage others granted by the legislature or retained by victims.

SECTION 3 SUPREME LAW OF THE LAND. The Constitution of the United States is the supreme law of the land.

SECTION 4 DUE PROCESS OF LAW. No person shall be deprived of life, liberty, or property without due process of law.

SECTION 5 RIGHT OF PETITION AND OF ASSEMBLY. The right of petition, and of the people peaceably to assemble for the common good, shall never be abridged.

SECTION 6 FREEDOM OF SPEECH AND PRESS. Every person may freely speak, write, and publish on all subjects, being responsible for the abuse of that right.

SECTION 7 OATHS AND AFFIRMATIONS. The mode of administering an oath, or affirmation, shall be such as shall be most consistent with and binding upon the conscience of the person to whom such oath, or affirmation, may be administered.

SECTION 8 RIGHT TO PRIVACY. No person shall be disturbed in his private affairs, or his home invaded, without authority of law.

SECTION 9 IRREVOCABLE GRANTS OF PRIVILEGES, FRANCHISES OR IMMUNITIES. No law granting irrevocably any privilege, franchise, or immunity shall be enacted.

SECTION 10 SELF-INCRIMINATION; DOUBLE JEOPARDY. No person shall be compelled in any criminal case to give evidence against himself, or be twice put in jeopardy for the same offense.

SECTION 11 ADMINISTRATION OF JUSTICE. Justice in all cases shall be administered openly, and without unnecessary delay.

SECTION 12 LIBERTY OF CONSCIENCE; APPROPRIATIONS FOR RELIGIOUS PURPOSES PROHIBITED; RELIGIOUS FREEDOM. The liberty of conscience secured by the provisions of this Constitution shall not be so construed as to excuse acts of licentiousness, or justify practices inconsistent with the peace and safety of the State. No public money or property shall be appropriated for or applied to any religious worship, exercise, or instruction, or to the support of any religious establishment. No religious qualification shall be required for any public office or employment, nor shall any person be incompetent as a witness or juror in consequence of his opinion on matters of religion, nor be questioned touching his religious belief in any court of justice to affect the weight of his testimony.

SECTION 13 EQUAL PRIVILEGES AND IMMUNITIES. No law shall be enacted granting to any citizen, class of citizens, or corporation other than municipal, privileges or immunities which, upon the same terms, shall not equally belong to all citizens or corporations.

SECTION 14 HABEAS CORPUS. The privilege of the writ of habeas corpus shall not be suspended by the authorities of the State.

SECTION 15 EXCESSIVE BAIL; CRUEL AND UNUSUAL PUNISHMENT. Excessive bail shall not be required, nor excessive fines imposed, nor cruel and unusual punishment inflicted.

SECTION 16 CORRUPTION OF BLOOD; FORFEITURE OF ESTATE. No conviction shall work corruption of blood, or forfeiture of estate.

SECTION 17 EMINENT DOMAIN; JUST COMPENSATION FOR PRIVATE PROPERTY TAKEN; PUBLIC USE AS JUDICIAL QUESTION. Private property shall not be taken for private use, except for private ways of necessity, and for drains, flumes, or ditches, on or across the lands of others for mining, agricultural, domestic, or sanitary purposes. No private property shall be taken or damaged for public or private use without just compensation having first been made, paid into court for the owner, secured by bond as may be fixed by the court, or paid into the state treasury for the owner on such terms and conditions as the legislature may provide, and no right of way shall be appropriated to the use of any corporation other than municipal, until full compensation therefore be first made in money, or ascertained and paid into court for the owner, irrespective of any benefit from any improvement proposed by such corporation, which compensation shall be ascertained by a jury, unless a jury be waived as in other civil cases in courts of record, in the manner prescribed by law. Whenever an attempt is made to take private property for a use alleged to be public, the question whether the contemplated use be really public shall be a judicial question, and determined as such without regard to any legislative assertion that the use is public.

SECTION 18 IMPRISONMENT FOR DEBT. There shall be no imprisonment for debt, except in cases of fraud.

SECTION 19 BRIBERY OR ILLEGAL REBATING; WITNESSES; SELF-INCRIMINATION NO DEFENSE. Any person having knowledge or possession of facts that tend to establish the guilt of any other person or corporation charged with bribery or illegal rebating, shall not be excused from giving testimony or producing evidence, when legally called upon to do so, on the ground that it may tend to incriminate him under the laws of the State; but no person shall be prosecuted or subject to any penalty or forfeiture for, or on account of, any transaction, matter, or thing concerning which he may so testify or produce evidence.

SECTION 20 MILITARY POWER SUBORDINATE TO CIVIL POWER. The military shall be in strict subordination to the civil power.

SECTION 21 FREE AND EQUAL ELECTIONS. All elections shall be free and equal, and no power, civil or military, shall at any time interfere to prevent the free exercise of the right of suffrage.

SECTION 22 BAILABLE OFFENSES. All persons charged with crime shall be bailable by sufficient sureties, except for:

Capital offenses when the proof is evident or the presumption great.

Felony offenses, committed when the person charged is already admitted to bail on a separate felony charge and where the proof is evident or the presumption great as to the present charge.

Felony offenses if the person charged poses a substantial danger to any other person or the community, if no conditions of release which may be imposed will reasonably assure the safety of the other person or the community and if the proof is evident or the presumption great as to the present charge.

SECTION 23 TRIAL BY JURY; NUMBER OF JURORS SPECIFIED BY LAW. The right of trial by jury shall remain inviolate. Juries in criminal cases in which a sentence of death or imprisonment for thirty years or more is authorized by law shall consist of twelve persons. In all criminal cases the unanimous consent of the jurors shall be necessary to render a verdict. In all other cases, the number of jurors, not less than six, and the number required to render a verdict, shall be specified by law.

SECTION 24 RIGHTS OF ACCUSED IN CRIMINAL PROSECUTIONS. In criminal prosecutions, the accused shall have the right to appear and defend in person, and by counsel, to demand the nature and cause of the accusation against him, to have a copy thereof, to testify in his own behalf, to meet the witnesses against him face to face, to have compulsory process to compel the attendance of witnesses in his own behalf, to have a speedy public trial by an impartial jury of the county in which the offense is alleged to have been committed, and the right to appeal in all cases; and in no instance shall any accused person before final judgment be compelled to advance money or fees to secure the rights herein guaranteed.

SECTION 25 BILLS OF ATTAINDER; EX POST FACTO LAWS; IMPAIRMENT OF CONTRACT OBLIGATIONS. No bill of attainder, ex-post-facto law, or law impairing the obligation of a contract, shall ever be enacted.

SECTION 26 BEARING ARMS. The right of the individual citizen to bear arms in defense of himself or the State shall not be impaired, but nothing in this section shall be construed as authorizing individuals or corporations to organize, maintain, or employ an armed body of men.

SECTION 27 STANDING ARMY; QUARTERING SOLDIERS. No standing army shall be kept up by this State in time of peace, and no soldier shall in time of peace be quartered in any house without the consent of its owner, nor in time of war except in the manner prescribed by law.

SECTION 28 TREASON. Treason against the State shall consist only in levying war against the State, or adhering to its enemies, or in giving them aid and comfort. No person shall be convicted of treason unless on the testimony of two witnesses to the same overt act, or confession in open court.

SECTION 29 HEREDITARY EMOLUMENTS, PRIVILEGES OR POWERS; PERPETUITIES OR ENTAILMENTS. No hereditary emoluments, privileges, or powers shall be granted or conferred, and no law shall be enacted permitting any perpetuity or entailment in this State.

SECTION 30. INDICTMENT OR INFORMATION; PRELIMINARY EXAMINATION. No person shall be prosecuted criminally in any court of record for felony or misdemeanor, otherwise than by information or indictment; no person shall be prosecuted for felony by information without having had a preliminary examination before a magistrate or having waived such preliminary examination.

SECTION 31 DAMAGES FOR DEATH OR PERSONAL INJURIES. No law shall be enacted in this State limiting the amount of damages to be recovered for causing the death or injury of any person.

SECTION 32 CONSTITUTIONAL PROVISIONS MANDATORY. The provisions of this Constitution are mandatory, unless by express words they are declared to be otherwise.

SECTION 33 RESERVATION OF RIGHTS. The enumeration in this Constitution of certain rights shall not be construed to deny others retained by the people.

SECTION 34 INDUSTRIAL PURSUITS BY STATE AND MUNICIPAL CORPORATIONS. The State of Arizona and each municipal corporation within the State of Arizona shall have the right to engage in industrial pursuits.

Index

abandoned mines, 135
adobe, 9
African Americans, 77, 157–158
agriculture, 9–10, 50–51, 87, 205–206
Agua Fria Freddie, 55
Agua Fria National Monument, 211
Agua Fria River, 66, 175
AIMS Testing, 212
air conditioning, 10–11
air crashes, 68, 211
air quality, 55
airports, 11, 168
Ajo, 11
Ak-Chin Indian Community, 14, 15–16
Alamo State Park, 184
Alpine, 204
American Indians, 11–20; arts, 147–149;
    casinos, 45–46; Cochise, 55;
    Geronimo, 95; population, 77; pow
    wows, 165; prehistoric people, 12–15,
    21, 109, 114, 154–156; "Thunder in
    the Desert" Fair, 210; trading posts,
    17; tribes and reservations, 14. *See also
    names of specific peoples*
amphibians. *See* reptiles and amphibians
Anasazi people, 12–13. *See also*
    prehistoric indigenous people
Apache County, 21–22, 58–59, 60, 160
Apache Junction, 20
Apache people, 14, 16, 19, 20, 55, 95, 149
Apache-Sitgreaves National Forest, 91
archaeology, 20–23; map, 21; prehistoric
    peoples, 12–15, 21, 109, 114, 154–155
architects, 25, 189
architecture: Biosphere II, 31–32; hogans,
    117–118; San Xavier del Bac Mission,
    179; Taliesin West, 189
area codes, 23–24
Arizona Constitution, 215–217
Arizona-Sonora Desert Museum, 193,
    197–198
Arizona State University, 199–200
Arizona Strip, 24
Arizona Territory. *See* territorial years
Arpaio, Joe, 166
artists, 24–25
arts, 24–27; artists, 24–25; Native arts,
    147–149; performing arts, 25–27;
    Phoenix, 156; Tucson, 198

Asian Americans, 77, 158
astronauts, 137
astronomy, 27–28
authors, 126–128
auto racing, 28–29
Avondale, 164, 203–204

Baron of Arizona, 113
Bartlett Dam and Reervoir, 67, 124
baseball, 29–30
basketball, 30–31
Battleship *Arizona*, 31
Benson, 31
Besh-Ba-Gowah Park, 22–23
bibliography, 213–214
Biosphere II, 31–32
birds, 32–33, 74–75
Bisbee, 33–34, 67–68
Blewster, Barbara, 212
botanic gardens, 184, 193, 197–198, 208
Boyce Thompson Arboretum, 184
Buckeye, 203–204
Buckskin Mountain, 42, 43, 184
Buffalo Soldiers, 34–35
bugs, 120–121
Bullhead City, 35
Butterfield Overland Mail, 35

cacti, 35–37
calendar of events, 37–41
caliche, 41
Californians, 165
camel experiment, 41–42
Camp Grant massacre, 67
camping, 42–44
Canyon de Chelly, 21, 143
capital on wheels, 44–45
cartoonists, 25
Casa Grande (city), 45
Casa Grande Ruins, 23, 45, 143
Casa Malpais Archaeological Park, 21
casinos, 45–46
Catalina (town), 157
Catalina State Park, 184
Cattail Cove State Park, 184
cattle ranching, 87, 170
caves, 55–56, 67, 122, 185
Central Arizona Project, 46
Chandler, 50, 164

Chemehuevi people, 14, 16
chiles, 50–51
Chiricahua National Monument, 146
Chloride, 95–96
chronological history, 114–117
cities: chambers of commerce, 46–49;
    ghost towns, 95–96; map, 48; mileage
    between, 110–111; population,
    164–165; retirement communities,
    172–173. See also names of specific
    cities
citrus groves, 87
Civil War, 51, 196
Clifton, 51–52
climate, 52–55; air quality, 55; drought,
    211; economics of, 87–88;
    precipitation, 52–55; snowfall, 43, 53;
    temperature, 8, 53–54, 192; zones, 52
Cochise, 55
Cochise County, 22, 59–60
Coconino County, 22, 60, 160, 187
Coconino National Forest, 91
Cocopah Indian Tribe, 14, 16
coldest temperature, 52
colleges and universities: Arizona State
    University, 156, 199–200; community
    colleges, 202–203; libraries, 126;
    Northern Arizona University,
    200–201; state universities, 199–201;
    University of Arizona, 105, 198, 199,
    201
Colorado Plateau, 94
Colorado River, 66, 173–174, 188–189
Colorado River Country, 95
Colorado River Indian Tribes, 14, 16
Colossal Cave, 55–56
community colleges, 202–203
congressional delegates, 56–57, 72;
    representatives, 56–57; senators, 56.
    See also elected officials
congressional districts, 57
Coolidge Dam, 66, 67
copper mines, 86–87, 134–135, 175
Coronado, Francisco Vasquez de, 58
Coronado National Forest, 91
Coronado National Memorial, 146
cotton farming, 87
Cottonwood, 58
counties, 58–64, 160
courts, 74, 182–183
cowboys, 64–65; cowboy hats, 76;
    rodeos, 177

crafts, 147–149
crime rate, 65

dams, 66–67; Central Arizona Project, 46;
    collapse, 68; lakes, 123–125; rivers,
    173–175; Salt River Project, 178–179
day trips, 192–195
daylight savings time, 87
de Coronaado, Francisco Vasquez, 58
de Nisa, Marcos, 15
Dead Horse Ranch State Park, 184
Declaration of Rights, 215–217
deserts, 94; heat, 192; plants, 162
disasters, 67–68
Doubtful Canyon, 161
Douglas, 68
drought, 211
dude ranches, 68–69

ecological zones, 93–94
economy, 69–71; agriculture, 9–10;
    chambers of commerce, 46–49;
    employment, 71; Five C's, 86–88;
    labor force, 123; Phoenix, 155; top
    employers, 71; tourism, 191–195;
    Tucson, 198; unions, 198
education: AIMS Testing, 212; libraries,
    126; superintendent of public
    instruction, 72, 182. See also colleges
    and universities
El Mirage, 203–204
El Niño and La Niña, 52, 54
Elden Pueblo, 22
elected officials, 70, 71–72; governors, 99;
    politicians, 125–126; politics,
    163–164; state representatives, 73–74,
    212; state senators, 72–73; U.S.
    representatives, 56–57, 72;
    U.S. senators, 56, 72. See also
    congressional delegation; politics,
    state government
elevations, 8
employment, 71, 123, 198
endangered species, 74–75
energy, 75–76; Central Arizona Project,
    46; dams, 66–67
entertainers, 76–77
epidemics, 68
Esteban, 15
ethnic distribution, 77. See also
    population
European Americans, 160

events. *See* festivals and events
exports

Fairbank, 96
fairs. See festivals and events
famous Arizonans, 83–84; Blewster,
    Barbara, 212; Cochise, 55; Earp,
    Wyatt, 102; Geronimo, 95; Goldwater,
    Barry, 98, 163; Grey, Zane, 101–102,
    127, Hall, Dick Wick, 127; Hunt,
    George W.P., 119; Luke, Frank, Jr.,
    132; McCain, John, 56, 209; Mecham,
    Evan, 141; Poston, Charles Debrille,
    165; Reavis, James Addison, 113;
    Rogers, James E., 199
federal lands, 144–145
festivals and events, 37–41, 77–83
fires, 68, 154
fish, 74–75, 84–86
Fives C's, 86–88. *See also* cattle ranching;
    citrus; climate; copper mining; cotton
Flagstaff, 79, 88, 161, 164, 194–195
Florence, 88
foods, 50–51, 88–90
Fools Hollow Lake Recreation Area, 184
football, 90
forest. *See* national forests; state parks
Fort Bowie National Historic Site, 22,
    146
Fort McDowell Indian Community,
    14, 16
Fort Mojave Indian Tribe, 14, 16
Fort Verde State Historic Park, 184
Fort Yuma-Quechan Tribe, 14, 19
forts, 132–134
Fountains Hills, 91–92
Four Corners Monument, 94

Gadsden Purchase, 92–93
Gadsden Treaty, 88
gambling, 45–46
gardens, 208
gemstones, 175–177
geoglyphs, 154–155
geographic features, 93–95; elevations, 8;
    map, 92; mountains, 137–178
Geronimo, 95
ghost towns, 95–96
Gila County, 22–23, 60, 160
Gila Pueblo, 23
Gila River, 66, 174–175
Gila River Indian Community, 14, 17

Gila Trail, 96–97
Gilbert, 97, 164
Glen Canyon Dam, 66
Glen Canyon National Recreation Area,
    146
Glendale, 97–98, 164, 203–204
Globe, 98
gold, 98, 129, 134–135, 176–177
Goldwater, Barry, 98, 163
golf, 99
Goodyear, 203–294
government. *See* state government
governors, 72, 99, 119, 181, 183
Graham County, 60–61, 160
Grand Canyon, 63, 68, 99–101, 146
Grand Canyon-Parashant National
    Monument, 211–212
Green Valley, 101
Greenlee County, 60, 61, 160
Grey, Zane, 101–102, 127
Guadalupe Hidalgo Treaty, 102
Gunfight at the OK Corral, 104, 152
gunfighters, 102–104

Hall, Dick Wick, 127
Hance, Cap, 63
Havasupai Tribe, 14, 17
health care, 104–108
Heard Museum, 140, 156
heat, 192
highways, 102, 110–111; map, 108; speed
    limits, 181; trips, 192–195
Hispanic population, 77, 159
historical societies, 142–143
history: chronology, 114–117; prehistoric
    era, 12–15, 21, 109, 114, 154–155;
    Spanish exploration, 112, 114;
    pioneers and settlers, 157–160;
    mining, 134–135; territorial years,
    44–45, 56, 112–113, 114, 183;
    statehood, 113–114, 116, 187–188;
    World War II, 204–205; Japanese
    Internment, 121; 1999–2000 news
    highlights, 209–212
hockey, 117
hogans, 117–118
Hohokam people, 13–15. *See also*
    prehistoric indigenous people
Holbrook, 118
Homolovi Ruins State Park, 23, 184–185
Honeymoon Trail, 118
Hoover Dam, 66

Hopi Tribe, 14, 16, 17–18, 148
horse racing, 118
Horseshoe Dam and Reservoir, 67, 124
hospitals, 105–108, 160
Hualapai Tribe, 14, 18, 149
Hunt, George W.P., 119
hunting, 119–120

insects, 120–121
Internet voting, 210–211

jackass mail, 121
Japanese Internment, 121
javalinas, 58
Jerome, 96, 97, 121–122
Jerome State Historic Park, 185
Jewish pioneers, 158
Judd, Winnie Ruth, 65

kachinas, 16, 148
Kaibab National Forest, 91
Kaibab Paiute Tribe, 14, 18
Kartchner Caversn State Park, 122, 185
Kingman, 123
Kino, Eusebio Francisco, 112, 114

La Niña, 52, 54
La Paz (town) 96
La Paz County, 60, 61, 160
labor force, 123
labor unions, 34
Lake Havasu, 124
Lake Havasu City, 123, 128–129, 164
Lake Havasu State Park, 185
Lake Mead, 123–124, 146
Lake Mohave, 124
Lake Powell, 124
lakes, 123–125; dams, 66–67; map, 174
land ownership, 70, 144–145
lawmen, 102–104
leaders, 125
legislature, 72–74. See also state
    government
libraries, 126
life zones, 93–94
Litchfield Park, 203–204
literature, 126–128
London Bridge, 128–129
Lost Dutchman Mine, 129
Lost Dutchman State Park, 185–186
Luke, Frank, Jr., 132
Lyman Lake, 21–22, 125, 186

magazines, 129–130
mammals, 74–75, 130–131
maps, 6–7; cities and towns, 48;
    congressional districts, 57; counties,
    59; federal lands, 144–145; geographic
    features, 92; highways, 108; Indian
    reservations, 13; military posts,
    132–134; prehistoric people, 21; rivers
    and lakes, 174; otate parks, 185
Marana, 157
Maricopa County, 23, 60, 61, 160
Maricopa people, 14, 15, 19
massacres, 67
McCain, John, 56, 209
McFarland State Historic Park, 186
Mecham, Evan, 141
media, 149–151; magazines, 129–130;
    news highlights, 1999–2000, 209–212;
    radio stations, 167–169; television
    stations, 190
medical care, 104–108
Mercer, Jacque, 80
Mesa, 131–132, 164
meteorites, 67, 132, 137
Mexican Americans, 77, 159
Mexican gray wolves, 130
mileage, 110–111
military: air crashes, 211; bases, 132;
    Buffalo Soldiers, 34–35; camel
    experiment, 41–42; Civil War, 51,
    196; historical military posts,
    132–134; Mormon Battalion, 96
mining, 86–87; gold, 98; history,
    134–135; Lost Dutchman Mine, 129;
    mine inspector, 72, 182; mining camp
    fires, 68; Pioneers Home and Disabled
    Miners Hospital, 160; rocks, minerals
    and gemstones, 135, 175–177
Miranda v. Arizona, 135–136
miscellaneous facts, 8
Miss Americas, 80
Mix, Tom, 139
Mogollon people, 15. See also prehistoric
    indigenous people
Mogollon Rim, 94
Mohave County, 23, 60, 61–62, 160
Mohave people, 14, 16, 17, 149
monsoons, 54–55
Montezuma Castle, 23, 136, 146
Monument Valley Tribal Park, 136–137
moon walkers, 137
Mormon Battalion, 96

Mormons, 118, 159
mountains, 137–138
movie stars, 76–77
movies, 138–140
museums, 140–142
musicians, 76–77

national forests, 90–91
national parks, 143–147, 211–212
Native Americans. *See* American Indians
Navajo County, 23, 60, 62, 160
Navajo-Hopi Land Dispute, 210
Navajo Nation, 14, 16, 18–19, 148;
    basketball, 31; hogans, 117–118;
    Navajo rugs, 78, 148
Navajo National Monument, 23, 146
news highlights, 1999–2000, 209–212
newspapers, 149–151
Niza, Marcos de, 15
Nogales, 151–152
Northern Arizona University, 200–201

Oak Creek Canyon, 152
Oatman, 96
OK Corral, 104, 152
Old Tucson, 139, 198
Old West: cowboys, 64–65; forts,
    132–134; ghost towns, 95–96;
    gunfighters, 102–104; movies,
    138–140; OK Corral, 104, 152;
    pioneers and settlers, 157–160;
    reenactments, 104; rodeos, 177;
    Thieving Thirteen, 183
Organ Pipe Cactus National Monument,
    42, 44, 146
Oro Valley, 157
outdoor recreation, 152–153; camping,
    42–44; fishing, 84–86; hunting,
    119–120; mountains, 137–138;
    national forests, 90–91; skiing and
    snowboarding, 180–181; state parks,
    184–187; tennis, 190–191; tourism,
    191–195

Page, 153
Pah-Ute County, 62
Painted Desert, 153
painters, 24
Paiute people, 14, 18, 19
Papago people, 15, 19–20
Park of the Canals, 23
parks, 143–147, 184–187, 211–212

Pascua Yaqui Tribe, 14, 19
Patagonia Lake, 42, 43–44, 186
Payson, 153–154
Peoria, 154, 164, 203–204
performing arts, 25–27
periodicals, 129–130, 149–151
Petrified Forest, 22, 147
petrified wood, 91, 176
petroglyphs, 154–155
Phoenix, 155–157; origin of name, 161;
    population, 164; suburbs, 203–204;
    trips, 193–194; USAA, 209–210
photographers, 24–25
Picacho Peak, 186
pictorgraphs, 154–155
Pima Community College, 198
Pima County, 60, 62, 157, 160
Pima people, 14, 15
Pinal County, 23, 60, 62–63
Pinetop-Lakeside, 204
Pioneer Arizona Living History Museum,
    194
Pioneer Hotel fire, 68
pioneers and settlers, 157–160
Pioneers Home and Disabled Miners
    Hospital, 160
Pipe Spring National Monument, 23, 147
place names, 160–161
plants, 74–75, 161–162, 195–196
Pleasant Valley War, 68
politicians and politics, 125–126,
    162–164, 210–211
Polygamy Creek, 161
ponderosa pines, 94, 196
population, 8, 60, 77, 164–165
postal service: Butterfield Overland Mail,
    35; Jackass mail, 121; zip codes,
    206–208
Poston, Charles Debrille, 165
pow wows, 165
power generation. *See* energy
precipitaion, 52–55
prehistoric indigenous people, 12–15;
    history, 109, 114; map, 21;
    petroglyphs, pictographs and
    geoglyphs, 154–155
Prescott (city), 164, 165–166
Prescott National Forest, 91
prisons, 166
private colleges and universities, 201–202
pronunciation guide, 167
public transportation, 167; air crashes,

68, 211; air travel, 11; railroads,
169–170; Tucson, 198
Pueblo Grande Museum, 23

Quechan people, 14, 19, 149

racing, 28–29, 118
radio personalities, 76–77
railroads, 169–170
rainfall. *See* precipitation
ranching, 170–171; cattle, 87, 170;
cowboys, 64–65; dude ranches, 68–69;
sheep, 170–171
Reavis, James Addison, 113
recreation. *See* outdoor recreation
Red Rock State Park, 186
representatives: state, 73–74, 212; U.S.,
56–57, 72
reptiles and amphibians, 74–75, 171–172
retirement communities, 172–173
Rio Salado, 173
rivers, 173–175; Central Arizona Project,
46; map, 174; Salt River Project,
178–179. *See also* dams
roads. *See* highways
rocks, 175–177
rodeos, 177
Rogers, James E., 199
Rogers, Will, 67
Roosevelt Lake, 124
Roper Lake State Park, 186
Rustler Park, 44

Safford, 177
saguaro cactus, 177–178
Saguaro National Park, 147, 177–178,
198
Salt River, 66–67, 175
Salt River Pima-Maricopa Indian
Community, 14, 19
Salt River Project, 178–179
San Carlos Apache Tribe, 14, 19, 149
San Francisco Peaks, 94–95, 137–138
San Juan Southern Paiute Tribe, 14, 19
Santa Cruz County, 23, 60, 63, 160
Scottsdale, 164, 179
Sedona, 180
senators: state, 72–73; U.S., 56, 72
settlers, 157–160
sheep ranching, 170–171
sheriffs, 102–104, 166
Show Low, 160–161, 204

Sierra Vista, 164, 180
Skeleton Cave, 67
skiing, 180–181
Slide Rock State Park, 186
snowboarding, 180–181
snowfall, 43, 53
Snowflake-Taylor, 204
Sonoita Creek, 186–187
South Tucson, 157
spadefoot toads, 171
Spanish exploration, 112, 114
speed limits, 181
spiders, 120–121
sports: baseball, 20–30; basketball, 30–31;
football, 90; golf, 99; hockey, 117;
hunting, 119–120; skiing and
snowboarding, 180–181; tennis,
190–191
Springerville-Eager, 204
state chambers of commerce, 47
state emblems, 8
state government: Arizona Constitution,
215–217; Arizona Court of Appeals,
183; Arizona Supreme Court, 74, 182;
attorneys general, 182, 184;
corporation commission, 72, 182;
elected officials, 72–74; governors, 99,
181, 183; internet voting, 210–211;
legislative branch, 182; legislature,
72–74; politicians, 125–126; politics,
163–164; secretary of state, 72,
181–182, 183; superintendent of
public instruction, 72, 182; Superior
Court of Arizona, 183; taxis, 189–190
state parks, 184–187, 185
state universities, 199–201
statehood era, 113–114, 116, 150,
187–188
steamboats, 188–189
stolen explosives, 209
summer heat, 192
Sun City, 164, 203–204
Sunset Crater, 67, 147
Surpise, 203–204

Taliesin West, 189
taxes, 189–190
telephone area codes, 23–24
television stars, 76–77
television stations, 190
Tempe, 164, 190
temperature, 8, 53–54; air conditioning,

10–11; coldest day, 52; summer heat, 192
tennis, 190–191
territorial years, 112–113, 114; capital on wheels, 44–45; delegates, 56; first officers, 45; Thieving Thirteen, 183
Theodore Roosevelt Dam, 67
Thieving Thirteen, 183
threatened species, 74–75
"Thunder in the Desert" Fair, 210
timeline, 114–117
Tohono O'odham Nation, 14, 19–20, 149
Tolleson, 203–204
Tombstone, 154, 161, 187, 191
Tonto Apache Tribe, 14, 20
Tonto National Forest, 91
Tonto National Monument, 23, 147
Tonto Natural Bridge, 187
tourism, 191–195. *See also* outdoor recreation
towns: chambers of commerce, 46–49; ghost towns, 95–96; map, 48; mileage between 110–111; population, 164–165; retirement communities, 172–173. *See also names of specific towns*
transportaion. *See* public transportation
treaties, 88, 102
trees and shrubs, 195–196
Tubac (town), 197, 201
Tubac Presidio, 23, 187
tuberculosis, 68, 87
Tucson, 197–198, 201; origin of name, 161; population, 164; South Tucson, 157; trips, 192–193
Tumacacori, 23, 147
turquoise, 1776
Tusayan Ruin and Museum 22
Tuzigoot National Monument, 23, 147

unions, 198
University of Arizona, 198, 201; Program in Integrative Medicine, 105; Rogers donation, 199; University Medical Center, 105

Van Dyke, Vonda Kay, 80
Vasquez de Coronado, Francisco, 58
Verde River, 67, 175
Verde River Greenway, 187
volcanic eruptions, 67

Walnut Canyon, 22, 147
Walnut Grove Dam disaster, 68
web sites, 214
western Maricopa cities, 203–204
White Mountain Apache Tribe, 14, 20
White Mountains, 138, 204
Why, 161
Wickenburg, 203–204
Williams, L.A., 31
Window Rock, 204
Winslow, 204
World War II, 204–205
Wright, Frank Lloyd, 189
writers, 126–128
Wupatki National Monument, 22, 147

Yaqui people, 14, 19, 149
Yavapai-Apache Tribe, 14, 20
Yavapai County, 23, 60, 63, 160
Yavapai people, 16, 67, 149
Yavapai Prescott Reservation, 14, 20
Yodaville, 134
Yuma, 164, 205
Yuma County, 60, 63–64, 160
Yuma Crossing Historic Park, 187
Yuma Missions massacre, 87
Yuma people, 67
Yuma Territorial Prison, 187

zanjeros, 205–206
zip codes, 206–208
zoos, 208